"A GREAT STORY." —*Sir Edmund Hillary*

THE LAND OFFERED NO MERCY. AMONG THE STARK,
AWESOME PANORAMAS, ON A TRAIL SHARED BY
WANDERERS AND BANDITS, A YOUNG AMERICAN PURSUED
A DREAM, WALKING TOWARD A DESTINY HE COULD NOT
QUITE COMPREHEND. IN THIS CLASSIC TALE OF ADVENTURE,
PARKER ANTIN RECALLS HIS EXTRAORDINARY EXCURSION
ACROSS THE HIMALAYAN RANGE ON FOOT—A JOURNEY OF
REMARKABLE, HEART-STOPPING DANGER AND EVEN MORE
REMARKABLE REWARDS....

"An odyssey on the thin edge of
survival...an engrossing tale."
—*Publishers Weekly*

"Well-written, classy adventure.
Refreshingly human."
—*Kirkus Reviews*

LAUREL EXPEDITION

"Gripping adventure."
—*Library Journal*

THERE ARE NO CONQUERORS,
ONLY SURVIVORS.

Exhausted, disheartened, I could not force my mind to hold more than one thought at a time. And my obsessive thought was *We must find Sangdak*. Somehow we must get to the other side of the river, we must find a way to do it. I could not imagine our condition getting any worse. We were lost, without food, a raging snowstorm blew around us. It seemed a miracle to me that Prem was still alive, but how much longer could his iron will carry his ailing body?

Despairing utterly, I didn't know where to turn. We were abandoned in the fury of the wilderness that we had the temerity to enter, to challenge. Man, nature, the gods—all had withdrawn their help; none offered us refuge or even hope. Alone now, just the five of us, how much longer could we struggle? The snow swirled white around me, but blackness possessed my soul.

—*Himalayan Odyssey*

"A magnificent, little-known setting . . . A well-written story of physical endurance and spiritual growth."
—*Lincoln Journal-Star*

"A candid and infectious account of a truly remarkable journey."
—Joe Kane, author of *Running the Amazon*

LAUREL
EXPEDITION

HIMALAYAN ODYSSEY

THE PERILOUS TREK TO WESTERN NEPAL

PARKER ANTIN with PHYLLIS WACHOB WEISS

"AMONG THE YEAR'S BEST...AN ACCOUNT OF GRUELING, DRAMATIC ENDEAVOR."—*The New York Times Book Review*
WITH 8 PAGES OF PHOTOS

A LAUREL BOOK
Published by
Dell Publishing
a division of
Bantam Doubleday Dell Publishing Group, Inc.
666 Fifth Avenue
New York, New York 10103

ISBN: 0-440-21125-5

Reprinted by arrangement with Donald I. Fine, Inc.

Printed in the United States of America

Published simultaneously in Canada

November 1992

10 9 8 7 6 5 4 3 2 1

OPM

For Nora

ACKNOWLEDGMENTS

This is a true story, presented with minor changes of some names and places—minor in that they camouflage the truth only when necessary to protect those with whom I shared these experiences.

I wish to express my sincerest thanks to Phyllis Wachob Weiss for persuading me to begin this project. Her boundless enthusiasm buoyed us through many difficult months of writing. Don Weiss gave up both the serenity of his home and the companionship of his wife to the singular task of writing this book. For those sacrifices, and for providing helpful advice concerning the choice of photographs, I thank him. I am also indebted to Jerry Athearn for arranging the initial meeting between Phyllis and me.

The many insecurities and doubts that accompany the writing of a first book were eased by the early interest and encouragement of our editor, David Gibbons. My parents, Tony and Jean, were equally supportive, and patient. For only in reading this book did they finally learn the "whole story." My father, a writer by trade, tirelessly edited our many manuscript drafts and added much, but not himself, to the book.

Of those who helped put this book in its final form, I am

grateful to the late Hugh Swift, who lent his extensive knowledge of the Himalayas and their peoples to a critical reading of the final manuscript, and to Niranjin Koirala, who patiently corrected the grammar and spelling of my "tourist Nepali," with little more than an occasional smirk and raised brow.

My debt to Prem Tshering Lama, Akaal Bahadur, Jeet Bahadur and Pema Tshering Sherpa is best expressed in the text that follows. Their enthusiasm and spirit of adventure kept us constantly veering toward the less trodden routes. I also wish to thank the many fellow travellers who influenced my thoughts, among them Randy Smith, Mark Castagnoli, Andre DeCary, Charlie and Debbie Weinberger and Peace Corps volunteers Sean Gaffney and Robert R. Bell, Jr.

Finally, I wish to express my deepest gratitude to J.B. Gross; friend, Sensei, and world class wanderer.

The box outlines the area of Parker Antin's journey. See map on following pages for detail.

0	5	10	15	20	25

Scale in Miles

----------- Parker's Route
················· Other Trekking Routes

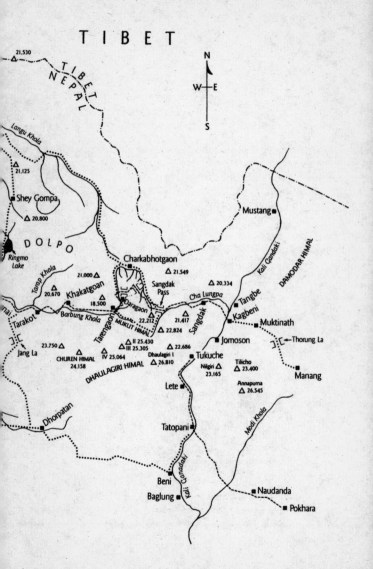

PROLOGUE

▲

In the high mountain forest, the late afternoon sun cast a golden light onto the green of hemlock trees. As I climbed towards 12,000 feet, the air cooled. In the stillness of the afternoon I heard no sounds except an occasional shrill whistle from the yak herders on the slopes somewhere below me. Prem, my *sirdar*, had moved ahead of me, the porters had fallen behind. The trail contoured along the hillside curving into four deeply forested side canyons before again emerging onto an open ridge.

I saw her sitting on a grassy knoll beside the trail. A young Tibetan woman, startling in her beauty. No more than eighteen, she held a suckling infant at her breast. Her long jet-black hair fanned out around her, enveloping the child in dark gossamer. With half closed eyes, a smile of enchanting radiance lit her rosy-cheeked face as she turned it towards the warmth of the sun's last rays. I stood mesmerized. Despite poverty, hunger, disease, ignorance, this woman-child who held life itself in her arms personified the quietly persistent will to live of these mountain people, especially their elemental ability to experience each moment just as it came to them. The guileless smile on her exotic Asian face captivated me—and, for a moment, I saw my Clara as we said goodbye in Kathmandu.

The encounter lasted less than a minute, but it lingered with me as I strolled on in the forest. The amber hue of the setting sun dappled light onto the forest floor. Huge masses of moss hung from the oak trees forming a canopy over my head. I sat on a lichen-covered rock that beckoned me.

I held my breath and heard . . . nothing. At that time of afternoon, the wind had died, leaving the forest at peace. The earth was silenced. I sat for several minutes, motionless, barely breathing, challenging the magnificence of nature around me to blink, to break the spell.

My eye caught a movement on the trail ahead. An animal had bounded onto it and was coming towards me. Perhaps four feet from nose to tail, marten-like but huskier, with chestnut-red fur and a raccoon face; a red panda, one of the rarest of Himalayan animals. He leapt gracefully in undulating strides until barely thirty yards away. Then he picked up my scent and stopped, looking directly at me through the camouflaging foliage. Rearing up slightly, he inspected me for several seconds with an odd, dancelike swaying motion, and then was gone, off the trail and out of sight.

I sat for several more minutes and felt a deep sense of melancholy overtake me. My eyes moistened and filled, and, surprised, I brushed tears from my cheeks.

I'm not sure why the tears came. This was not what I expected when I came to Nepal. The pull of the Himalayas for many is a religious quest, a search for enlightenment, personal fulfillment, a guru, the Way. Having scoffed at all that, I now began to understand, to feel the essence of life as I never had before. By coming halfway around the world, by removing myself in multiple cultural and physical layers from my upper-middle-class existence in America, I was beginning to learn a lesson in what it meant truly to *live* on this earth. The lovely young Tibetan mother, the red panda, the moss-laden trees, the magnificent mountains; the spirits of all of them were inextricably tied together, and so was I. This connection between man and the earth on which he lives was a link missing from my experience of life. The tears made me suspect that Asia, in all its unfathomable complexity, was profoundly altering my life; something was happening to me on this journey to western Nepal.

CHA LUNGPA GORGE, DOLPO, WESTERN NEPAL
Wednesday, April 11, 1984, 3:00 P.M.

My foot touched but did not hold on the sloping sand-covered rock, and I slipped off into the void.

Instinctively, I spun around as I fell, arresting my fall by bearhugging the rock I had slipped from. My chest and chin slammed into the boulder, knocking the wind out of me and driving my teeth into the side of my tongue. I sucked for breath that wouldn't come. My feet flailed in empty space. I started to slip.

Frantically grabbing for a more secure hold, my hands met only grit, sliding across the uneven rocks. Sand trickled onto my face. Then torn fingers clutched something firm and I stopped slipping. My feet dangled, and I swung them around blindly, wildly searching for purchase on anything.

Nothing below me. Realizing the futility of searching for nonexistent footholds, I put everything I had into pulling myself up. Forearms shaking, I hauled myself up until the side of my face pressed against the crumbling wall. With a contortionist's maneuver I dragged one foot onto the rock. With shallow, painful gulps of air, I pulled and pushed myself to my feet.

Prem and the porters watched in utter silence, their mouths agape. Auri Bahadur, who was closest to me, finally spoke, *"Bistaari, Sahib."* ("Go slowly, sir.")

I stood on the rock embedded in the compacted dirt conglomerate until my breath returned and my forearms uncramped. Looking down was inconceivable, I didn't want to know what I had missed this time. A fall to my death. Or worse, a fall that would have left me bone-broken deep in the gorge, wishing I had died quickly.

Hacking pink globs of blood and spit into the air, I tentatively explored the damage to my tongue, which felt numb. Along with the blood came bits of a front tooth. After a few minutes I gathered enough control to make my way, ever so cautiously, back the remaining ten feet to where the others waited.

San Francisco, California

February, 1990

I returned from Asia five years ago, but it has taken most of the intervening years to truly come back. In 1983, when this story begins, I was twenty-seven, fresh out of graduate school and eager to see the world. One could say with some truth, given the pattern of my life till then, that I was looking for a rite of passage. In my youthful ignorance and arrogance, I challenged the greatest mountain range on earth—the Himalayas. With my friend J.B. Gross, I formed the "Everest K2 Trans-Himalayan Expedition." Our avowed purpose: to traverse the entire Himalayan range, from Sikkim to Pakistan.

I did not set out to prove my manhood or to risk my life. I had nothing in mind to conquer. I meant simply to trek, walk up and down the mountains, see exotic cultures. But by March 1984, six months into the trip, the expedition had been reduced to one sahib (myself), a *sirdar* (guide) and two Nepalese porters. I was in Dolpo, the most remote, most inaccessible part of western Nepal. I didn't have the proper permits, enough money or enough food; and information about what lay ahead was nonexistent. I had good reason to fear the Tibetan nomads, the villagers, the police and military, not to mention the mountains themselves.

I found myself extended to my physical limits; lost, starving, facing death itself in the stark haunting mountains. I had plunged myself into a world totally dissimilar to what I had known. A world with life stripped of its pretenses, where man coexists with and does not attempt to compete with nature. Dolpo, in the winter of 1984, also brought a new consciousness of the mental, emotional and, most unexpectedly, the *spiritual* center of myself. An awareness that alternately made me exalt and despair, laugh and sob, understand and wonder. A spiritual core that I had never allowed anyone to see or sense, even myself.

Although I returned from Nepal physically unscathed, the spiritual odyssey continues.

HIMALAYAN ODYSSEY

CHAPTER ONE

▲

KATHMANDU LAY WRAPPED IN A DARK GRAY CLOAK EXCEPT FOR soft lights on Swayambhunath, the Monkey Temple. I could see them quite clearly from my window on the fourth floor of the hotel. Voices came from the big room at the head of the stairs, and hearing them, I downed my cup of coffee and went to join J.B. and the others.

Although Prem and our porters, Akaal Bahadur and Jeet Bahadur, had walked three miles from Prem's place clear across town, they had arrived only twenty minutes after J.B. and I had wakened at 4:00 A.M. The night before, Prem had carefully directed the packing of our equipment into the funnel-shaped bamboo *dokos* (baskets) the porters would carry. Now, in the early morning hours, they whispered to each other as they shouldered their loads and stepped quickly down the stairs.

Clara, accompanied by her friend Sera, had come to say goodbye. In May, I would see Clara again in Darjeeling, but that seemed a long, uncertain time away as we moved into the darkened stairwell. She pressed a round pendant into my hand, a good-luck charm.

"Good luck, I will miss you." Her soft voice and averted eyes said more. Our bodies moved closer and she grabbed my shoulder. "Parker, please, you must come to see me in Darjeeling."

Incapable of expressing what I felt, I only nodded my reply. Awkwardly we kissed in the predawn twilight.

I ran down the concrete staircase to the open courtyard below. I carried one porter load in a *doko* on a tumpline around my forehead, not something I would recommend to anyone who, like myself, had never done it before. At the far side of the courtyard I paused and looked back to the fourth-floor balcony where Clara stood. I waved. She raised her hand slowly, then turned and was gone. With an ache I knew that I would think of her often in the days ahead.

The cool, forty-five-degree February morning was damp and overcast, the sky a pearl gray. We piled into the back of a minitruck, and creaked through the awakening streets. Sweepers with long brooms made piles of yesterday's trash and set them on fire, leaving smoking mounds every few yards along the streets. Porters carrying produce-filled baskets hurried through the narrow alleys, stopping at their favorite shrines with offerings before delivering their loads to the early morning bazaar and setting out vegetables for sale. We met the bus near the post office, and after securing our gear on the roof we left, more or less on time, at 5:30 A.M. Eight hours later we arrived in Pokhara, Nepal's second largest city, and our first stop on a much longer road trip towards Nepal's western border with India.

The next morning, Prem and I walked for an hour from the Himalayan Hotel near the airport to the Tibetan camp. With the passing years and the continued Chinese occupation of Tibet, the refugee camp had become a permanent village of stone and mud houses. Here we hoped to hire an extra porter who also was knowledgeable about the routes through the Karnali, Mugu and Dolpo regions of Nepal's far west. Neither Prem nor our Kathmandu porters had traveled further west than the Kali Gandaki River Valley of central

Nepal. For two weeks before leaving the Kathmandu Valley, we had searched vainly for such a porter around the great stupa of Bodnath, a winter gathering place for Tibetans from the far reaches of the Himalaya. We had found no one, but hoped for better luck in Pokhara.

Prem stopped and spoke with some young Tibetan women. We were in luck, for extreme cold had driven many people out of the Himalaya and south along the Kali Gandaki. Porters from Dolpo would arrive soon, possibly tomorrow.

We continued our search through the scattered village houses. A man dressed in a black *chuba*, the voluminous Tibetan topcoat, stepped forward and offered to guide us. He hesitated, however, when told of our intention to bus to the western border with India and then travel back towards Kathmandu along the crest of the Himalaya. He outlined another plan: walk north out of Pokhara up the Kali Gandaki to Jomoson, then west into Dolpo. Both Prem and I had already rejected this option, as the 18,000-foot passes into Dolpo would be buried under snow this time of year. Also, since the final 1975 shootout with the anti-Chinese Khampa rebels in Dolpo, this area was closely guarded. We became suspicious, as our would-be guide must have known that we would never make it past the police and military checkposts. He would just make a few easy rupees before we were turned around. Our suspicions grew when bystanders whispered to us that he stole from the trekkers he guided. Disappointed, we returned to the Himalayan Hotel, still without an extra porter.

I suspected that Prem was secretly relieved. He didn't like or trust these Tibetans, considering them a shiftless, dirty lot. As in our crossing of eastern Nepal last fall, he was our *sirdar*, and would continue to be no matter who we took on here. Even though I might choose who we hired, he would have to establish his authority and a porter who ranked also as a guide had him a little worried.

I, too, felt relieved. The Everest K2 Trans-Himalayan Expedition, never a well-financed one, could certainly use the money saved in salary and bus fare. Now, rather than return to the Tibetan camp, we decided to wait until we got to the west to hire any porters.

We spent our last day in Pokhara writing letters, repacking and doing last-minute shopping in preparation for our three-day bus ride two hundred and fifty miles to the west of Nepal.

I first met James Bernard ("J.B.") Gross at the Philadelphia Judo Dojo. In 1978 I had moved to Philadelphia to begin graduate school in biology at the University of Pennsylvania. Although I had begun studying judo at the age of ten, I dropped it when I started college. Now, in the summer of 1981, I had been invited to the Olympic Training Center in Colorado Springs. But I hadn't been on the mat in several years.

Panicking, I looked in the phone book and called the only listing, the Philadelphia Judo Dojo on North Broad Street. A recorded message gave the hours of the classes.

At six o'clock the following Wednesday, in the war zone of North Philadelphia, I opened the battered yellow metal door with *JUDO* stenciled on it and climbed four flights of grimy wooden stairs. A worn white canvas-covered mat, twenty-five by forty feet, covered most of the big room. The dojo was empty. I walked around the mat and looked into the office. I found J.B. sitting behind the desk.

I introduced myself and explained why I needed to get into shape quickly. He nodded. "Locker room's in the back."

My first impression was *big*. An understandable assessment of a man with a neck as wide as his head, standing six foot two and weighing anywhere from 225 to 280 pounds, eight inches taller than I and nearly twice my weight. In his early thirties, he had short light-brown hair and wore a military-issue green T-shirt. I soon learned that J.B. had recently returned from five years studying judo in Japan and had just taken over as the sensei (teacher) of the dojo.

We got to know each other over the requisite beers after practice and I learned that his early years differed markedly from mine. He had grown up along the south Jersey shore. Although quiet and unfailingly well-mannered, he had always been bigger than his classmates and never quite fit in. His father's stories of the South Pacific during World War II planted the seed of wanderlust. At sixteen, J.B. graduated from high school and immediately shipped out with the Merchant Marine. He returned two years later to attend Annapolis. But at the last minute, he broke his mother's heart by enlisting in the Marines instead. He wanted to fight in Vietnam, and four years of officer training was too long to wait.

War wounds put him in the hospital for twenty-two months and the doctors said he would never walk again without canes. He proved them wrong, not only walking but returning to judo and even playing professional football.

Almost from the beginning he talked longingly of getting back on the road. I didn't take him seriously until late one night in a bar.

"Parker, I'm tired of the kind of people we get at the dojo. And I'm bored to tears with Philadelphia. I want to get out of here."

"I never understood why you left Japan," I countered.

J.B. sighed. "The culture's hard on foreigners. For a year it's not so bad, but then you realize that you're forever a second-class citizen. But I've been to a lot of other places in Asia that I'd like to get back to." He turned to me. "You'll be through with grad school in a year. You're the only one around here that I'd consider going with. Parker, let's *do* something."

In a deep corner of my mind a similar notion had been banging around, as yet it was nebulous, nothing more than a faint feeling of discontent. My life until then had been school, vacation, college, vacation and graduate school. I was supposed to be set for life, on the track to a career, family, mortgage and the proverbial white picket fence. But something seemed missing. Life couldn't possibly be so simple, so pat, so superficial. I didn't know, and the more I thought about it, the more elusive the answer became. So perhaps in search of something, perhaps for the sheer thrill of the thought, I was willing to follow J.B. to Asia.

I received my Ph.D. in biology in July 1982. That same week we started planning—a 4,000-mile walk across China, from Harbin in the northeast to Kashgar in the far west. J.B. was a dreamer, and he dreamt big thoughts. And he yearned to follow in the footsteps of the characters in his oft-read books. Men who had traipsed the barren plateaus and steppes of Asia. Heinrich Harrer and Peter Aufschnaiter. Wilfred Thesiger. And who was I to suggest that we start with something just a bit shorter?

For several months our preparations continued at full speed until one day we received a phone call from our contact at Mountain Travel. China, having just opened its doors to foreigners, was also embracing the capitalist philosophy. Our "permit fee," the China expert informed us, had been set at something in excess of $100,000, payable in cash directly to the Chinese government.

So we pulled out a map of Asia and looked again. If not China, then how about something further south—perhaps a traverse of the Himalayas? At first glance our qualifications seemed impeccable. J.B. had spent a month trekking in Nepal a few years earlier, and I had once climbed New Hampshire's Mount Washington—all 6,288 feet of it. Who needed more experience than that?

Thus the Everest K2 Trans-Himalayan Expedition was born.

We both set to work researching and organizing. Despite its humble origins, our expedition soon took on the trappings of a serious undertaking. Johnson Camping Incorporated gave us Eureka tents. Because It's There, an expedition equipment outfitter in Seattle, gave us sleeping bags. Nike supplied shoes.

That spring and summer I had papers to finish for my postdoctoral work. Pressure mounted from my friends, my colleagues and my professors, who frowned and shook their heads. "You'll ruin your career, you know, dropping out like this." The trip organization took time and long nights stretched me thin. I extricated myself from a sound relationship with Susan, my girlfriend of two years. I found it difficult trying to tell her that it had nothing to do with her. Not that I was afraid of commitment (*Just keep telling yourself that, Parker*), but I wasn't "husband" material just then.

In April, I injured my back in a judo accident. It hurt. For three weeks, I lay in the University of Pennsylvania hospital, not two hundred yards from the lab in which I had been working. Sadly I watched solid muscles turn to flab from inactivity. Exactly six weeks before I left I had disc surgery, but was up and walking the same day. I told my body there simply was no time for a leisurely recovery.

Three days before leaving, I moved back to my parents' house in Darien, Connecticut, sick with the flu. Three days in which I tried to ignore the largely unspoken concerns of my parents. My mother quietly seemed to accept my going with more grace than my dad, somehow sensing better than I the need for this "adventure." My father, always the one to worry, shook his head. How could his only son, armed solely with some Boy Scout merit badges and not a single day of serious mountain climbing, plunge himself into the vast maw of Asia, to trek across the most daunting mountain range in the world? I suspected he felt it was all "damned foolish," that I would fall off a cliff or be gored by a rhinoceros and never come home.

Before I had time to think I stood at the Air India desk at JFK. Four hundred Indians, 1,600 oversized suitcases, the bewildering screech of a dozen languages and the exotic smells of curry. And me. My father stood transfixed and mumbled, "Oh my God." There wasn't time to say proper goodbyes, I was gone so quickly.

To pluck myself from the entanglements of my family, my job and my expected course in life, and to fly off to Asia so suddenly was hard—the second hardest thing I have ever done.

Since the Himalayan Hotel in Pokhara stood a mile out of town, we made arrangements for the bus to Butwal to pick us up. At 5:30 A.M. we piled our supplies along the side of the road and waited. Just before 7:00 A.M., a particularly aged and dirty TATA bus wheezed to a halt across the road, already overloaded with passengers and cargo. Akaal Bahadur and Jeet Bahadur immediately climbed onto the roof and, deftly untying and rearranging cargo, secured our loads in the safest center spot.

We squeezed inside the bus to find our reserved seats occupied. We argued, we righteously waved tickets, Prem threatened the driver. But we lost. Four of us, one of whom was J.B., squeezed into a space meant for three small Nepalese.

Murphy's Law worked without a hitch all day, a very long day. At a tea stop in a dingy village of squalid hovels we ate *daal bhaat* (lentils and rice) from filthy metal plates. For two hours, we waited as six boys pried one of the bald tires from its rim, found and then patched the leak and, after a break for tea and a smoke, rebolted it to the bus. An agonizing procedure to watch because we had witnessed the same protracted exercise on each and every bus trip of the last six months. We piled back onto the bus . . . and sat for another thirty minutes. Exasperated, J.B. leaned out of the window to berate the lazy driver, but stopped in midsentence.

"No, no," he muttered. "Parker, take a look, you're not going to believe this one."

I stuck my head out the window just in time to see a young Nepalese boy empty the contents of a large beer bottle into the bus's gas tank. Then he turned and ran to a fifty-five-gallon drum twenty yards away, where he refilled the bottle.

Refueling, one beer bottle at a time.

Cramped and desperate for some fresh air, J.B. and I pushed our way outside and climbed a ladder at the back of the bus to the roof rack. Just then the bus lurched forward, and quickly we found comfortable spots amidst luggage and large bales of wool. Except for inhaling an occasional bug, we found the roof a refreshing place to ride in good weather. A rumor had made the rounds (J.B. claimed that if it weren't for the unending stream of rumors, Nepal would have dried up and blown away a long time ago), that on this same road a low wire had neatly sliced off half of a roof-riding foreigner's head. We saw picture-postcard images of the Himalayas to the north, but no wires.

Twelve and a half hours after leaving Pokhara, the bus ground to a halt in the town of Butwal. Like all *terai* towns, its single main street was lined with poured concrete buildings, the kind that seemed to be taking over the Third World. We had passed through this border town only the month before while playing the visa extension game. Now, with twelve hours to kill until our next bus heading further west to Nepalganj, we found a filthy, windowless room in a filthy hotel on the second floor of one of the concrete boxes. I threw my pack on the jaundice-colored mattress with suspicious stains in suspicious places, and eyed the hovering mosquitos warily. Having lived above 3,000 feet continuously for the past several months, I had stopped taking antimalarial drugs.

To speed the hours, we sent Prem to the bazaar for a bottle of Kukri rum, which we drank out of greasy water glasses with Coke, real Coke. At least we weren't across the border in India and forced to drink our rum with Campa Cola, a sickly sweet brown liquid whose color is its only relation to The Real Thing.

I lit a mosquito coil and J.B. pulled out a worn deck of cards. We played hand after hand of our ongoing gin rummy game. After midnight, we pulled tattered mosquito nets down around us and tucked them in. We fell asleep, but not for long.

I guess just about every American kid has heard, "Sleep tight, don't let the bedbugs bite." But no one I knew in grade school had ever seen one, let alone been bitten by one. And a good thing. As hardened Third World travelers, we thought we could handle a few bedbug bites. We were wrong. These unsavory mattresses crawled with the evil little beasties. Scratching and cursing, we tore the mosquito nets down and wrapped ourselves in them. Unfortunately, tattered mosquito nets don't stop bedbugs. We slept intermittently between the scratching.

At four-in-the-middle-of-the-night, a bus horn blasted us awake and kept on blasting. A cup of sweet, milky tea and a couple of *rotis* (unleavened flatbread) did for breakfast, then we stumbled into the dark to find our bus. The "navigator" on our overbooked bus told us the road between Butwal and Nepalganj was closed for repairs and had been for weeks. The bus driver/owner, however, had sold every seat twice over, so he was willing to have a go. Chaos reigned as we hoisted our loads to the roof and then found our seats. We felt lucky to get seats, but then cursed our luck when the driver popped a tape into his tape deck, and the incessant wailing of Hindi songs began to emanate from a cheap plastic speaker right above our heads. We cringed at the screeching female voice, but our fellow passengers seemed to love it.

Our companions were a hodgepodge of locals, rich and poor. Three ex-Gurkha soldiers, a group of wild-looking Nepalese of an undetermined tribe, women weighed down with silver ankle and wrist bracelets, coin necklaces and nose rings. Some men wore the dress of typical hill tribesmen; baggy white jodhpurs, *topees* (hats) of multicolored cloth and large *kukris* (Nepalese knives) in wooden scabbards stuck into dark waist sashes.

Four wild-eyed Tibetans in greasy black chubas pushed down the aisle and took up residence on the floor just behind us. The "navigator" came back and told them in Nepali that they couldn't block the door with their piles of belongings. The Tibetans merely fingered their silver-handled knives, stared through the boy and smiled wild, demented smiles. The navigator backed away, the Tibetans and their bundles stayed put for the entire trip.

With a blast of horns that would have brought down the walls of Jericho, the bus lumbered out of Butwal and immediately came to the first obstacle, a two-hundred-yard-wide river. The water rose to the axles as the bus churned over the rocky river bottom. Just upriver we saw the disintegrating concrete pilings of an unfinished bridge. On the far bank, a gravel road ascended into the green Siwalik hills. As dawn broke misty gray we saw that the road sliced a bloody gash into the steep mountainsides of red clay. Workers stopped and stared as we drove past. Where an entire hillside had washed away, we dropped back down to a dry riverbed and followed its course over the rocks and sand in the narrow canyon. With the monotonous sway of the bus, my eyelids closed. I woke a short time later to the sound of retching, and opened my eyes just in time to see the five-year-old in the seat in front of me heave a stream of chunky yellow vomit onto my left boot.

It began to rain. Soft mist rapidly turned into a downpour as we came out of the canyon and back onto the road. Soon the bus bogged down in a depression of soft clay turned to mud. The navigator told us that we might like to push, so we stumbled out into the pouring rain. Leaning into my piece of bumper, I found myself next to two of the still-grinning Tibetans.

"Tapaaiko gaarma kahaa ho?" ("Where is your house?") I asked, impressed with my imagined command of Nepali and eager to know where they came from. They merely grinned.

"Ek, dui, tin." ("One, two, three.") We pushed. Suddenly the bus lurched and swerved like a drunken hippo, sending a Gurkha and two jodhpured Nepalese sprawling facedown in the muddy quagmire. Laughs froze in our throats as the wildly spinning wheels sprayed the rest of us with flying globs of muck. The bus regained the firm roadbed and slowly picked up speed. Realizing that the driver had no intention of stopping, we chased after the bus and re-boarded on the run. As we continued through the gray afternoon, I dozed off.

A rock crashed into the side of the bus just below my window. I bolted awake. "What the hell . . . ?"

"Do not worry, Parker Sahib. It is just the road workers. They are attacking us," Prem answered nonchalantly.

Struggling to clear my head, I peered out. Through the rain-streaked window I saw groups of workers alongside the road ahead. They hurled rocks and mud and sticks as we sped by them at thirty miles an hour. Irate that we might destroy their half-finished repairs, they had erected barri-cades along the road.

A quarter-mile beyond one such barrier, we came to a halt. Prem and I went forward to investigate the commotion and witnessed a mutiny on the bus. Several passengers ar-gued with the driver, urging him to keep moving. He re-fused, fearing for his bus and/or his limbs. A round Newari in Western clothes dislodged the driver from his seat, and the other mutineers shoved him towards the rear. Taking the wheel, the Newari quickly accelerated back onto the road amidst a barrage of mud and cow dung. With a blaring of horns we crushed two dogs in our path, then flew down the embankment of a washout and jolted to a stop at the bottom. With a grinding of gears and the smell of burning clutch, our driver rocked the bus back and forth before we broke free and climbed the far side.

Both darkness and rain fell and we reached Nepalganj at 9:00 P.M. Yet another dirty transportation *terai* town. At this hour all of the shops were shuttered, so we dined on a bit of our yak cheese and warm vodka.

Once again, our wake-up call came at 4:00 A.M. with the blasting of horns. We gathered our gear as Prem searched for our bus heading west towards Dhangarhi. Ten minutes later Prem returned—with bad news. "The roads ahead, they are washed away. We cannot go farther west."

This news necessitated a major change in plans. Short of crossing the border into India, which would invalidate our visas, our only choice was to head for Surkhet, eliminating at least a hundred miles of trekking in the far west. Prem had already spotted the bus. We loaded our gear and climbed aboard for another eight-hour bus ride.

As we crested the final tortuous switchback, the bus belched billowing clouds of acrid gray smoke. From the top of the ridge, a broad flat valley lay before us. Surkhet was spread out at the far end, its whitewashed buildings shining like a beacon in the slanting afternoon sunlight. I stuck my head, then half my body, out of a window for a breath of fresh air. I squinted into the sun as the wind flattened my hair against my head. Imagining the warm wind washing away the sweat and dust that had accumulated during the last three days, I smiled to myself as we barreled the final few miles towards Surkhet. I eagerly looked forward to escaping this cramped, noisy bus and to getting back onto the trail.

The road was paved, barely, and lined with local villagers traveling towards the "city." The driver, perhaps emboldened by the sight of our destination, leaned incessantly on his horn as we maintained a continuous weaving course at forty miles per hour through the increasingly thick throngs of people.

Bright multicolored banners arched across the road every fifty yards for mile after mile, all the way into Surkhet. In gold letters they welcomed His Majesty King Birendra Bir Bikram Shah Dev, scheduled to arrive in Surkhet that afternoon! The people had decorated every roadway in the region on the remote chance that His Majesty might pass their way. For these isolated villagers, he is truly a god, a reincarnation of Vishnu.

Because our trekking permits did not include Surkhet, we nervously eyed the troops and police lining the road. We had hoped to keep a low profile, but lost that hope as soon as we stepped off the bus. We couldn't help attracting attention. Men in Nepal over six feet tall are a rare sight and revered in a way, as if they harbored unusual powers. J.B., as the biggest man most Nepalese had ever seen, was an attraction wherever we went. Our porters called him "Buddha." Naively we thought we could just slip into Surkhet and trek out on our merry way.

The bus had stopped in the midst of a large flock of bleating goats, seemingly abandoned in the central square. A crowd of onlookers instantly gathered to stare at Buddha while Akaal Bahadur and Jeet Bahadur straddled our baggage to prevent theft. A small band of pleading porters competed with the goats and onlookers for our attention, hoping to earn a rupee or two carrying our loads. Prem quickly took control and from the midst of the boisterous, beseeching crowd selected two of the sturdiest porters. J.B. and I hoisted the remaining loads and our entourage set off, trailing a stream of children and luckless porters to a small house a half-mile beyond the town center.

The house, a classic Nepali dwelling, was beautiful in its simplicity. Burnt orange covered the first five feet of mud walls, the rest was whitewashed. The floors were packed dirt, and rough beams supported the high-angle thatched roof.

We were settled into a small room on the second floor, surprisingly cool despite the heat outside. Leaning back against my pack, I looked out the window. A yellow moon rose above the surrounding hills.

CHAPTER TWO

▲

AS THE FIRST ORDER OF BUSINESS, AFTER A POT OF *CHANG* AND A plate of *daal bhaat*, we had to obtain information about the route between Surkhet and Jumla. We laid our purple ammonia-dye map out on the floor. It was entitled "Latest Trekking Map Jomoson to Jumla and Surkhet, showing whole of the Dhaulagiri Himal and Kanjiroba Himal."

With his finger, Prem traced our route north, then east to Jumla. We had heard rumors of food shortages to the north, which meant we would have to carry enough to be self-sufficient to Jumla.

J.B. studied the map, then questioned Prem. "What do you think, Prem? How long will it take us to reach Jumla?"

"Carrying all our food, ten or twelve days, I think. Walking long days and with good weather. And we will need two, maybe three more porters to carry the food."

J.B. thought for a moment. "That means eight people. Lots of rice. Fifty kilos ought to do it."

"Sixty at least, maybe more," replied Prem.

I leaned over the map and traced our route north further, beyond Jumla to the Tibetan border then east through 250 miles of the remotest region in the Himalayas, Dolpo. Thirty days, maybe more, with no chance of resupply. If we needed three more porters just to carry to Jumla, how did we expect to carry our food for thirty days? Speed would be critical. Our lives might depend on how fast we could move, and on not getting lost. The magnitude of our intended journey began to hit home.

Prem's voice brought me back to Surkhet. "We will have no problem getting porters, many were asking at the bus. We can find them in the bazaar."

But preparations could wait for another day. In thanksgiving for surviving the three-day bus ride, we bought two bottles of apple *rakshi*, the homemade distilled liquor found everywhere in Nepal, and a large jug of *chang*, the local beer made from whatever grain was available. Our guesthouse hostess cut her last strips of *suggotti*, dried buffalo jerky, from above the hearth, and soon the pungent smell of the meat frying with onions and garlic filled the room. We had designated tomorrow as a rest day to hire more porters and buy provisions, so we ate well and drank better before stumbling off one by one into the darkness and sleep.

I woke just before nine to the excited racket of Surkhet, already several hours into its busy day. The king's visit had swollen the town's populace by several thousand, and it seemed they had all chosen to execute their vociferous business beneath my window. J.B. and I had a quick snack of *chapattis* (unleavened bread) and tea, a light meal in deference to our pounding heads, and sent Prem and the porters to the bazaar.

Two hours later, they returned with three new dokos and three Thakuri porters. Two of them had carried our loads from the bus the day before, the other was an acquaintance from their home village near Jumla. Soon we found ourselves back in the bazaar to buy provisions, and also socks and the favored Chinese sneakers for the newly hired porters. If we expected our porters to make it through the deep snow we might have to cross in the mountains during the next two weeks, they needed something more than the usual bare feet or rubber flip-flops.

For an hour we peered into every stall in the market before Prem chose an especially small and decrepit one. Then began the lengthy bargaining process for our rice supply of sixty-five kilos. Prem, Akaal Bahadur and Jeet Bahadur fingered one lot after another, engaged in animated discussion about the relative merits of each. Because they came from a culture that survived on rice, this was serious business. J.B. and I were never once consulted, for it had been determined months and hundreds of miles before that we possessed unsophisticated rice palates, and thus were next to useless for making such important decisions.

As three pairs of watchful eyes confirmed that the correct amounts were weighed out, I peered into the dim interior from just outside. Above the shopkeeper's head hung a curved two-foot-long *kukri*, more sword than knife. The merchant's small child squatted and deposited a stream of yellow diarrheal feces on the flat stones of the street not eight inches from my foot.

After twenty minutes, Prem nodded his satisfaction that the correct quantity of rice was now safely stowed in our burlap bags. He paid the shopkeeper with crisp blue fifty-rupee notes. With a few deft jabs, using homespun thread and a large sewing needle, Akaal Bahadur and Jeet Bahadur sewed the bags shut.

At the local bank we converted several thousand rupees into five-, ten- and twenty-rupee notes. In the remoter regions of Nepal, bills of over twenty rupees (about U.S. $1) were seldom seen and sometimes impossible to change. In exchange for our large bills, the teller handed us several stapled bundles.

"Parker, we'd better check them all. You know how hard it is to get people to take torn bills around here," J.B. said, handing me a 500-rupee bundle of twenties.

I pried a brass staple out of the first packet. "Isn't it ironic that *nobody* wants old or torn money, but the banks start out by punching holes in every single note, even the new ones?"

The teller stood behind the counter and blinked at us as we carefully examined the stacks of bills. The bank's lone guard, brandishing his ancient twelve-gauge shotgun, sauntered over to peer over our shoulders.

"Here's one right in the middle of the stack. Sneaky bastards." J.B. held up a five-rupee note, nearly torn through a crease down the center, oily from hundreds of dirty hands and many shades darker than the rest.

I laughed. "What do you expect? The bank gets stuck with them like everybody else. They may as well fob them off on some other unsuspecting fools."

A half hour later, the teller smiled sheepishly and wobbled his head from side to side as we confronted him with more than two hundred rupees' worth of useless paper.

"I want *new* bills, *brand-new* bills," J.B. demanded, towering over the teller.

We got them.

Returning to the guesthouse, we spent the next several hours packing and repacking loads, carefully hoisting each one innumerable times to judge its weight. Our three new porters would demand loads of equal weight. Besides the rice we bought in the bazaar, we had two large buffalo salamis, a large wheel of yak cheese, cooking oil, Tibetan rock salt, tea, chilies, curry powder, garlic and two #10 cans, one each of coffee and hot chocolate. We planned to buy more rice in Jumla.

Surveying the gear spread out around the room, I realized that we had considerably less now than when J.B. and I arrived last summer. It would be a leaner expedition, this journey to western Nepal.

J.B. had arrived in Delhi on August 1, 1983. When I landed at 1:00 A.M. on August 31, he met me at the Delhi airport. Me and 390 pounds of extra gear. At the door of the plane, a wall of treacly monsoon humidity embraced me. Sweat gathered along my spine, trickled down and pooled in the small of my back; my underwear chafed.

First, I needed to shepherd my large pile of expedition gear through the inevitable tangle of customs paperwork. We had worked six months with the embassy in Washington and the consulate in New York accumulating the appropriate forms to avoid paying customs duty. Now, as I negotiated with the customs officials, all the carefully prearranged paperwork was "totally unacceptable." Two hours later, I capitulated and slipped the agent the requested *baksheesh* (bribe), a crisp fifty-dollar bill. Then I joined the battling throngs at the money exchange window before emerging into a monumental downpour. Standing under the crowded eaves, I counted my wad of multicolored bills. I was twenty-six rupees short. Cheated at the government exchange window. *Welcome to India, Parker.*

An Indian business associate of my father's, Vivian D'Souza, met us at the airport with his car. The aged but well-maintained Ambassador was a blessing, a lifeboat that sailed through the monsoon puddles while the taxis refused to travel the flooded roads into the city from the airport. We crammed our hillock of gear into the car with only breathing space to spare.

"You are staying in one of the hotels near the airport?" Vivian asked as he negotiated the throngs at the curb. Perhaps he was thinking of the Sheraton or the Hilton.

J.B. gave me a sideways smile and replied, "No, we're staying at the Hotel Chanakya. In Paharganj."

Vivian slowed, then brought the car to a squeaking stop at the side of the road. He turned and looked directly at J.B. "Surely you are joking?" he asked hopefully with a nervous giggle.

"No, really, Paharganj."

"Our expedition is just a bit tight on cash," I chimed in,

sensing Vivian's shock and knowing the kinds of places J.B. might find appealing.

After a long pause, Vivian replied, "It is no problem, really. I will take you wherever you wish to go."

That first ride through the dark streets was a fantastic nightmare, a hallucinatory journey into the abyss.

"This being your first exposure to Asia, I thought it only proper that you should dive right in, body and soul," J.B. announced as the car wound slowly through the narrow darkened streets. "Nonstop, JFK to the slums of Delhi."

"Looks like straight to the ninth circle of Hell," I muttered.

J.B., who had spent years in Asia, kept up a running commentary on the significance of the monstrous ghostly white cows with huge humps and curving horns that materialized from the gloomy side-streets. Dark forms covered the wet sidewalks, huddled onto thin bamboo mats. "Some of those people are probably beggars. They say they mutilate their own children so they'll have ugly scars and twisted legs and get more money."

"This is true, this is true," Vivian nodded. "Such a sad and evil thing in India."

Long after three o'clock we gingerly stepped over sleeping bodies to get into the hotel door. Later we referred to it as Fort Chanakya, in one of the oldest, dirtiest parts of Old Delhi.

A week's living and eating in Paharganj left me with an acute case of Delhi belly, and the heat kept us confined to our room under a slowly revolving ceiling fan. J.B. had time to fill me in on the planning he had been doing for the expedition.

"Last month, August, while I was waiting for you to get here, I went out to Rajasthan. I was staying at the Evergreen Guest House in Jaipur. A real traveler's hangout. People used to say they named it after the swimming pool, a real grungy green. Evergreen." He laughed.

"One day I was in the dining room and I saw this little brown man in the corner, sweating his nuts off. I thought he looked like a Sherpa. So I went up and introduced myself. His name is Pema Tshering Sherpa and he owns a shop in Kathmandu. He got himself into a brawl and had to lay low for a while, so he was hiding out in Jaipur. Nobody's going to look for a Sherpa in the desert in August."

"So he's going to help us?" I asked.

"He's our outfitter. He's a former high-altitude porter and climber. Knows everybody. He owns the International Mountaineering and Equipment House in Kathmandu and was really excited about us trying to traverse the Himalayas."

The journey from Delhi to Kathmandu was one of those Asian epics; an overnight train, a bus, another train, a horse-drawn two-wheeled *tonga*, spending the night (all three hours of it) in a shabby hotel on the border, another nine-hour bus ride with goats, people and plenty of noise. After uncounted switchbacks, at five in the afternoon we crested one last ridge and there before us lay the Kathmandu Valley. The Himalayas, glaciers gleaming yellow in the late afternoon sun, loomed over the lush green valley. I had looked forward for so many years to being in that fabled city, the mythical Kathmandu, exotic starting point for reaching into the Himalayas, the emperor of mountain ranges. In my naivete, I thought then that I had reached Nirvana.

Now Pema took over, organizing the first part of our expedition, actually two treks: the first from the eastern border west to Kathmandu, and the second from the western border east to Kathmandu. For the first part, we would bus to the eastern border of Nepal and then trek back to Kathmandu, stopping at Everest Base Camp to "touch go." We would leave about October 1 and be back in time for Christmas in Kathmandu. For the second part, on January 1, we would bus to the western border and trek back in an easterly direction to Kathmandu. Because of impassable snow in the region just north of Dhaulagiri in January, we would start our journey in the lower areas of the far west. That way we would reach the higher passes in late spring when the deepest snows had melted. Both of the Nepal portions of our expedition would be coordinated by Pema from his shop in Thamel.

The list of equipment and food supplies lengthened rapidly, and we soon realized that our expenses were rising far above our original expectations. We had not counted on buying *all* of the equipment for the trek. We also had to buy a sleeping bag, parka, boots and climbing gear for our *sirdar*. All this would be his to use on the trek and then to keep or sell afterwards. Our porters needed gloves, hats, sunglasses, socks, shoes, pants and specially made pullovers. We weren't going to eat *daal bhaat* every day, so the list of foodstuffs grew and grew. Pema sold us the leftovers from a British military Everest expedition; two boxes of high-altitude rations, which supplemented our local supplies.

After mornings of gathering supplies from shops hidden in narrow alleyways around Asan Tole, in the heart of Old Kathmandu, we had our afternoons free. Prem Tshering Lama, our *sirdar*, J.B. and I often had tea together in the garden of the Kathmandu Guest House where J.B. and I were staying. In leisurely, informal conversations, we learned about the man who was to be our guide and companion for the next eight months. He grew up in Darjeeling, India, and in Ilam in eastern Nepal. He weighed 110 pounds and stood a dignified five foot four under a full head of unusual curly black hair. Eyes so dark they seemed black offset a walnut-tan complexion. A well-educated man, Prem was intelligent, articulate and spoke excellent English as well as Nepali, Tamang and a little Tibetan. And he needed all these skills because a *sirdar* on a trek has a complicated and demanding job; combination travel guide, chief of staff, interpreter and liaison with the local population.

Quiet, with an impassive face, Prem didn't confide much

in anyone. In fact, like me, he was perhaps a bit too intro-spective. He worked in the mountains by choice. With his education and intelligence he could have found more lucra-tive employment, but he felt strongly the lure of the moun-tains. Months later I found that my earliest intuitions had been correct: the Himalayas were a Siren tempting him to deeds beyond those expected of him. As they did me.

On October 5, we left Kathmandu with nine porters, Prem as *sirdar*, a cook and two sahibs—thirteen in all. We took a bus to Ilam on the eastern border with India and started trekking west from there. The lush, corrugated hill country of the east, an area few foreigners ever reached, in-troduced me to life on trek.

After the two weeks fattening up in Kathmandu, I felt relieved to be out on the trail. I had spent so much of the previous year in a frenzy of preparation, work and emotional turmoil that I looked forward to immersing myself in physi-cal activity. It was also a time to rebuild my body and clear my brain. Four weeks in a hospital bed prior to my back surgery had turned my legs to jelly.

Walking alone for hours, I let my mind wander down un-expected paths, allowing myself to explore ideas for which I seemed to have no time back home. The beauty of nature and the daily physical exertion seemed to encourage creative thought, and my perspective seemed far clearer and health-ier.

The two-month trek in eastern Nepal, while not filled with death-defying excitement, nevertheless was more than just interesting. We crossed four hundred and fifty miles of rugged eastern Nepal hill country. By luck we happened upon the Mani Rimdu festival at Thyangboche Monastery in November. We did our duty to Everest Base Camp, our theoretical starting point, and thought about our destination at K2 Base Camp in Pakistan, fifteen hundred miles to the west.

But the most important benefit from the traverse of eastern Nepal was confidence gained in the art of Himalayan trekking. I went in green and came out seasoned, both physically and mentally. I learned the lay of the land, what to expect out of a day's journey. I learned rudimentary Nepali, enough to talk to the porters and communicate my needs, ask directions and receive information. Our routine was laid down as a team, Prem's duties as *sirdar*, the porters' duties along the trail and in camp.

Then, a half day north of Lukla on our way out, we temporarily lost J.B. His service in Vietnam, plus years of football and judo, had left him with legs both literally and figuratively shot. He had walked across eastern Nepal without a misstep. Now, in a moment of careless levity, while racing one of our porters into camp, he stepped on a loose stone and sprained his ankle badly. He limped into Lukla, and that ended his trekking for the time being.

As we said goodbye at the Lukla airport from which he would fly back to Kathmandu, I realized for the first time that I had, indeed, become seasoned. Last August, J.B. had brought me to Asia; I was a neophyte, he had lived for more than eight years in various parts of the Orient. He showed me many things: how to hold my place in a line of two hundred clamoring Indians, the finer points of bartering, and the judicial, lubricating use of *baksheesh*. He told me to watch closely as my letters were franked in the post office, lest my stamps be stolen and my letters remanded to the "never send" pile. He showed me his favorite haunts in Kathmandu, the westernized restaurants, the local gin joints, places like the Momo Cave. As I watched him hobble to the plane, I thought, *See you later, you lucky bastard. In less than an hour, it will be beer, pizza, steak, apple pie . . . and women.*

I stayed behind with Prem and the porters and we walked, or more accurately, we ran eighty miles and 60,000 vertical feet out of the Khumbu region. Hospitably waylaid in the village of Mugli, home of five of our porters, we feasted on chicken and chang. It would have been impolite to refuse anything. How could we spend time in one man's house and not another's? How could we drink only one bottle of *chang* and not three? In a bloated, drunken stupor, Prem and I were held captive for three days as I grew increasingly frustrated in my yearning to return to the delights of the city of Kathmandu.

Finally we got underway, but missed the early bus out of Karantichop because Akaal Bahadur had to pay one last conjugal visit to his wife. The later bus unloaded at Ratna Park well past midnight. Because I had only one rupee left, we jogged through the dark streets towards Thamel. The narrow, dirty alleyways in the old parts of the city were quiet as we headed to the Kathmandu Guest House where I had a rendezvous with J.B.

Thuli, the desk boy, peered sleepily at me from beneath his blankets.

"I'm looking for J.B. Gross. Where is he?"

"Sorry, Sahib. No J.B. here," Thuli murmured.

"I know he's here. Let me see the ledger!"

As Thuli blundered through stacks of paper to find the ledger, I continued fuming and mumbling about life on the Indian subcontinent. "Two and a half months on the trail. The only thing that's kept me sane the last week was the thought of getting here, of having a bed, a hot shower, a beer."

Fortunately, Thuli had worked at the KGH for several years and was well acquainted with foreigners gone berserk. I flipped through the pages—no J.B.

"Sorry, Sahib. But no rooms here."

"What?"

Thuli was also a swift thinker and had a ready answer. "But next door there are rooms."

As I walked up the stairs to my assigned room, coincidentally directly over Pema's trekking shop on the main drag of the district of Thamel, I heard the barred front door close behind me and a lock scrape. I was hungry, filthy, exhausted and had an overwhelming craving for one of those gassy Golden Eagle beers.

When we had left Kathmandu in early October, Thamel had been a sleepy area. Shops were shuttered by eight, and there was no night life. But now I heard raucous music coming from across the street, a song I hadn't heard before. Prying open my window, I peered through the iron bars and listened.

"Do you come from the land down under?" What in the hell was that? (I later learned that this was a new album from the Australian band Men at Work.) Crazed people on the second floor of the shabby white building across the way stomped and yelled and screamed this song like some newfound national anthem.

This cannot be happening, I thought. A mirage with a sound track, the final hallucination before total mental cave-in. Locked in my hotel, and not forty feet away I could hear and see the action I craved—and I couldn't get to it.

In desperation I swallowed ten milligrams of Valium, lay down on the bed fully clothed and turned out the light. Finally, at 4:00 A.M., the music ended.

At 7:00 A.M. I roused myself to look for J.B. Christmas season in Kathmandu filled the hotels, including the KGH, so J.B. had booked a room in another hotel just two doors down. Now, with the company of friends we had made the previous September, the hotel's fourth floor became ours. Although it was mid-December, the weather in the valley was pleasantly warm during the day and we had a large sunny balcony. That first afternoon I found a comfortable chair in the sun and lined up four ice-cold, twenty-two-ounce Golden Eagles. Rags (Californian Randy Smith), the quintessential party man with a serious spiritual bent lurking somewhere just below the surface, punched on the boom box. With the first strains of Roxy Music's "Avalon" drifting off towards Swayambhunath, I poised on the brink of the most outrageous partying of my life.

My goal in preparation for our journey through western Nepal was to pack on as much weight as possible. So I ate four or five meals a day, plus generous slabs of cake and pie. After a few days, I ate alone. No one could bear to watch!

Crazy times reigned in Kathmandu. A series of seemingly unrelated political events had combined with the inherent corruptibility of Third World bureaucracies to turn this Himalayan backwater into a wide open country. For a few brief months, the green light blinked on for smugglers of all descriptions. Electronics, gold, heroin, money—with the apparent complicity of the government—flowed into and out of the country. U.S. dollars by the millions, bought on the black market from tourists, went to Hong Kong, then were converted into gold and smuggled back into Nepal or India for a tidy profit. Heroin from the Golden Triangle of Burma, Laos and Thailand came overland across the Tibetan Plateau and down into Nepal. From there it was smuggled out to corners of the drug-craving West, including the U.S. Lots of money, lots of risk. In all my naivete, months passed before I realized that many of my good friends survived by muling contraband through Tribhuvan International Airport.

For those so inclined, drugs were everywhere. The pharmacies conveniently supplied Valium, Quaaludes and little white Dexedrines at five or ten rupees for twenty-five tabs. Hashish was ubiquitous. The Pheasant Lodge next door sported a thirty-foot marijuana tree in its central courtyard. Although not as flagrantly advertised, heroin was available and addicts swarmed into Kathmandu. Though they played it close to the vest, they apparently played it very seriously. I woke one morning to the news that John, a regular at our fourth-floor parties, had O.D.'ed on heroin and almost died the night before.

"You mean John, the quiet accountant from Oklahoma?" Only then did it dawn on me how many of my acquaintances had intimate knowledge of the stuff.

Kathmandu was an odd sort of place, at the end of the line, not really on the way to or from anywhere. Within the sanctuary of this idyllic valley one could wear any mask, play any role. Thus it attracted an eccentric amalgam of would-bes and has-beens, outcasts, castoffs, con artists, mercenaries and dope smugglers, in addition to the standard trekkers, climbers and pajama-wearing nirvana seekers. Within the cheap hotels in Thamel, they all swam in the same social soup.

The wild party I had heard my first night back had been at a new bar, the Up and Down, which I took to calling the Bar at the End of the Universe. In addition, the Marine Bar, open only on Friday nights, K.C.'s Bambooze Bar and Restaurant and the Copper Floor, a particularly sleazy establishment, were favorite hangouts for foreigners, and we frequented them all. These places were not in any way Nepal, but rather an intrusion of the worst degenerate customs of the western world, endured and condoned because of the insatiable lust for the tourist dollar. The mixing of East and West in the bars, with the ignorance of accepted norms of social behavior on one side and intolerance on the other, occasionally precipitated serious altercations.

Barroom brawls were commonplace. One night just before Christmas, it turned bloodier than even the bloody norm. The Up and Down's proprietor, a slight, bearded man who owned an immaculate two-tone 1956 Chevrolet, had hired a crew of bouncers to maintain order and to turn away most of the Nepalese who tried to get in. By a system indecipherable to me, the bouncers knew exactly which of the locals were permitted. This screening was for the safety of all, as the majority of fights could be traced to friction between well-meaning but wasted Nepalese and unenlightened foreigners.

One of the bouncers was Sita Ram, a twenty-year-old just five foot four but solidly built. With a short stubble covering his recently shaven head, he looked like a misdirected remnant of Genghis Khan's Mongol hordes, fearsome-looking but unfailingly polite. I liked him and we had started to meet several times a week in the afternoon. I taught him English; he helped me with my Nepali.

On this particular night Sita Ram had tangled with a Manangi, refusing to let him into the bar. The Manangis came from the small isolated village of Manang, high in the Himalayas behind Annapurna. Tagged with the reputation as an unfriendly, aggressive people, they were now, rumor had it, deeply involved in the heroin trade. Rolling in money but new to the sophisticated social whirl of Kathmandu, they had no idea how to conduct themselves. The Manangi that Sita Ram turned away had recently indulged in the latest fad, a Kawasaki motorcycle. When refused admission to the Up and Down, he cracked Sita Ram on the head with his visored helmet, splitting open a long, deep cut in the bouncer's scalp.

Arriving moments later, I found Sita Ram covered with blood. The owner, whom I knew quite well, asked if I would help. I ran upstairs and grabbed a guy we called "Life," a Swedish doctor, bizarrely attired in a bow tie, white ruffled shirt and black dinner jacket. Throwing Sita Ram in the back of the owner's Chevrolet, we screamed through the streets, our patient bloodying the floor like a drain gutter in a slaughterhouse. We stopped at Life's house, gathered up sutures and sped on to Bir Hospital.

The emergency room was a scene from a Hieronymus Bosch painting. In the open dingy green room with a dirty floor, cots and gurneys held people in silent agonies. We asked the hospital staff for needles and they pointed to an old stainless steel tray of translucent bluish liquid. Some needles rattled at the bottom, thrown there when someone had finished with the previous job. We laid Sita Ram on his stomach on a table and, with no anesthetic, started sewing him up with Life's sutures. We wouldn't let anyone else touch him, although it was doubtful that they would have known what to do anyway. Life and I took turns sewing up his head; it was hard work forcing the needle through the skin on his scalp. There weren't any clamps and we pulled the needle through with our hands. The atmosphere seethed with infectious bacteria, and when I asked for antiseptic, I was handed a can of white powder which we sprinkled liberally on Sita Ram's head.

Throughout the whole ordeal Sita Ram never made a sound. Alternately, depending on who was stitching, one of us held his hand, and with every stitch he would nearly crush the hand holding his. After forty-odd stitches, I stepped back to admire our handiwork. Sita Ram looked pretty good, in a Frankenstein monster sort of way, and he thanked us for sewing him up. We took him back to the Up and Down and he returned to his station by the door.

To show his thanks, the owner led me upstairs, cleared a stool and told the bartender to start pouring—on the house. Three quick shots of Johnnie Walker Red brought me to an appropriate frame of mind to enjoy the rest of the evening. I ordered a beer chaser and turned to peruse the crowd.

The Aussie kayakers who had led the fracas the night I arrived were already stoked, pounding beers and making time with some fine-looking Norwegian women, new arrivals in town. On the dance floor a growing crowd of sweating bodies moved to the throbbing beat of Bob Marley. Just as the scotch began to kick in, I spotted Rags, J.B. and the rest of the group just across the room. Which reminded me that Rags, he of the golden tongue, had arranged a date for me that night. I signaled the bartender and he slid me a final peg, this time of Kukri rum. Not the most appealing stuff, but I downed it anyway. Grabbing my beer, I waded through the mass of people. Rags met me in the middle of the dance floor with two nurses from New Zealand on holiday. One of them slid her arm around me and I began to see that the evening, for all of the earlier blood and gore, was shaping up nicely. A pipe appeared out of the crowd. I took a long drag and passed it on. The music switched to Men at Work, the Aussies hit the dance floor and the energy level popped up a couple more notches. The music pounded, the crowd was in a frenzy. I was flying. And it was only a quarter to nine.

Several hours and many beers later I turned at the sound of another argument. A drunk Manangi, reeling around the floor, bumped into a girl dancing with an SAS soldier (British Special Forces in Nepal to train the crack Nepalese troops). The SAS man whacked the Manangi just once, and that did it. Confederates from both sides jumped in. Prudently we backed into a corner and watched. Bottles smashed through the mirrored shelves behind the bar; barstools, fists and bodies flew everywhere. And in minutes the brawl grew from the Nepalese fighting the British to an authentic riot in the streets outside between rival Nepalese factions. A law in Nepal says that in self-defense, you can shoot an attacker below the waist. One of the Nepalese turned to me.

"Parker, you're a foreigner, you can get out of here. There's a Winchester rifle in my car. Please go and bring it back for me."

I declined as politely as I could. Unfortunately his lackey got it for him. Someone called the police, but it seemed like hours before they arrived. Meanwhile, we kept drinking beer. We had friends in all factions. And, despite our condition, we still had enough sense to stay away from flying fists and bottles. When the police arrived, they cleared everybody from the street in front of the bar, and we moved the party to the fourth floor of our hotel. Just another night in Kathmandu.

The three Thakuri porters we had hired arrived at our guesthouse in Surkhet promptly at six on the morning of February 14. They were three of the filthiest human beings on earth. Their tattered homespun clothes had accumulated sweat and oils from continuous wear and were encrusted with the dirt of daily living. In contrast, Akaal Bahadur and Jeet Bahadur stood out markedly because of their cleanliness.

Golden rays of sunshine filtered through the sparkling morning mist as we followed a rutted dirt track to the edge of town. At six-thirty, dawn had just arrived, fresh, sweet, the start of a new journey. All of our porters, especially Akaal Bahadur and Jeet Bahadur, carried excessively heavy loads. Lingering behind to take some photos, I watched our small band spread out two hundred yards ahead of me, mist swirling at our feet, green hills surrounding us.

Our crossing of eastern Nepal had been in many ways just a rehearsal for the journey confronting us now. We had planned a venture into the unknown, a trip to legendary places. In hushed whispers in the back of Pema's Kathmandu shop, we had thrashed through several difficult decisions about our passage through western Nepal. While the trails in the east had been mapped and traveled by our companions, this journey to the west would lead us into unfamiliar territory. Where would we find food, porters? Would the trails be passable? We had concluded that our only hope of making it in, around, through and, if necessary, over the Himalayas and back to Kathmandu was to go as fast and as light as possible.

Pema had insisted we leave ropes, climbing gear and crampons behind. We argued with him and won only on the issue of ice axes. I wondered, as I watched our porters carrying our meager supplies down the trail in front of me, what this might mean in the weeks ahead. Would we have need of our ropes, our crampons? What use would we make of our ice axes? Food weighed us down now, but would we be able to resupply?

Once the sun had burned away the mist, the day turned clear and hot. The porters' loads slowed our steady ascent, but to my surprise I found my climb really no chore at all. Five months ago, during our first days trekking in eastern

Nepal, I had been so out of shape that just about any small hill had filled me with consternation. Glad to be back on the trail, putting one foot in front of the other, I found myself deep in thought, pondering innumerable ideas, ending the mental stagnation that had become habit in Kathmandu. The hedonism of Kathmandu had been necessary after two and a half months on the trail, but I was ready once again for some physical work as well as some cerebral activity, which for me go hand in hand.

The second day out of Surkhet, we ascended the first major ridge and dropped back down to camp for the night. The porters still moved slowly, though we knew their loads would lighten as we continued to eat our food supplies. We were also slowed by snow and ice along the trail. As we headed north, we would move further into spring, but we also would go higher into the Himalayas.

I could feel the history of the trail we followed, one of the oldest trading routes in Nepal. Before the Chinese takeover of Tibet, the Tibetans and Nepalese traded actively. Each year, the Tibetans collected rock salt from lake beds in central Tibet and made the long journey down through Mugu and Jumla. They traded with the Nepalese for grain and other food supplies. This trading relationship, which over hundreds of years linked individual families of Tibetans and Nepalese, was drastically curtailed by the Communist Chinese. The trade had not stopped altogether—the Chinese had not been willing or able to police the high border passes —but it had diminished greatly.

Hindus of various castes and tribal groups inhabited the region we passed through now. The Nepalese easily identified one another as belonging to a certain group by dress, language and facial features. Further north, in the high mountains, the people were Buddhists, mostly of Tibetan stock. The Tibetans had moved gradually south into Nepal over the last two hundred years. In some areas where the valleys were easy to reach, lowland people moved north and adopted Tibetan Buddhism, even though they were ethnically Nepalese. This trail was used by all of these people, Tibetans and Nepalese, Hindus and Buddhists.

That night, the full moon rose white and brilliant. With us far from any artificial light, it shone brighter than I had ever seen. I took my heavy, bound journal, the one embossed on the front with *Everest K2 Himalayan Expedition* and my name in gold letters, and recorded the day's events by the glowing light.

I recalled now that I had spoken to Clara for the first time by the light of the full moon. I first saw her in late December. One sunny afternoon as I lazed on the fourth floor balcony, I saw two women come up the stairwell.

The first held my glance. Only slightly shorter than I, she had shoulder-length, raven black hair and shining black eyes. Her attire seemed inappropriate for her Nepalese features, a plaid pleated skirt, white knee socks and red wool sweater. She faced me briefly, then started up the open stairs to the roof with her friend.

I called out to them, "Hello."

She turned to me and smiled, deep dimples in her cheeks, warmth in her wide-set eyes. "Hello," she answered. Then they continued up.

I watched her disappear behind the low wall along the roof's edge. Something in that first look drew me towards her.

One evening a few days later, I stood on the balcony as the huge yellow orb of the moon rose out of the Himalayas far to the northeast around Everest. Just at that moment, Clara and her friend Sera came up the stairs.

"Come and look at this." I pointed to the moon. "Isn't it beautiful?"

Clara came and stood next to me, leaning out to see the moon. I could feel her body's warmth near me. I looked at her thick black hair caught in a clip at the nape of her neck and watched the expressions flit across her clear, fresh face, the color of warm honey.

Though it had only been two months before, now I couldn't remember the rest of the conversation. Small talk baffles me and this conversation had been trite, inane, not overly coherent, words spoken only to make contact.

The thoughts of Clara broke my concentration. And so reluctantly I left the moon and my journal and crawled into my sleeping bag.

CHAPTER THREE

▲

THE MOON PLAYED FUNNY TRICKS ON ME THAT NIGHT. I DREAMT I was a professional baseball player. That image segued into watching the rock group The Who play in the basement of K.C.'s Bambooze Bar and Restaurant, which has no basement. I gave no thought to the Jungian significance of descending into basements, but I did have to get up three times in the night to heed the call of nature. Each time the moon stared benevolently down on me, a cold, white, silent blessing on our journey.

Soon after breaking camp, J.B. and I moved out ahead of the porters along the broad, gently descending trail. The sun cleared a ridgeline, and with its first warming rays I stopped to strip off my gray bunting jacket and wool hat. Even this early in the day, J.B. wore only his green military-issue T-shirt, already sweatstained from his broad shoulders to the small of his back. Stopping to wait while I packed my gear, he wiped his brow with a small blue towel tied to one pack strap. A habit he picked up in the jungles of Vietnam, he had told me, when he was with the Marine Corps, First Force Reconnaissance. Secret, sensitive missions, with a life expectancy measured in weeks. J.B. had endured for months and was wounded twice, the second time nearly costing him his life.

An hour later, we stopped at a trickling stream and washed the sweat from our faces before resting in the shade of a teahouse. A barefoot girl in a tattered red smock offered us soothing glasses of cool *dahi* (yogurt). J.B. sat on a flat rock along the trail's edge. I found a low wicker stool on the porch of the hut.

From around a bend in the trail, a uniformed man and a woman on horseback approached us. Two policemen, burdened with weighty loads, followed hurriedly on foot. This was the first time I had seen anyone on a horse, which, along with the silvery bars atop the epaulets on the man's shoulders, denoted a high-ranking officer. I watched as he reined in a few feet from J.B.

He eyed J.B. intently for a few seconds before asking, in perfect English, "Where are you going?"

"To Jumla," J.B. replied offhandedly.

"And what is your purpose?"

"Trekking and to see the views."

Concentrating on the foreigner in front of him, the officer hadn't spotted me yet, obscured as I was by the low eaves of the porch. Certain that this police officer would detain us if he learned we traveled without the appropriate permits, I formulated a plan. If he asked to see J.B.'s trekking permit, I would walk through the door into the teahouse, and then out through the kitchen in the back. I knew J.B. would say nothing.

For fifteen seconds, the man stared down at J.B., then with a flick of his gleaming black riding boots, he nudged his horse back onto the trail. His wife followed and the junior officers trotted along behind them. For me, it had been an unsettling meeting; J.B., though, just shrugged it off.

At ten-thirty, we stopped at a group of bamboo and thatch huts built on stilts for our first meal of the day. While trekking we had formed the habit of eating as the Nepalese do, twice a day. We ate first in the late morning, after we had walked for two to four hours. In the evening, we ate our second meal, after the day's work.

Prem, both *sirdar* and cook, built a small fire to begin cooking as I unfolded my map of western Nepal. "Prem," I asked, "how many police checkposts do you think lie between here and Jumla?" Shopkeepers in Surkhet had said none, but J.B. and I hesitated to believe them.

Prem turned to our newly hired Thakuri porters and spoke quickly.

"They say three, perhaps four."

Four too many, I thought. J.B.'s encounter with the policeman, the hard stare and ominous tone of voice, had shaken me. I had not expected to be concerned about the police until we began trekking north of Jumla, into the Mugu region. Because we had no idea how we would cross western Nepal, when we applied for our permits in Kathmandu we had the only route available—through Beni, Baglung, Dhorpatan and Jarjakot—written on them. However, this route passed through hill country and our intent was to traverse further north, through the Himalayas themselves. Now we were trekking 250 miles west of where we were supposed to be and traveling without proper paperwork on this trail from Surkhet to Jumla.

After our meal, Prem spoke. "If we come to a checkpost, I think it will be best for you to split from us. You and J.B. stay together, the porters and I will go separately, one at a time."

I thought about Prem's words, trying to decipher his meaning. After five months together, I had become attuned to the nuance of his speech. "I think it best for you" meant Prem was certain of the course to take, but unwilling to explain further. Perhaps, in the Asian way, he would lose face, or he had learned something he thought it better we not know. Language and cultural barriers created many complexities. The phrase was one Prem used rarely, and I didn't ask for an explanation.

I recalled a conversation we had in Surkhet, in which Prem had suggested that the police might deal harshly with him and the porters for leading foreigners into restricted areas. Plainly he was afraid of getting caught with us, and I couldn't blame him for not wanting to find himself staring at the four walls of a Nepalese jail. *But what about us? What would J.B. and I do about not having the proper permits?* Before I could ask, J.B. came up with a plan.

"Parker, remember the police in Pokhara telling us about the banditry problems due to the Tibetan refugees in the area around Dhorpatan? We can just say that to avoid all that mess, we decided to hop on a bus and start from Surkhet. Maybe throw in a little of the 'lost and confused foreigners' routine."

"The best plan is to avoid the police checkposts altogether," I answered. "Prem, can we find out from the Thakuris where those checkposts are?"

"I will ask them, Parker Sahib, but I am not sure we should believe what they say. They do not lie to us, but they are very simple men. Sometimes they make up things just to please us."

The Thakuri porters still huddled on their haunches around the embers of their fire, cooking more of their flatbread rotis to be squirreled away for future meals. Prem squatted and talked casually with them.

He returned to our fire. "It is certain that one checkpost can be found in Dailekh, two or three days ahead. A big one, they say, with a military garrison. After that, they cannot tell me. They say the checkposts sometimes move from village to village."

"Then let's find a way around Dailekh," I replied. "I certainly don't want to walk right into the middle of an entire garrison."

With a belly full of rice, I reclined on my pack and watched J.B. leave. Thirty yards down the trail, three barefooted girls tumbled from a hut, intent on a secret game among themselves. The urchins were about six years old. They surrounded J.B. almost before he spotted them.

"*Namaste! Namaste!* What time? What time? Give me your pen!" one screeched at him, practicing her English and hoping for that most precious commodity, a pen to take to school.

I smiled at their innocent, unfettered gaiety. Not taught to be afraid of strangers, as yet untouched by the harsh existence that awaited them, they played happily, thinking of nothing but their current game.

J.B. stopped, leaned on his walking stick and namasted them back, speaking a few words of Nepali. Startled, their chattering stopped, and their large eyes stared from dirty faces at this impossibly huge human being. J.B. resumed his pace and left them huddled together, three little girls on a dusty trail, wondering who this light-haired giant could be. A ghost? A yeti? A mythical personage from out of the past?

I noticed that J.B. favored his left ankle, the one he had injured in the Khumbu and then reinjured in a pothole in Kathmandu. Fearing he would hold us back, he left before the rest of us in the morning, and again now, after our lunch stop. But our porters, laden with a two-week food supply, dictated our pace, and I thought it unnecessary for him to go ahead. Lingering with the slowest porter would have been kinder on his mending ankle. But I said nothing, deciding that he could take care of himself. Only later did I realize that J.B.'s absence at crucial decision-making times would become a problem.

I left last, after lazing in the midday sun. Soon, though, I caught and passed Prem and the porters. I pushed myself recklessly downward, straining to regain the timing necessary to rapidly negotiate the steep rocky trails. Six weeks of inactivity had softened my body, and now leaden thighs and burning feet screamed their protest. In preparation for this crossing of western Nepal, I had purchased a used green Tibetan pack. With my slight build, dark hair and brown eyes, I hoped to pass unnoticed as a foreigner. Now the pack, with its primitive suspension system, bounced awkwardly and scraped at my back.

As I sat resting on an exposed promontory, I saw J.B. 1,500 feet below approaching the village of Dungibara, fifty or more houses situated on a flat green expanse at the confluence of two rivers. Fearing he might go right through the village and run into a checkpost, I cut my rest short and hurried after him.

A hundred yards before the village, I found J.B. resting atop a boulder set in a rice paddy. He, too, had worried about the village and pulled off to wait.

Fifteen minutes later, several policemen materialized above us. They stared for half a minute, then slowly continued into the village. One, a black turbaned adolescent in oversized olive trousers, stopped several times to watch us before disappearing between the houses. J.B. pulled out his binoculars and scanned the village, hoping to spot them emerging from the other side. No one appeared.

Three-quarters of an hour later, Prem showed up with the porters, the Thakuris sheepishly admitting they had forgotten about the *chaulki* (checkpost) in the village center. A path led off to the left, skirting the village. Prem proposed we take this path, camping where the stream spilled into the Katia Khola river a quarter of a mile beyond the settlement.

We started along this trail, but just abreast of the village a policeman appeared on a rooftop, waving and yelling in our direction. He left no doubt that he wanted us to go into the village and visit his checkpost. Prem muttered a few obscenities and we conferred hurriedly to get our stories straight.

As we made our way along the narrow paths, balanced atop paddy dikes, Prem called back over his shoulder. "Do not be concerned, they can do nothing to us."

"Nothing but throw our butts in jail," I muttered to no one in particular, feeling none of Prem's confidence.

We entered the courtyard of the *chaulki* smiling, hands

pressed together. *Namaskar!* Eight officers in military green, wearing felt berets and with black wooden batons cradled in folded arms, stared sternly at us from the porch. In the middle of the slate courtyard, a short mustached man sat at a small table, scribbling in a notebook. The pungent smell of high-quality tobacco from his black pipe filled the air. He motioned me towards a small stool near the table. J.B. sat on the porch. Prem conversed with two officers, answering their questions. I understood just enough to hear him say he had met us on the trail only this morning.

"Passports," snapped an assistant.

J.B. handed me his and I handed both to the officer. He took them but, continuing his mad scribbling, handed them on to an assistant. The younger officer opened a large ledger and began to transcribe information. Our many entry and exit stamps perplexed him and he flipped back and forth, pulling out the extra accordion pages we both had in our passports. I helped him find the information for each column in his log: Name, Passport Number, Date of Visa, Purpose of Journey, Trekking Permit Number.

Damn, I thought, sweat trickling down between my shoulder blades. *They've got us now!*

But he didn't notice our trekking permits and continued his aimless flipping. I saw a glimmer of hope. Maybe he had never seen a trekking permit. Quickly I diverted him to the visa numbers, and he dutifully recorded them in the Trekking Permit column.

After all the paperwork was complete, the mustached man looked up from his writing and spoke softly in heavily accented English. "Where are you going?"

"To Jumla," I answered.

"And what is the purpose of your journey?"

"To view the scenery."

"Where will you go after Jumla?"

"Back to Kathmandu through Dhorpatan," I replied evenly.

His face softened. "I grew up in Kathmandu. I have spent time in Hong Kong. Now I have been here in Dungibara since three years. So boring here. I wish I could go with you! Okay, you can go after signing the book." He pointed to the ledger. We signed it, hoisted our packs and bid them farewell. We had made it through the first checkpost!

We set camp just beyond a large wooden bridge spanning the Katia Khola. After a wash in the river and a meal of *daal bhaat*, we were joined by Prem in our tent.

Our relief at bluffing our way through the checkpost was promptly shattered by Prem's first words. "The police have sent a runner to Dailekh, three days to the north. They will ask to see your trekking permits when you get there."

"How do you know?" I asked.

"At the checkpost they did not know what to do with you. First they thought they would keep you there while they sent word to Dailekh. I told them to wait and let the police in Dailekh find you, you would walk there anyway. But they talked and then the head officer ordered one man to leave for Dailekh to warn them of you. So now I think we must go through Dailekh."

That night I lay awake for a long time, staring at the tent walls. Late-night doubts took over, and for the first time I thought of what lay ahead, what might happen to us if we were taken by the police. Traveling quasi-legally through these areas was one thing; playing hide-and-seek with a military police force was another. We could avoid Dailekh, try to bypass the checkpost, try to outrun the police. But with our heavy loads we would lose for sure. The other option, to go brazenly to the checkpost, present ourselves with bravado and confidence, also worried me. What if they didn't buy our story? What if they threw us in jail?

At dawn three days later, gunmetal gray storm clouds scudded low across the sky, threatening rain below, still more snow above. A morning's climb brought us to within a half mile of Dailekh, its whitewashed buildings straddling the ridgeline.

We opted for the role of innocent, disoriented trekkers. The same passport game we played in Dungibara would be our strategy. And if the situation turned against us, we could always try spreading *baksheesh* around.

The wind rose as we approached the first clusters of houses on the outskirts of town. Dust devils swirled and the first large drops of rain spattered on the cobbled streets. Hurriedly, we jogged with bodies bent against the rising winds. We passed an ancient stone fortress, the remnant of an earlier era fifty or more generations past, when Nepal lay fragmented into small kingdoms, each struggling to defend itself against the others and against periodic waves of marauding invaders. Now the weathered stonework lay abandoned and covered in vine, a relic slowly returning to the soil.

In the central square, the police post appeared on our right. Two uniformed men watched us. We walked to the far side of the square and stopped next to a huge banyan tree. Just then, with a flash and a thundering boom, the skies let loose a torrential downpour. Searching for shelter, we retreated two hundred yards through nearly horizontal sheets of rain to a small lodge.

Within fifteen minutes the storm had passed. Prem told the porters to go ahead, one by one. J.B. and I followed five minutes behind; Prem brought up the rear.

As we walked, J.B. suggested a different plan. "Look, they know we're here, and they haven't paid us much attention so far. Maybe we can just walk by."

As we entered the square, we could see that the porters had passed through unchecked. I glanced across to the checkpost forty yards away. Policemen inside talked with one another, but no one emerged.

I was still calculating our chances of being chased down and thrown into some grimy jail cell when J.B. queried again, more insistently. "C'mon, Park, what do you think? Should we give it a try?"

"No balls, no glory," I replied with a shrug. "Let's go for it. Just keep looking straight ahead."

With that, we casually strolled side by side past the checkpost to the far end of the square, between two houses and out of sight. We looked back. No one followed. Prem caught up with us a few minutes later near the edge of town; he had not been stopped either. Our prospects looked good. We found the porters waiting just beyond the last buildings.

"Why don't we camp near here?" suggested J.B. "That'll give the police a chance to check on us if they really want to."

Although we had decided not to try to outrun the authorities, nonetheless I felt that we should at least keep moving, if not actually running. But instead of voicing my opinion, I merely shrugged. There wasn't a suitable camping place, anyway.

So with a decision made by default, we all kept moving and left J.B. standing alone. We climbed to an exposed ridge, then stopped for a rest. J.B. caught up with us and once again suggested we camp, this time in the lee of a large wall surrounding a water works. Despite the wall, the site was exposed, and the winds still whipped around close to thirty miles an hour. Once again I said nothing, but looked at Prem. I sensed he didn't like J.B.'s choice of a site either, although he was reluctant to contradict the sahib who paid his wages.

Prem hesitated, kicked a few stones around, then looked up and down the trail. He beckoned to Akaal Bahadur and whispered a few words in his ear. Akaal Bahadur dropped his load and went on ahead—to check for a better campsite, I assumed. He returned in a few minutes and conferred with Prem. The porters then hoisted their loads and went down the trail. The decision had obviously been made to go on a little further.

J.B.'s mood turned dark. "Hell, if we go on a little further, we might as well walk the whole damn afternoon!" He grabbed his pack with an angry jerk, and stormed off.

Prem and I caught up with him an hour later as he sat on a stone wall in the small village of Khursanbari. Prem poked his nose into one of the houses and, wishing to give J.B. a wide berth, suggested to me that we camp in a nearby field for the night. As we cleared a space for the tents, a middle-aged man in jodhpurs and topee talked to Prem, urging him not to camp outside in the fields.

Prem translated his grisly tales of recent robberies and murders, the last incident occurring only the night before.

"A man who lives just there," Prem pointed to a thatched-roof house not two hundred yards away, "asked a Gurkha soldier to stay in his house for the night. After going to bed, the Ghurka had a bad feeling. So he got up from his bed and went out of the house. Then, a little while later, the man's son came home from drinking and slept in the same bed. Later, the man, his father, went into the room to cut and kill the Gurkha, but killed his own son instead. He says this happened just last night. Parker Sahib, I think we should do as this man says, stay inside tonight."

I agreed. Throughout our conversation J.B. sat on the wall thirty yards away. When I told him of our change of plans, he exploded.

"Who's making the decisions around here anyway? Prem's job is to take orders, not give them."

I struggled to maintain an outward calm, but my quavering voice betrayed me. "I didn't like the campsite you chose this afternoon, either. It was too close to town, it was exposed."

"Then why didn't you say so? You could have said something earlier instead of making it look like our *sirdar* was calling all the shots."

Anger simmered on both sides, and we went to bed with the issue unresolved.

* * *

We had had this sort of argument before. While J.B. and I were good friends, we were not perfectly matched to take this trip together. We came from different backgrounds and had differing views on decision-making.

More than once, J.B. complained that I was not forceful enough in expressing my opinions. In a sense he was right, but I had my reasons. For the last five years, I had spent my time first in graduate school, then in a high-powered biomedical research lab. Day after day, long hours, stress, conflict. The last six months had emptied me completely. Back surgery, relationships left hanging, unfinished scientific manuscripts, leaving my job, reducing my worldly possessions to a backpack and a duffel, family fears of never returning home—all had sapped my mental energies. I embraced the idea of finding myself on the trail with nothing more to do for the next year but walk. I sought peace, not conflict.

I had imagined that one could take a motley group of six to thirteen people of two nationalities and put them on the trail for two months without trouble. I was wrong. There had been conflict. And J.B. disagreed with me on how to handle it. His approach, born of the Marine Corps, was one of active leadership, of being on top of and involved with each decision, a firm hand on everything. Although I had exercised my share of leadership in the past and could adopt this style when necessary, I found a laissez-faire approach more effective with Prem and the porters.

Prem, as *sirdar*, had charge of the details of everyday life: cooking, setting and breaking camp, keeping the porters moving, purchasing food. Because of the language barrier and his authority over the porters, I found it best to let him do his work. Only if I disagreed with or questioned a decision would I intervene.

I was never quite sure whose style was more effective, J.B.'s or mine. But clearly our attitudes differed and this difference caused friction and then outright arguments during months on the trail.

Two days later, we pushed above 9,000 feet, and here, on a broad trail through intermittent rhododendron and conifer forest, we found snow. Towards late afternoon, Prem went ahead in his daily task of selecting our campsite for the evening and I walked on alone.

The trail became steeper as it followed the ridge crest, and having lent my ice axe to Jeet Bahadur, I negotiated the slippery descents cautiously, sidestepping on precarious footholds. On one stretch I found myself reduced to backing down on all fours. I topped a knoll and my altimeter recorded 9,200 feet, our highest altitude thus far. Another slippery descent brought me to a broad saddle that dropped off on either side into steep, tortuous ravines. Far below and to the west, clouds clung to a broad valley floor. Nearer, a succession of deeply forested side canyons dominated the landscape.

I stopped briefly and fished out my Nikon to take some photographs. As I removed my pack, I heard a brief muffled yell from somewhere back up the trail. I listened but heard nothing more, and wondered if I might have imagined the sound. I took a number of photos, then hoisted my pack and continued on down the trail.

Prem waited for me at a squalid farmhouse a short ways ahead. A small boy, incongruously dressed in a red wool jacket and matching red and white striped hat, played with a decaying corn cob. His sister, barefoot and wearing a homespun smock, leaned against the doorway clutching an empty metal bowl. From between her legs a wizened mongrel growled and showed his teeth.

A half hour later, J.B. hobbled into view on the trail above us. Prem and I hurried to help him the last few yards. We sat him down on a low wall.

"I fell on one of those steep places. Think I whacked it a good one this time." J.B. grimaced as he spoke.

"I heard you yell. Here, let me get your boot off." Gingerly I pried the heavy boot from his foot, then cut through two layers of socks. The ankle seemed okay, but his Achilles tendon was pulled bowstring tight with pain centered on two spots. "You might have partially torn your Achilles, J.B. Not the best news."

"Jesus, it's starting to really hurt. Where are those Demerols?"

I gave him two fifty-milligram tablets, then wrapped his foot and ankle in a compression bandage. By the time the Demerol had taken effect, we had the tents set up. Carefully, four of us helped him into our tent.

Just at dusk, it began to snow, and Prem brought mugs of tea into our tent.

"What do you think we should do, J.B.?"

"We don't have a whole lot of options, do we?"

"No, I don't guess we do." I lit a candle and handed Prem my map. Unfolding it, we traced our route to Jumla. "How long do you think it will take us, Prem?"

He marked out distances and thought. "I cannot tell, Parker Sahib. Maybe five days if we all are in good health. Now, I think seven or eight if J.B. Sahib can walk."

"That puts us equal distance to Surkhet or Jumla. But Marbu Lekh is between us and Jumla. With this weather moving in, getting over that mountain could be quite a chore." I paused, then suggested the obvious. "It would be easier to retrace our way back to Surkhet. From there you can bus to Nepalganj, then fly back to Kathmandu."

J.B., who had been lying flat, now struggled unsteadily onto one elbow. With his fur hat pulled down over his head, and with his sun-grayed beard, he looked and smelled every bit like a burly eighteenth-century trapper. "There is no way I am going to make the rest of you backtrack to Surkhet. That would waste two weeks and jeopardize this entire segment of the expedition. I don't care if I have to crawl, we're going to Jumla. Supposedly planes fly in there several times a week carrying rice. I can hitch a ride on one of the rice charters."

"It is a long way, J.B. Sahib. We must cross Marbu Lekh the next two days with deep snow, then go 7,000 feet down to the Tila Khola." Prem pointed out the route to J.B. "Then three more days along the river to Jumla."

J.B. remained unswayed. "You said yourself that it's about the same distance, north or south. We're going to Jumla. Period. No back talk from either of you."

Prem and I remained silent. We had nothing to say. I felt grateful to J.B. for his willingness to continue north instead of returning south. Backtracking always depressed me, and I wasn't sure I would have the drive, once reaching Surkhet, to turn around and cover the same ground a third time.

Finally Prem set forth the plan. "If you cannot walk in the morning, J.B. Sahib, we *must* go south. We will need many porters, maybe thirty or more, to help carry you. And we will find no one on Marbu Lekh."

"Then I will walk tomorrow," replied J.B. with finality as he fell back onto his sleeping bag. I prayed he was right.

So J.B. would head back to Kathmandu. He would have up to four months to heal before we started through the Himalaya of northern India. But where did that leave me now?

Alone.

We had meant this section between Surkhet and Jumla in western Nepal as a warmup, to hone our bodies and our team for the far more treacherous crossing of the regions to the north and east of Jumla. Through Mugu and Dolpo, one of the most remote inhabited regions on the planet. Surprisingly, I was more excited than frightened. I had never thought of doing it alone.

Snow and high winds rocked our tent during the night. For more than an hour during the darkest period I lay awake, unable to sleep as the curved tent poles bent towards the ground. Worried that our tent might fail, I lay in my sleeping bag fully clothed.

When Akaal Bahadur brought us "bed tea" to start the day, my thoughts immediately turned to J.B. Could he walk? The drugs had left him groggy, and it was after eight o'clock when he finally unzipped the tent door and tested his leg. I helped him upright, then handed him his walking stick. Cautiously, he placed some weight on his left foot and took a tentative step, then another. He could walk. We would head north towards Jumla.

The snowstorm had turned to rain in the night and cleared the trail ahead. J.B. moved steadily with surprisingly little pain until we hit snow once more just before noon. We stopped for a quick meal, then continued. Because few braved this route in the middle of winter, we laboriously cut our own trail through two feet of wet snow. At one-thirty, on a narrow ledge engulfed in clouds, J.B. pulled up.

"This is about as far as I can go today, Park. It's tightening up fast."

I called ahead to Prem and suggested we find a place to camp. He disappeared into the windblown whiteness as I dropped off the ridgeline to search for a suitable flat spot. Twenty minutes later, I found Prem waiting.

"No place to camp above," he said. "The trail goes up and down steeply."

"The slopes below seem to drop off for quite a way. I couldn't find a flat place either," I replied.

J.B. interjected. "I can go on a bit. Let's keep moving up, so we'll have less to climb in the morning."

The trail became steeper and the snow deeper. I remembered my gaiters, the one extra item I had allowed myself, and stopped to put them on. Removing my pack, I rummaged deeply into it, extracting the brand-new, bright green gaiters. Just then, I looked up and saw one of our Thakuri porters laden under his thirty-kilo load. Clad in thin pants and torn coat, summer socks and shoes woven from old string, he sank with each step almost to his waist. Only the day before, I had learned that even before leaving Surkhet the porters had given the Chinese sneakers we had bought for them to their families. As I watched our porter struggle through the snow, my hands tightened around the gaiters. Ashamed, I hastily shoved them deep into my pack and quickly moved on through the snow.

Prem and I alternated in the lead, laboriously kicking steps in the steeper sections for the others to follow. Although J.B. said nothing, he leaned heavily on his walking stick and grunted with each step. His pace slowed and I worried that we might be forced to bivouac out in the open. At one near vertical descent, I turned to J.B. and asked him to give me his pack.

"No. I can carry it."

"Dammit, J.B., now is not the time to let your ego get the best of you. It's not just you I'm worried about. If you tear that Achilles tendon right through, it's going to mean trouble for all of us. Now give me your pack!"

Reluctantly, he passed it to me. I put it on backwards so it rested on my chest.

At 10,580 feet, as the trail switchbacked up a steep exposed slope, J.B. slowed and then stopped. He could go no further. His Achilles tendon was tight, and an ominous knot appeared midway between heel and calf.

Prem and I searched through blowing snow and cloud for a small patch of level ground. We found a spot just where the switchbacking trail turned on itself. Using cooking pots as shovels, Akaal Bahadur and I cleared away the snow and fashioned a ledge from a mixture of rock, ice and dirt—an area just large enough for the two tents. The swirling gusts raked the unprotected site.

With a final, gargantuan effort, J.B. hobbled the last two hundred feet and we quickly settled him inside a tent.

Earlier in the day I had noticed three local men trailing us.

Afraid to cross the lekh (mountain) alone, they had attached themselves to us, and now they huddled without any form of shelter just outside our tents. Fearing for their survival, Prem and I used our blue cooking tarp to construct a lean-to, and then stacked the porters' loads to close off the open side. After we finished, our friends crawled in and silently hunkered down for a long, cold night.

Just before dusk, the wind slackened. Hoping to take some photos, I scrambled a short way above our encampment. The clouds rose vertically around me and intermittent breaks gave spectacular views of forested ridgelines stretching south towards the plains of India. Closer, I glimpsed sunlit fields 8,000 feet below, just as the clouds settled in once again. The winds came up stronger than before, driving horizontal sheets of freezing rain and snow across the sky. I retreated to the relative warmth and dryness of our tent, exhausted after a long, hard day.

At daybreak, my thermometer showed just four degrees Fahrenheit. I unzipped the tent door and peeked out. Despite the bitter cold, the skies were clear and half a foot of fresh snow blanketed the surrounding mountains. Pulling on my boots, I clambered outside just as our hangers-on emerged stiffly from their makeshift shelter, like bears arising from a winter's hibernation.

In the brittle morning air, Prem prepared large mugs of sticky sweet tea for everyone. The porters sat on their haunches around the small fire, slurping loudly and warming their hands on the steaming metal mugs.

Hoping to take advantage of the good weather we broke camp hastily, without eating. In foregoing food, we committed ourselves to reaching the pass and descending to treeline on the north side of Marbu Lekh before stopping for our first meal. I wondered if J.B. could make it up and over the top in one push. He seemed more agile than the day before, but we had more than 1,500 feet of steep snowy trail above us. Before setting off, I distributed sunglasses to the porters. Snowblindness was one malady we could prevent.

We followed the faint impression of the switchbacking track beneath two feet of snow. Soon the trail narrowed and then climbed for several hundred feet up a near-vertical face before opening out into a series of large open bowls. Spectacular alpine scenery unfolded before us: rocky, snow-laden peaks, vast cirques of unmarked snow, bright sun and azure sky.

Suddenly J.B. stopped. "Parker, listen."

Standing still, I heard it, the *wupp-wupp* of a helicopter. With a mixture of amazement, amusement and horror, we saw a white helicopter, only half a mile away, clear a notch in the ridge to the north.

"Good God, it's the king," J.B. exclaimed.

I, too, recognized the helicopter from the times I had seen it parked in its special hangar at Tribhuvan International Airport. An experienced pilot, the king often took to the air to visit the remoter regions of his kingdom, much to the consternation of his security forces. Close behind, two green military helicopters also cleared the ridge, and the three flew in a triangular formation, passing us at eye level just a quarter of a mile away.

I pointed to the white helicopter and exclaimed to our porters, "*Sri Paanch, Sri Paanch!*" The king's nickname meant "five sirs," in reference to the five honorifics that preceded his name. Our Surkhet porters stood wide-eyed at the sight of their god-king, he of the same Thakuri caste, in a great white flying machine. As the choppers receded, the porters pressed their palms together and, bowing slightly, raised them to their foreheads in salute.

The top of the pass now seemed just a few hundred feet above us. Another delicate traverse across unstable snow and another series of steep switchbacks. At the top, a summit cairn, its windward side and lone prayer pole caked with several inches of windblown snow, stood in stark defiance of the harsh elements. By my altimeter, we stood at 12,300 feet, with surrounding peaks rising another thousand feet above us. To the south our entire route was laid out behind us, to the first ridge just north of Surkhet, and beyond to the Gangetic plain of India sixty miles away. To the north stood the broad snow-capped ridge of Chuli Lekh.

Relieved to have reached the top before eleven o'clock, and that the skies had remained clear, we turned our thoughts now to getting down below treeline before the regular afternoon winds began. As I set out behind the rest, I saw that the north slope opened onto a broad gentle valley. Our toil seemed largely behind us, for now we began the 7,000-foot descent to the Tila Khola, followed by an easy thirty miles along its banks to Jumla.

Just fifty yards below the cairn, I saw how premature my relief had been. For on this gentler north-facing slope, the trail disappeared beneath chest-deep snow, a slick veneer of breakable crust glistening under a midday sun. I watched our laden porters break through up to their waists with each step, one foot buried, the other jammed up against their buttocks. Then a slow roll to one side and a struggle to right their loads. Only to repeat the process with the next step. "Postholing," I found, proved as exhausting as it looked. For J.B. with his injury and the porters with their loads, it proved a colossal effort.

Half a mile from the pass we hit the treeline and rested on the exposed trunk of a fallen fir. Looking to the north and east, I glimpsed for the first time the Himalaya of western Nepal. An unbroken wall of snowbound peaks stretched across the horizon. Forty miles away, beyond Jumla at the far end of the Tila Valley, stood the Sisne, Patrasi and Kanjiroba Himal. Further east, hardly more than a mirage on the horizon, shimmered the 25,000-foot peaks of the westernmost portion of the Dhaulagiri range.

This, then, was the challenge, this jumble of mountains that lay between us and Kathmandu. Somewhere amongst those jagged spires of rock, snow and ice, over high mountain passes, through steep canyons, across churning rivers of glacial waters, we hoped to find a passage. But first, we had to deliver J.B. safely to Jumla.

We continued down in deep, soft snow through conifer and rhododendron forest until 1:00 P.M. Exhausted, we hacked out a campsite in the drifted snow. From a standing dead pine we collected mounds of firewood for a large fire and a hot meal.

With great relief I unrolled my sleeping bag and fell back onto it. We had crossed Marbu Lekh without a major mishap. J.B. had found the downs much easier on his ankle than the ups, although he confided that he thought the day's efforts had further damaged his ankle. The pain had worsened as soon as he stopped. He took another one hundred milligrams of Demerol and was asleep by 7:00 P.M.

The crossing of Marbu Lekh had invigorated me. Having seen our destination, the big peaks of western Nepal, I yearned to be there quickly. But I thought about J.B.'s injury and the porters' struggle through the deep snow, and kept my yearnings to myself.

The next day we continued under sunny skies, but deep crusted snow slowed us to a crawl. With clear weather, Chetri and Thakuri men in twos and threes passed us on their way up to Marbu Lekh. Soon after we stopped for our first meal, I spotted three such porters, each carrying a heavy basket, approach from below. It seemed late in the day to try for the top. Still 3,000 feet below the pass, they would have another 2,500 feet down on the south slope before finding shelter. At 1:30 P.M. the winds had already picked up, and clouds formed over the peaks. As the men passed, stepping in each other's footsteps in the snow, I saw they walked on nothing more than the thick callouses of their bare feet.

Late in the afternoon, the highest village on the north side of Marbu Lekh appeared below us; its natural beauty captivated me. Thatch-roofed houses sat in picturesque disarray,

backdropped by the snowy Chuli Lekh. The first shoots of
spring turned the terraced fields a tender green,
patchworked with the brilliant yellow of flowering mustard.
As we approached, the sounds of village life rose up to greet
us: roosters and dogs, the high-pitched chatter of children at
play.

The pastoral beauty of Dillikot, however, like many villages in Nepal, was best appreciated from afar. For upon
entering, the idyllic vision disintegrated. The villagers, children and adults alike, were filthy with soot-blackened skin,
covered with tattered and unwashed clothes. A thick stench
from rotting garbage and human excrement greeted me. I
swatted ineffectually at clouds of flies.

As we threaded our way through narrow passageways between houses, the villagers' stern, unfriendly faces glared at
us. Suddenly and without warning, a black mongrel leapt
silently from a darkened doorway. Reflexively, I sidestepped
the blur of black fur and flashing teeth that hurled itself at
me and swung the flat blade of my ice axe, catching the
animal a glancing blow to the back of his head. He hesitated,
momentarily stunned, then with a terrifying growl turned to
renew his attack. Prem, twenty yards ahead, grabbed a broken length of fence post and rushed to my aid, crashing the
stave down on the dog's back. Yelping, the beast fell to the
ground, and in an adrenaline-induced rage I closed in, intent
on making this day his last. Just as I swung my ice axe, he slid
under a fence, and the sharp blade embedded itself in the
fence post inches from his rear leg. Taken aback at my intention to maim this animal, I pulled the blade from the wood
and turned to see two young women and a grizzled old man
standing, expressionless, in the doorway from which the dog
had leapt. With Prem at my rear, we continued cautiously
and found J.B. at a campsite just beyond the village.

The next day, we followed a silty stream downwards towards the Tila Khola. Preoccupied with calculations of
money and food supplies, I hardly noticed when I entered a

hamlet of thatch-roofed huts. A small girl stood by the trail, and as I passed, she fell in step beside me, grasping my hand in both of her grubby ones.

"Hello, Japanese. Whoayou? Whoayou?" She giggled and skipped along at my side for a few steps, giving my hand a gentle tug, as if beckoning me to follow. Then she wheeled and darted on chubby little legs back towards her home.

Unprepared for this gesture of communion with her world, a spontaneous touch from this Asian child's sphere, I stopped. I experienced a momentary tightness in my throat, then a deep smile came from within. My world of finances, food, petty concerns of the trek, had made me forget for a time the joys of life, the laughter, the pleasure of another's company. She had come from nowhere to change my day, this child of the Himalayas.

I turned back; the tiny face disappeared in the shadow of the door. I called, *"Namaste!"* ("I greet the god within you!")

She reappeared, still half hidden in the darkness and placed her hands together gravely in front of her oval face. *"Namaste!"* Such a tiny voice.

Early the next morning, we crossed the Tila Khola on a cantilevered wooden bridge. Formed of tremendous rough-hewn planks pegged together like some child's oversized toy, the posts on either end stood adorned with grotesque carvings; incongruously, one was capped by the wooden likeness of an airplane. On the south-facing slope of this deep gorge at only 5,800 feet, the sun had baked the earth brown. We stopped in the shade of granite boulders to study our map. Jumla, we estimated, lay only two long days ahead. For the first time, I felt confident J.B. would make it under his own power.

We hoped to cover ten miles or more on this hot afternoon, but after waiting impatiently at a rest stop, Prem confided angrily that the Surkhet porters deliberately lagged behind. The Tila trail was virtually flat, and since we'd eaten most of our food, the loads were now half their original weight. Suspecting trouble, Prem had instructed Akaal Bahadur and Jeet Bahadur to stay close to the Thakuris. We would pass close to their village tomorrow, and Prem worried they might slip off with our supplies. At the least, by going slowly they could squeeze an extra day's wages from us.

Finally they arrived, Akaal Bahadur and Jeet Bahadur at the rear as if herding them along. The Thakuris fiddled sheepishly with their loads as Prem chastised them, announcing that we would make Jumla tomorrow, no matter what. With our slow going that day, I privately doubted that we could cover the distance.

At six-thirty the next morning, J.B. packed his gear and headed out. "I'm making Jumla today, come hell or high water."

I didn't understand his reasoning, and after our misunderstandings at Dailekh, I resolved to voice my concerns. "J.B., I don't think that's a smart move. It would be a lot better on your ankle if you took it easy."

"No, Parker, I know I can make it. I'll see you there."

"But the porters are carrying your gear and all of the food. And you probably won't get there until well after dark. If the rest of us don't make it, you'll be stuck. Where will you sleep?"

"The sooner I get to Jumla, the sooner I get to Kathmandu and have this foot looked at."

"The faster you go, the more likely you are to do more damage." I was exasperated at his obstinacy. "Besides, you can't leave for Kathmandu until the porters reach Jumla. We're not going to haul your gear hundreds of miles through the mountains."

"I'll see you in Jumla. I'm leaving." With that, J.B. started off down the trail.

Prem and I left an hour later with the porters, but given Prem's desire not to lose J.B., he and I walked without a break for three hours. Where the marble black waters of the southward-flowing Sinja Khola blended into the Tila, we came upon the village of Nangma. Here we found J.B. resting at a teahouse. Prem and I ordered a meal of *daal bhaat*, but as the shopkeeper hefted his *kukri* to go find the wood to build the fire to cook our rice, we realized the delay this would cause us. J.B. said little and, impatient, ate just a small snack and left.

We lounged amidst dusty midday heat and meddlesome flies, in the shade of a tremendous ancient pine. An hour and a half drifted by, and still no food. The porters, as slow as our cook, also languished somewhere behind. Frustrated at trying to appease J.B. and keep the porters moving, Prem suddenly rose to his feet and jammed his ice axe defiantly into the soft earth.

"This is not good! We should not get so apart! I do not understand, why is J.B. Sahib far ahead, when the porters are still behind? I am the *sirdar*. It is my job to organize food, the camp, to make certain you and J.B. Sahib are safe. How can I do this when we are everywhere at one time? First rule, Parker Sahib: stay together!" As he talked, Prem, more angry than I had ever seen him, pulled his ice axe from the earth and swung it around wildly.

Finally our rice arrived, the pinkish long-grained Kashmiri variety brought ages ago to this region near Jumla, and a tasty yellow *daal*. We finished quickly and greedily licked our fingers clean.

After our meal, Prem and I continued eastward along the Tila Khola, not waiting for the porters. We trusted Akaal Bahadur and Jeet Bahadur to keep an eye on our gear. As we neared Jumla, the gorge opened into a valley. Under a disorienting white sun, we traced a broad flat trail as it paralleled the riverbed. We walked steadily for several hours, scanning ahead in hopes of spotting J.B.

At the village of Raku we stopped at a decrepit teahouse to escape the sun. This rough village, though typical, looked even more primitive and dirty than any other we had seen in western Nepal. Dark-skinned Thakuris watched us intently as Prem ordered two glasses of tea, ladled from a large open kettle, a pale liquid in oily metal cups. Ash and fragments of sticks floated on the surface. Prem caught my eye, and, of a single mind, we surreptitiously emptied our glasses onto the thirsty earth. From the bottom of my glass fell a crumpled black beetle.

The trail wound past crude two-story dwellings; the bottom levels housed livestock, the upper ones, unwashed humanity. Locals stared silently from the flat roofs as we passed. From somewhere behind us, a stone was launched, then another. They landed and rolled just a few feet in front of us. Enraged, I whirled to confront the throwers. Two dozen faces glared at me.

"Do not stop, Parker Sahib. We should get away."

I stared for a moment longer, recording indelibly the scene of these uncharacteristically inhospitable people. Turning, I jogged a few steps to Prem's side and we strode quickly past the last buildings.

Two school-age boys fell in a few feet behind us, laughing and taunting us with rapid staccato bursts of Nepali.

"They think we are both foreigners and cannot understand their language," Prem whispered.

We endured the slurs for several minutes, then Prem had heard enough. With a speed that surprised even me, he whirled and confronted them with his ice axe. The boys backpedaled, wide-eyed and silent, out of his range. Prem raged at them for thirty seconds before we continued on our way.

Several minutes later, in a subdued voice, Prem commented on the incident. "They were poking fun at us because we were strangers. Calling us stupid and worse. Calling us stupid! They who live as animals, so backward and lazy, and still we are the stupid ones. Never have I seen such people in Nepal, Parker Sahib."

Except for the villagers at Dillikot, neither had I.

Towards late afternoon, a soft golden haze settled across the sky, but the heat and stultifying humidity remained. A dull ache crept up my legs, and my feet burned from the long day's walk. Drawn to the gently tumbling waters, I veered and sat at the river's edge. I removed my boots and socks, then plunged my feet to mid-calf in the icy waters. Prem stopped and we soaked our feet together.

"I do not understand, Parker Sahib, why we must go to Jumla today. It is a very old village, and surely it will be there tomorrow and the next day."

"Prem, I have no idea why J.B. insists on reaching there today. Even if he goes on, I am sure he won't make it much before midnight."

Passersby kept us informed that the *tulo maanchhe* ("big man") walked thirty minutes ahead of us. Although we increased our pace, we could not catch him.

Two hours later, as a purple-gray dusk settled on the valley, we rounded a bend along the river and spotted J.B. on the trail a half mile ahead. Head down, supported by his stave, he plodded purposefully along. Helpless to stop him, we merely watched in frustration and anger as his form slowly faded into the growing darkness.

Why didn't he stop? He knew as well as we that the next village was still two hours ahead, Jumla easily another hour beyond that.

"To hell with it. We'll spend the night at the teahouse just ahead. Let J.B. fend for himself," I muttered.

"Yes," Prem said wearily. "I can do only so much. Let him find his own way."

We ate a spartan meal of *daal bhaat* and *alu* (potatoes), then were shown to a room upstairs. A lone wooden bed hugged one wall, and Prem insisted I take it. The proprietor gave us each a single blanket. Prem found a spot on the earthen floor and lay down. In this chimneyless house, the oily pine fire below soon filled our room with acrid, sooty smoke. Around three o'clock, I fell into a fitful sleep.

At dawn, Prem shook me awake. A thin layer of soot covered everything and had darkened our faces and hands by several shades. Our heads pounded from inhaling the smoke. After a quick cup of tea, we set out towards Jumla. Both Prem and I felt terrible, with headaches and grumbling bowels. Our progress was interrupted by frequent dashes into the bushes.

Within three hours, the river valley opened into a broad plain of gently terraced fields. Twenty miles in the distance, the valley abruptly ended in a wall of towering glaciered peaks, the Himalaya of western Nepal. Several miles ahead on the left bank of the river, mustard-and-white flags on four towering poles rose above the main temple of Jumla. For an hour, we trudged towards them. Spitefully they seemed to recede before us. I had run out of drinking water and with incessant diarrhea, I became weak and disoriented.

As we approached the first building less than a mile before Jumla, we found J.B. waiting on a small wall. Depleted of all energy, I felt dehydrated, my feet hurt, my guts hurt and I hadn't eaten since the night before. I exploded with the frustrations of the last two days.

"What was the goddamned rush for?"

J.B. sighed. "I wanted to get the walk over with."

"But what about the rest of us? The porters aren't even here yet!"

"I thought they would get here even if they had to walk all night. Prem told them we were going to Jumla yesterday. I got here last night about nine, and I didn't think they would be too far behind. Where were you?"

"Don't ask!"

"Well, I was attacked by one of those Tibetan mastiffs at the edge of town. I just managed to hold him off with my walking stick. Where were you?"

"Fighting off smartass boys in Raku."

"Yeah, I had a run-in with those little bastards myself. They bounced a rock off my shoulder, but I managed to knock one off his feet with my stick. So where did you spend the night?"

"In a cold, smoky teahouse about ten miles back. We saw you ahead of us just at dusk, but couldn't catch up. Why didn't you stop when it got dark?"

"Because I want to get back to Kathmandu to get this foot looked at. The sooner the better."

I was exasperated. "If you could walk thirty miles in a day, it must not be bothering you so much that an extra day would make any difference. Yesterday probably did more damage than taking three days to cover the same distance."

Speechless and drained, I wondered whether I might be seeing this in the wrong light. J.B. and I had never experienced such conflict before. What had gone wrong here?

Then I realized that tomorrow or the next day J.B. would be on a plane back to Kathmandu and that would resolve the whole issue. Enough said.

I shouldered my pack and stomped the last few hundred yards to Jumla.

CHAPTER FOUR

▲

Jumla

Tuesday, February 28, 1984

A FADED METAL SIGN HUNG FROM THE SECOND-FLOOR BALCONY of the weathered wooden building: "Sherpa Hotel." *How had a Sherpa ended up in Jumla, hundreds of mountainous miles from his native Khumbu?* Whatever the answer, the sign brought back memories of the good food and sincere friendliness we had enjoyed in the Sherpa inns of eastern Nepal.

I waited in the shadow to catch my breath. Feeling anger and frustration from my encounter with J.B., I had half run the last third of a mile, leaving him and Prem far behind.

Now I took a hard look at some buildings clustered behind a barbed-wire enclosure about a hundred yards ahead.

Just then, J.B. arrived and nodded towards the buildings, "That's the police garrison. I passed it late last night. This morning when I came back to wait for you, they seemed pretty interested but didn't stop me."

"Damn. I was hoping we could get around to the other side of town without running into the police. We're already getting the once over from those two in bush hats."

By the route on our trekking permits, we should have entered Jumla from the east instead of the west, the direction from which we now walked. Our permits had not been stamped since leaving Kathmandu, and I had hoped that by skirting around the checkpost and approaching from the opposite direction, we might avoid additional permit hassles.

"We should stay here," Prem said. "Let them come and find us."

The Sherpa's name was Pema, although he called himself a Tamang, the same caste as Prem, Akaal Bahadur and Jeet Bahadur. A gregarious and diverse group of people who inhabit the hill country north and east of Kathmandu, Tamangs, like Sherpas, are of Tibetan descent—some say descendants of the Tibetan cavalry of centuries past.

Pema's lodge, although spartan, was typical of Sherpa inns in the Everest region. The hotel business in Jumla, however, was far from booming. We registered as his first guests in more than a month, then followed him to the second floor and along the balcony. Removing two oversized padlocks from the door, Pema led us into a darkened, musty room. Half a dozen wooden beds, strewn with colorful Tibetan carpets, cluttered the room. Silk-framed *thangkas* (religious paintings) lined the walls, and a Buddhist altar filled the far end. Three large golden statues, butter lamps, prayer books, cymbals and drums, and at the center, a small postcard likeness of the Dalai Lama draped in white prayer scarves. Pema said we could have the whole room to ourselves. Before leaving, he lit the row of butter lamps lining the altar.

Within minutes, a boy appeared at our door, a runner sent by the police to request our presence at their compound. Immediately!

J.B., Prem and I entered the compound and were shown to three wooden chairs in the middle, just opposite a small school desk. We sat in our own sweaty stench under the hot noonday sun for almost a half hour before a stocky man in crisply pressed military greens approached from a nearby building.

He stopped next to the desk and spoke in excellent English. "Good morning. I am Narayan Shrestha, the head officer here in Jumla."

An assistant held the chair as he sat down. He asked Prem several questions before turning to J.B. and me. "Passports, please, and your letters for trekking."

He leafed through both sets of documents, flipping back and forth, checking them against each other. Finally figuring out that we had permits to trek from Dhorpatan, but not from Surkhet, he directed a frowning question in Nepali at Prem. Although a fool might have guessed the topic, for our benefit Prem answered Narayan in English. "In Pokhara, they heard of much banditry just near to Dhorpatan. The police in Pokhara said they should change the route and go from Surkhet. And not to worry about the permits."

Narayan screwed up his face and looked incredulously at Prem. Sensing his skepticism, Prem quickly added, "Of course, I know just what they have told me. They hired me only in Surkhet as their cook."

Narayan shot back another question in Nepali. Prem again answered in English. "The police along the way saw us but just waved at us. They did nothing."

Narayan shook his head in obvious disgust at the ineptitude of the village police, then, thankfully, moved on to the subject of our travel plans after leaving Jumla. He launched into a rambling ten-minute monologue that left us glancing quizzically at one another.

"Please, you must understand my professional duties here in this city of Jumla. I am the chief officer here, but not anywhere else. I do not have any control outside of this place. If someone were to stop you, the police in another village, what can I do? Even if you have the proper paperwork, this has nothing to do with me." He leaned forward and eyed us intently. "I can do nothing to help you." I sensed hidden meaning in his tone, but did not understand what he was trying to tell us.

After a weighty pause, he continued. "Now, your permit

says that you wish to visit RaRa Lake. This is four days to the north. You must understand that you cannot go further into the restricted areas of Mugu or Dolpo. I can have no control over what happens if you do."

He asked us if we had a map, and I pulled out our slowly disintegrating ammonia-dye trekking map.

"The best way back to Pokhara," the officer said, tracing the route with a pen, "is to cross these passes and follow this river here, to the Bheri River, then south to Jarjakot and east to Dhorpatan. It is faster to go over the Jang La, but to do this you would need to go to Dolpo, and this is forbidden. The best way for you is through Jarjakot." He stood, signaling the end of our interrogation.

"Before you leave Jumla, you must come to me again to tell me the date of your departure. *Namaste.*"

An assistant showed us to the gate.

"I got it," I announced as I returned late that evening to our second-story room in the Sherpa Hotel. I waved the plane ticket in the air.

J.B., lying on a bed, smiled broadly. "Good going, Park. How'd you do it?"

"Not easy," I replied, slumping onto a bed, still wearing the same clothes I had arrived in that morning. "It took a while to find the RNAC office, and they were hopelessly overbooked for tomorrow. I've been arguing for hours. Finally I told the clerk that I would pay tourist rate, which came to 1,575 rupees—the Nepalese pay 375 rupees. Plus 100 rupees 'surcharge.' A seat just suddenly materialized."

"Money talks."

To our immense relief, the Thakuri porters had appeared late that afternoon, shadowed closely by Akaal Bahadur and Jeet Bahadur. After dropping their loads, the Thakuris disappeared into the Jumla bazaar. Akaal Bahadur and Jeet Bahadur crashed on the extra beds in our room.

Now my conversation with J.B. turned to the possible

routes through Mugu and Dolpo, and how J.B. might organize a search party if we didn't show up in Kathmandu. We
didn't speak about our conflicts of the last three days, and I
felt a subtle shift of attitude. A rapprochement of sorts had
occurred as soon as I had arrived with the ticket. Although
both still simmering, we seemed tacitly to agree to leave our
misunderstandings behind us along a thirty-mile stretch of
the Tila Khola.

Twenty feet off the ground a Pilatus Porter, the single-engine workhorse aircraft of the Himalayas, gunned its engines
and still barely cleared the barbed-wire fence before setting
down on the bumpy pasture that served as a runway. Although the plane brought precious rice supplies from the
terai town of Nepalganj, its arrival was always uncertain. But
that day the flight arrived on time at 8:00 A.M. and a crowd
mobbed the airport's tiny open-air building. Beyond the fifteen or so ticketed passengers, a group of clamoring
Tibetans had descended upon a waifish Nepalese in white
jodhpurs who held the day's manifest aloft. I assumed they
were attempting to cajole or bribe their way on board, the
same tactic I had used.

After an hour of milling around, the jodhpured Nepalese
led his entourage towards the runway gate, where a vague
semblance of a queue formed. J.B., as the only foreigner on
board, was permitted to board last. The rest of the passengers, Mugulis from the region just to the north, seemed intent on thwarting the tight weight restrictions necessary on
the short-takeoff-and-landing runway. One at a time, they
were allowed onto the runway where an attendant asked
each one to raise his arms. From deep within their oversized
black *chubas*, a veritable cascade of hidden treasures—bowls,
knives, jewelry, half-eaten pieces of meat and assorted bric-
a-brac—tumbled onto the ground, to the great amusement
of the onlookers.

Finally, after sorting out the Mugulis and their seat assignments, J.B. was called to board.

"Best of luck, Parker, see you in Kathmandu," J.B. said with a firm handshake. A quick wave at the plane's doorway and he was gone.

I had mixed emotions about seeing J.B. leave. I knew things would go easier without him. A residue of anger remained and I actually felt relieved to see him go, but also guilt at feeling that way. I also felt sorry for him. He had endured so many physical injuries, bouncing back again and again, only to be injured one more time.

The engines revved to full throttle, then the plane shot forward down the runway, lifting off only thirty yards shy of the fence. As I watched the tiny plane rise into the sky and disappear into the snowy peaks to the east, I felt a twinge of loneliness and apprehension. I would go on alone, with Prem, Akaal Bahadur and Jeet Bahadur.

A cheerful female voice with an American accent caught me off guard. "Hello. You look like you could use a shower."

I spun around, but she continued before I could reply. "I have the only hot shower in western Nepal. Would you like to use it?"

Too tired and not in the mood to brave the Tila Khola's icy waters the day before, I smelled worse than a week-old pair of gym socks. By the time I could manage a reply, the tall woman in her fifties had already loaded the packages she had received on the plane into a backpack, and had begun walking towards town.

"I guess I *could* use a shower," I called after her. "Thanks for the offer. Where do you live?"

"Over by the RNAC office. I saw you leaving there yesterday. Just ask around for the Youngkins' place."

An hour later, I reveled in my first hot shower since leaving Kathmandu. Afterwards, Anita invited me in for homemade muffins and coffee, and, as I was leaving, asked me to dinner that evening with some United Mission workers.

Anita proved an old hand at adapting recipes to the supplies at hand. Dinner was excellent, and dessert an indescribable treat, angel-food cake topped with real whipped buffalo cream. Anita and Frank Youngkin had worked for twenty-seven years as missionaries in Asia—twenty-three in Thailand, the last four here in Jumla. In Nepal, where proselytizing was strictly forbidden and swiftly punished, they built schools, taught and worked on forestry and agricultural projects. After dinner, we talked of their experiences living in Jumla, and their efforts on behalf of the Nepalese. And we talked of religion.

Throughout my life I had sustained a uniformly negative view of Christianity. At Sunday school, my earliest memories were of well-meaning teachers presenting fantastical stories, which seemed as plausible to me as Santa Claus or the tooth fairy. I was too young to perceive them as allegories. And the elders of our tribe offered no help, presenting these stories as truth "because the Bible tells us so." Their insistence on belief in the Bible without question turned me away from religion. If religion meant embracing the kind of dogma peddled by the Sunday morning Presbyterians, then I called myself an atheist. Unfortunately, in my homogeneous environment, alternative approaches to religion did not exist.

The Youngkins, however, had infused reality into their brand of Christianity. I thoroughly enjoyed my evening with these people, who worked selflessly to better the lives of others.

Later that night, back at the Sherpa Hotel, Prem and I discussed the next day's tasks; hiring porters and resupplying for the long push ahead.

As we talked, Prem and I drank fiery apple *rakshi*. Soon, Prem emptied his glass and turned in. I sat up for a time, finishing the last of the bottle in the soft light of two butter lamps. Their yellow glow bathed the altar in an eerie flickering light that left mysterious shadows. The Buddha's eyes watched me.

Did they just blink? I thought so. Under their benevolent gaze, my thoughts turned to what lay ahead. An unknown route through remote and forbidding Dolpo. Could I handle it? Would these mountains defeat me, or would I conquer them? Just before leaving for Asia I had finished Rick Ridgeway's book, *The Last Step*, about the first American ascent of K2. One phrase in particular, Barry Bishop's statement about the first American ascent of Everest, stuck with me: "There are no conquerors—only survivors." Alone in the far outback of western Nepal, I sensed that at best there would be only survivors. In the past, my anxieties and fears had been about such things as passing a test, winning a judo match, finishing graduate school. Contrived goals. If I failed, life would go on. What I faced now was far more visceral— survival itself.

Then, late at night, three sheets to the wind, staring into the eyes of that blinking Buddha, I ran head-on into the question, *What was I doing here?*

I was doing what I had always done. That is, doing instead of talking about it. My parents approached life with a "can do" attitude and made sure that I acquired this same air of confidence. Fearing that I, small for my age, would become withdrawn or feel insecure, my father involved me in the martial arts and joined in the learning experience. A neighborhood football team was organized and, recognizing that I was being left out, my father quietly suggested I be given the ball to run with. Being fast and agile, I soon became a star running back. Without his guidance, I might have languished on the sidelines, in sport and in life.

As I grew older, through intense physical training in both scholastic sports and judo, I glimpsed what the martial artist has always known: that spiritual development is attained through physical discipline. That true insight is acquired by doing rather than by thinking. That clarity and vision come spontaneously, often at wholly unexpected times and from

oblique angles. That when we are totally extended, stretched
to the limits of both body and mind, the barriers to understanding seem sometimes to drop and we glimpse some
truth, if only for a moment. Thus it is that humans strive
upwards, to be the first, the best, to perform the task in the
purist way, risking their lives to stand for a moment or two
on a mountaintop. Willing to die for the reason of being.

And thus I found myself, on February 29, 1984, about to
set off into the unknown. As I finished the gritty residue in
my glass, I had an uncanny feeling, as if I had always known I
would find myself here, on this day and at this time. J.B. had
been the early driving force behind our expedition that had
brought me to Asia. Now he was gone. It frightened me a
little, but I never entertained any doubts about my continuing. It was as if I couldn't *not* go.

Pulling myself up, I stumbled to the altar. A smile creased
the corners of my mouth as I gazed a final time into the eyes
of the golden Buddha. *Would we make it, Siddhartha?* No
answer, just the silent serenity of that all-knowing expression. I leaned down and extinguished the butter lamps.

The next morning, we set off for Jumla's bazaar. One of the
largest towns in western Nepal north of the *terai*, Jumla was
nonetheless smaller and more primitive than I had expected.
Although it was the starting point for most of the trekking in
western Nepal, there were virtually no tourist facilities there.
A government official had told us that only fifty trekkers had
registered with the police during the past year. The Sherpa
Hotel, the only trekker's lodge in town, rarely housed
guests, and the town lacked electricity and any semblance of
sanitation facilities.

The bazaar lay at one end of a two-hundred-yard cobbled
"main street." A mixture of rough Nepalese hill people and
Tibetans loitered in front of the squat flat-roofed buildings
lining the street. As Akaal Bahadur and Jeet Bahadur set off
through the throng, searching for trustworthy porters, Prem

and I bargained for food supplies. We quickly learned how scarce and expensive foodstuffs were in this region. After scrounging through stall after stall, we gathered only minimal supplies. Thirty kilos of rice at thirteen rupees per kilo; twenty-two mannas of sugar, which came to eleven kilos, at twenty-four rupees per kilo; packets of instant noodles, soap, kerosene and the small red screaming-hot chilies without which Prem and the porters could not eat their meals.

Foolishly, perhaps, I thought also of adding to my disguise in hopes of passing myself off as a Tibetan. In Kathmandu, I had discarded my western pack in favor of the external-framed, faded green canvas variety popular with Tibetan traders. Pema had found a tailor to make me a billowing black Tibetan *chuba*. Now I spotted a tall Tibetan wearing a Chinese army-green hat with fake-fur flaps. This hat, available only in Tibet, would place the owner as Tibetan. I approached the man and, through hand signals, bartered on fingers for several minutes. We settled on 120 rupees and a packet of Yak cigarettes, not available in Jumla but which the Tibetan had seen sticking out of Prem's pocket. The cigarettes I cared little about, although Prem parted with them grudgingly.

After paying the 120 rupees, however, I realized I had forgotten to collect J.B.'s extra money from him before he left. I had spent valuable cash on his plane ticket and we had yet to pay off the Surkhet porters. Now, by my calculations, it seemed that my money might not last us to Kathmandu. I sighed. Nothing I could do about it now.

On the way back to the hotel, I stopped at the police garrison. Narayan greeted me cordially. "Ah, yes, Mr. Parker, the American. Are you leaving us?"

"Yes, we're heading north to RaRa Lake tomorrow."

"Very good. When you come back to Jumla, please check in once again. I will look for you in two weeks. Goodbye."

After washing the caked black dirt from my new fur hat, I sat down to write J.B. a letter. I outlined our prospective

route. We would go north several days and then east to the
village of Dalphu, then continue east along what we came to
call the "high route." This would take us across the northern
reaches of Dolpo, near and parallel to the Tibetan border.
Once into Dolpo, our route would depend on trail conditions—or even finding trails—and food supplies. One option
took us south past Shey Monastery, then east to the Kali
Gandaki, over the Thorung La to Manang and back to
Kathmandu by early May. Perhaps four hundred miles in all.
J.B. had agreed that if we didn't show up in Kathmandu by
late May, he would organize a search party.

By early afternoon, Prem returned to the hotel with good
news. He had found two porters who knew the region well,
and he had brought one back with him, a wiry, bronze-
skinned man with high-cheekboned Tibetan features. He
greeted me with a smile, and I was astonished at how remarkably like a Native American he looked. Smiling, he
proudly showed us a photo of himself and Bob Adams, a
former Peace Corps volunteer in Jumla whom J.B. and I had
met by chance on the trail in eastern Nepal. In broken English, he told us of a French photographer from Kathmandu,
a man whom he had guided several times through Dolpo and
who planned to return in two months' time to make another
foray. This information cross-checked with what Bob Adams
had told us.

This Tibetan guide, however, was pessimistic about our
proposed route. The trail north and east beyond Dalphu lay
under deep snows—up to eight feet, he said, with many dangerous glacier crossings. To attempt to go along the high
route through Dolpo to the Kali Gandaki was certain death.
He spoke rapidly in Nepali, and I caught only fragments of
the conversation. Anxious to know for myself, I pointed to
our route and asked him, *"Baato jaanasakchha?"* ("Trail is
possible to go?")

"Sakdaaina! Sakdaaina!" ("Not possible!") came the em-
phatic reply.

I didn't know how to gauge such comments. Although this man apparently had extensive experience traveling through Dolpo, I knew of no areas north of the Dhaulagiris where we might encounter "many glacier crossings." What little snow fell generally evaporated quickly in the arid, high-altitude desert. I had read that the peoples of the Himalayas were poorly adapted culturally to their high, cold environment, and remained remarkably fearful of the elements. Perhaps they also feared disturbing the local deities, and used the threat of snow and glaciers as an excuse.

The Tibetan, however, remained adamant in his assessment. After conferring, Prem and I both remained skeptical, but decided to go to Dalphu and reassess the situation there.

Later, a little after eight, the Tibetan returned with our other newly hired porter. We shut the door to our room and talked in hushed tones. Our topic: the police and military presence in the region. The porters told us of a large garrison in Gum Gadhi and another in Mugu. But the police did not venture far from these villages because the Tibetan people in the area didn't like or trust the authorities. Stories abounded of Tibetan *drokpas* (nomads) setting upon police traveling between villages. So, they assured us, as long as we could skirt the villages of Gum Gadhi and Mugu, we should encounter no problems. But while I felt hesitant to believe their assessment of the trails in Dolpo, I was reluctant to believe we would pass through that area so easily.

They repeated stories—actually rumors which circulated in the bazaar—that shed some light on the police chief's odd monologue. One involved a French couple who had hired two Dolpo men to guide them back to Kathmandu. Deep in the mountains, the Tibetans murdered the French couple, burying them in a shallow grave. With cameras, money and traveler's checks, the Tibetans headed towards Kathmandu. The police in Jomoson were alerted, and apprehended the murderers as they attempted to sneak through town at night. They confessed to the police chief in Jomoson, but convinced him to take a bribe in exchange for their release. The Tibetans then continued on to Kathmandu, where they tried to cash the traveler's checks. That undid them and, upon their arrest, they told the entire story to the authorities, who subsequently arrested the Jomoson police chief. He was sent to prison in Jumla, under the watchful eye of his good friend, Narayan Shrestha, Jumla's chief of police.

Now the rambling oratory of two days earlier began to make sense. Narayan was telling us that, should we run into any trouble, he could no longer be bribed into helping us because the authorities were watching him.

Our new porters told us another story that troubled me more than the first. Prem translated as they spoke.

"Just last year, a French trekker on his way to RaRa Lake, with proper permits, was taken in by the police in Gum Gadhi. Even with the permit, they put him in jail. It was months before his friends found out. They came to Gum Gadhi and had to pay big *baksheesh*, many rupees, before they let him out. These police, they are so far away, they can do as they want, like a king."

Permits or not, I decided to avoid all police. I had heard yet another story about trouble in Dolpo from Bob Bell, a Peace Corps volunteer stationed in far western Nepal. He got the story directly from the chief of police in Silgarhi, who conducted the investigation. According to this story, another Peace Corps volunteer, proficient in Nepali and well-traveled in other parts of Nepal, went alone into Dolpo. Two months later, he was reported missing, and the U.S. embassy applied pressure on the Nepalese government to investigate the case. The police chief of Silgarhi himself went into Dolpo and came upon a local woman wearing one western-style sneaker. Asked where she got the shoe, she replied that she got it from her sister, who had the other one, and whose husband had removed the pair from the body of an American. The husband confessed to dropping a rock on the American's head while he slept, because he wanted his shoes. The body was found in a superficial grave, fully clothed, the pack still on his back. Inside the pack they found an expensive camera and camping gear, untouched.

All of these stories naturally disturbed me and made me resolve firmly to stay close to our group and to avoid all villages containing police or military posts.

By eight the following morning, four bulging *dokos* leaned against the balcony railing outside our room. Prem had carefully directed their packing, for the new porters had given hints they might balk at carrying heavy loads. The loads of Akaal Bahadur and Jeet Bahadur weighed close to thirty kilos. I hefted the other two loads a few inches off the floor and estimated their weight at twenty-five and twenty kilos, respectively.

The new porters arrived, and as they mounted the stairs their cheerful smiles turned to somber frowns at the sight of the *dokos*. The posturing began.

"Parker Sahib," Prem reported. "They say the loads are too heavy."

"Ridiculous," I answered. "They are less than our porters' loads and much lighter than the ones the Thakuri porters carried from Surkhet. Even I am carrying twenty kilos."

"I know, Parker Sahib. I have told them, but they think because they know the way that they can get us to make their loads smaller."

The conversation escalated to a heated argument. A Tibetan woman stepped forward, offering to carry for us. One of the porters—her husband, we later learned—backhanded her across the face. At this, Prem took a step towards the man and the argument rapidly degenerated into a shoving match. The two men advanced on Prem. Akaal Bahadur, Jeet Bahadur, Pema and I stepped in to turn the numbers in our favor. We backed them down the steps but they didn't leave, sullenly conferring twenty yards away. From a small crowd that had gathered to watch the altercation, a stocky man in his late thirties came forward and quietly offered to work for us. The two disgruntled porters angrily threatened him with a beating and chased him away.

Prem, whose normally reserved manner hid a hot temper, exploded. With the rest of us behind him, he advanced on the two troublemakers, warning them to leave or he would find the police. Waiting only for the would-be porters to melt into the crowd, Prem, Akaal Bahadur and Jeet Bahadur set off for the bazaar. They returned within a half hour with two new porters.

One was Puraba, the man who had offered to carry for us during the altercation. With only a hint of a smile, he introduced his companion as eighteen-year-old Shera Punzo. The chubby-faced boy looked no more than fifteen. Both lived in a village near Dalphu, our immediate destination. To avoid another unpleasant encounter, we arranged to meet our new hirees at the northern edge of town. Within the hour, we were off.

Porter problems came as nothing new to us. In eastern Nepal, we had up to nine Tamang porters with us. Tamangs are a gregarious caste, quick to laughter but also explosive if provoked. One memorable fight broke out after forty days on the trail.

We had just entered the Khumbu region from the east, and had eaten enough of our supplies to no longer need one porter. Prem had asked Akaal Bahadur to split the porter's remaining equipment among the rest of the loads. Akaal Bahadur did this, including a few kilos for our deaf cook boy, Buddhiman. An argument immediately broke out as Buddhiman objected to carrying anything not belonging to the "kitchen." A shoving match ensued, and Buddhiman, about five foot five inches and unusually muscular, quickly gained the upper hand against Akaal Bahadur. Shiro, Akaal Bahadur's brother and also one of our porters, picked up a rock and advanced on Buddhiman. J.B. and I had watched all of this unfold from the sidelines, but now we intervened. I jumped Shiro and quickly pinned him to the ground. Meanwhile, behind me, Buddhiman had grabbed Akaal Bahadur by the hair and thrown him to the ground. Grabbing a nearby ice axe, Buddhiman made a wild swing, adze end first, towards Akaal Bahadur's head. Fortunately, at the last second, Akaal Bahadur twisted his head to the side. The ice axe stuck in the ground inches from his face. Buddhiman had raised the ice axe overhead for a second blow when J.B. rushed to Akaal Bahadur's rescue. Arresting Buddhiman's swing, J.B. applied an armlock and almost broke Buddhiman's arm before the boy cried out and dropped the weapon.

That ended the actual fight, but tensions remained high and minor altercations occurred during the next few days. Finally, we threatened to dock their wages or even fire any porters caught fighting again. I never found out, and Prem would not tell me, what had started the incident. But I could never believe that just a few extra items loaded in a *doko* had precipitated such a nasty feud.

In planning for our trip to western Nepal, we consulted with Prem and selected two of the porters to go with us. Endless stamina, trustworthiness and spirit of adventure were the attributes we sought. Every one of our eastern Nepal porters wanted to go. For them, it meant a long period of employment with almost no opportunity to squander their earnings. The experience might also lead to other portering jobs, or even the chance to become a *sirdar*. Ultimately, we chose the two who showed the most promise of becoming *sirdars* themselves someday.

Akaal Bahadur was taller than most Nepalese, almost five foot eight, and a bit huskier, although still weighing less than 140 pounds. Because of his robust, outgoing personality, matched by his square-jawed good looks, women often hovered around him. He had a ready laugh and a wild sense of humor, but could become quite volatile at times. Jeet Bahadur was not only unrelated to Akaal Bahadur, but in many ways he was his total opposite. At five foot three and not much over 110 pounds, he was neither as strong nor as outgoing. He had thick, almost bushy, black hair, and was more Tibetan than Nepalese in feature. He spoke little, and I could remember stretches of two or three days when I did not hear him utter a single word. But what Jeet Bahadur lacked in physical size and strength, he possessed in character; I would trust him with my life. And he could carry, on what often seemed sheer will power, any load, all day long, albeit sometimes at a slow pace.

Both Akaal Bahadur and Jeet Bahadur, who together knew no more than two hundred words of English, expressed eagerness to learn more. And their desire to speak English complemented my desire to learn Nepali. So we taught each other. They both spoke Nepali, the umbrella language for the country, and Tamang, a Tibetan dialect, often confusing me by combining both within the same sentence and creating a pidgin language.

Their sense of humor surfaced when they took advantage of my eagerness to learn by teaching me nonsense phrases, telling me they were everyday expressions. They told me *musalai kaideo* meant "very good." When my repeated attempts to use this phrase backfired, leading to shocked expressions (and barely concealed guffaws from the porters), I began to suspect some subterfuge. Several months later, one of my Peace Corps friends told me it meant "The mouse ate it." *The sneaky bastards.* Thereafter I began to use the expression in more appropriate situations, and to plot my revenge.

We followed a stream due north out of Jumla, ascending gradually towards the 12,000-foot Danphya La pass. A half hour out of town, we came to a stone-walled compound containing several large, beautifully constructed slate-roofed stone buildings, the finest buildings I had seen in Nepal outside of the Kathmandu Valley. On the spacious grounds, twenty boys happily played volleyball. Prem translated the sign on the front gate, and I realized this was the school only recently completed by the United Mission workers. The Youngkins had told me the school was completely self-sufficient, and as we climbed past the main cluster of buildings I saw greenhouses and cultivated fields.

At midafternoon, we crossed an open pasture known as Charya Chaur. Just beyond, in a stand of pine with magnificent views of snow-covered peaks to the south, we set camp for the night.

An hour after first light, on our fourth day out of Jumla we topped the final pass separating us from the gorge of the mighty Mugu Karnali River. Forty miles to the north, a spine of snowy peaks marked the Tibetan border. Gum Gadhi and its police garrison lay far below on this south side of the Mugu Karnali watershed.

The trail descended through dense stands of Himalayan fir and pine. First imperceptibly, then precipitously, the track steepened as we wound down into the gorge of the north-flowing Lumsa Khola, a tributary of the Mugu Karnali.

Although having passed this way many times, Puraba remained unsure of the exact location of Gum Gadhi. He stopped two girls as they passed us. They pointed to a ridgeline rising above the dark depths of the Mugu Karnali. Gum Gadhi lay there, they said, two and a half hours away. Not wishing to go closer until late in the day, we stopped in an open field for our first meal.

Since leaving Jumla, Prem and I had talked often about how we would approach the checkpost at Gum Gadhi. Questions laced our plans with uncertainty. Did the checkpost lie within the village? How vigilantly did the police watch the main trail that skirted several hundred feet below the village? Could we make our way along this trail in the dark? Would our new porters balk at moving at night?

The stories we heard in Jumla had convinced me of one

thing: to avoid the police at all costs. With or without proper paperwork, they could stop us and very well might detain us. To avoid being seen, we decided to time ourselves so as to pass rapidly just at dusk below Gum Gadhi, where the Lumsa spilled into the Mugu Karnali. Then, following the Mugu Karnali east, we would walk for an hour or two in the dark before setting camp. Hoping to disguise myself, I took out my Chinese cap and borrowed back my Tibetan *chuba* from Puraba, to whom I had lent—or more likely given—it two days earlier.

In a barren rice paddy hidden from the trail, we languished in the warm sun, waiting. Then, as the amber sunlight rose off the west-facing slopes, we set off, following the Lumsa Khola steeply down towards its confluence with the Mugu Karnali. Small hamlets clung to the trail.

Although I wore my Chinese cap pulled down over my head, to my dismay it did little to disguise me. From a hundred yards and more, locals spotted me and stared. *What part of my appearance, what movement labeled me a foreigner?* I wondered. I wore drab gray pants, a tan shirt, my Chinese cap, and carried a weathered Tibetan pack, and still something shouted my presence off the canyon walls. I became alarmed.

"Prem, what is it about me that makes me stick out? I wear clothes the same as yours. My pack is old and dirty. What is it?"

Prem stepped back and perused me from head to toe. Then, with a condescending smirk, he replied "It is everything, Parker Sahib, from the inside you are a foreigner. You cannot hide it from them."

Great, I have some kind of foreign aura! I pulled my black Tibetan *chuba* from my pack and began to put it on. Prem intervened.

"Parker Sahib, it is no use. This coat will not help."

"C'mon, Prem. The only thing left showing is a bit of my chin. I know I have a beard and nobody else does, but I can hide that." I hunkered down into the oversized robe.

Prem merely shook his head and continued.

At the next cluster of houses I hung close to Akaal Bahadur, using his large *doko* as a shield. Prem and Puraba had walked by without being noticed. But as we approached, a group of men raising the centerbeam of a new house stopped their chatter and watched us pass. Two young boys stepped out into the trail to stare at me. Guise or no, they could tell. Feeling like an overaged adolescent out on Halloween, I hurried out of their sight and took off the *chuba*. I caught up with Puraba and held it out to him. *"Linos"* ("Take it"), I said, embarrassed.

Soon the trail split. The upper strand led directly into Gum Gadhi. We followed the lower trail that continued along the Lumsa Khola. At dusk we found ourselves still an hour or more from the Mugu Karnali. We had miscalculated, or the young girls had not told us the truth. In any case, we wouldn't get off this steep trail until well after dark. We pushed on.

Negotiating the rock-strewn trail in the murky twilight became difficult for the porters. We stopped and Prem asked them. *"Ke garne?"* ("What to do?") "Should we go on? Can you make it?"

All agreed that we should keep moving—except Shera Punzo.

"It's too dark," he sniveled.

"You are a small child, a baby," Akaal Bahadur shot back.

Since leaving Jumla we had come to find that Shera Punzo often acted even younger than his true age of fifteen. At first his requests to carry less, or to rest more often, had been amusing. Quickly, however, we lost our patience, and no one more so than Akaal Bahadur.

Shera Punzo cowered behind Puraba. "I cannot see. I will fall."

"We will be here, no one will fall," Prem said.

"What are you afraid of? It's dark every night!" Akaal Bahadur spat out the words in Nepali.

But nothing could sway Shera Punzo. Resigned to spending the night along the trail just below Gum Gadhi, we groped in the dark for a resting place. Behind a nearby stone wall, we cleared a small space of stinging nettles. Using long sticks as tongs, Akaal Bahadur and Jeet Bahadur collected the bristled leaves in our large pot. A half hour in boiling water would turn them into an unsightly but surprisingly edible green slurry called *sisnu*.

Fearing that our tents would be conspicuous, we used our kitchen tarp and ice axes to fashion a shelter close against the wall. With little available fuel, we ate half-cooked rice and *sisnu*, then settled in for several hours' sleep. I set the alarm on my watch for 3:00 A.M. Prem and I had quietly decided that no matter what, we would move out well before first light, dragging Shera Punzo if necessary.

Peering over the wall, we could see the lanterned windows of buildings along the ridge directly above us. Puraba identified them as the garrison barracks. This was *not* my idea of a good campsite. Worried that our cooking fire had been spotted, I slept only intermittently through the night.

By 3:15 A.M. we were on the trail. Surprisingly, Shera Punzo had put up no protest, although with the moon having set, the night was now pitch black. In Jumla we had bought two more Chinese flashlights, bringing our total to three. But to conserve our meager supply of batteries, we now used only one. This slowed us to a crawling pace along the precipitous rocky trail. A few feet to our right, the slope dropped away into the night—how far, we couldn't tell.

Suddenly, from behind, I heard Puraba's muffled yell and the scraping of body and basket. I rushed back to find him lying on a large rock, his *doko* half-crushed beneath him. Through skill or good fortune, he had twisted as he fell, avoiding serious damage. I bent to help him, but with injured pride he waved me off.

Prem, in the lead with the flashlight, had stopped at Puraba's outcry. To avoid more falls, we continued on as a human chain, each of us holding the load of the person ahead for guidance. Although slow, this method provided both stability for negotiating the trail and security for Shera Punzo, who by now was keeping up a constant litany about the blackness, his load, the rocky trail, his desire to stop and wait until daylight. We placed him second in line behind Prem, both to keep him moving and to make sure he didn't disappear into the night with our equipment.

After an hour, the trail flattened out along the Lumsa Khola. Here, on flat ground, other travelers had spent the night. Even at this early hour, people stirred. Ahead, the light of a fire lit the trail. I waited in the cover of darkness while Prem went ahead to check. He returned smiling. No police. Just travelers cooking an early-morning meal. Nevertheless, as we passed I hid behind Akaal Bahadur, his large *doko* providing a shield from inquisitive eyes.

Ahead, the persistent roar of the river grew louder. We crossed a small wooden bridge spanning the Lumsa Khola, and turned a corner. Below us rushed the dark waters of the Mugu Karnali, one of the few rivers to pierce the Himalayas completely. From its source somewhere to the north and east along the Tibetan Plateau, it runs as the Mugu Khola south where it merges with the Langu Khola, then turns due west to form the Mugu Karnali. From Gum Gadhi, the waters run another forty miles west before merging with the Humla Karnali and Kubori Kholas to create the Karnali River.

For two hours we headed east, contouring again along the sheer walls of the steep river canyon. Gradually, the eastern sky lightened. At dawn we stopped for tea and a quick meal.

I dropped behind some rocks, which partially hid me from the trail, feeling greatly relieved at having passed Gum Gadhi so easily. Maybe my worries were unfounded; perhaps we would have no trouble with police or permits. We had seen no one since reaching the Mugu Karnali. It seemed almost too easy.

Soon, however, Tibetans in groups of threes and fours began passing on the trail. As dawn turned to day, their numbers increased. And once again, with little more than my Chinese cap visible above the rocks, the *bideshi* (foreign) aura stopped them cold. Everyone paused to stare. I scrunched down lower, completely out of view, and waited for five minutes. Then I cautiously stuck up just an eyeball's worth of head, and incredulously counted twelve of them watching me. At my appearance, they commented and smiled, as if engaged in some spectator sport.

I had hoped to travel through this region quietly, causing only the merest ripple, slipping through the bureaucratic cracks, leaving nary a trace. *How was I supposed to do that when so many people knew I was here?* I could almost hear them saying, "Over there. Behind those rocks. Don't you see him slinking down, trying to make us think he is a local by hiding under that stupid hat? Doesn't he know we can smell him from half a mile away?"

I gave up and, like a kid found in a game of hide-and-seek, joined the others around the fire at trail's edge. With another checkpost in the village of Mugu several days ahead, there were bound to be officials as well as these Tibetans using this trail. Once again, the demons of doubt crept into my thoughts.

I might as well give myself up right now. Because probably sooner than later, the soldiers will come along and drag my ass off to some dingy jail cell. How many months will I languish, like that poor Frenchman, until someone realizes that I'm not coming back? What exorbitant price will they demand for my release?

I turned to Prem. "I thought there wasn't supposed to be any traffic along this trail. Who are all these people?"

He sensed my rising agitation and responded in a reassuring tone. "Only the local people, nothing to worry about, Parker Sahib."

"But they've seen me! All two hundred and fifty of them!"

"This is no problem, Parker Sahib. Come, let us go." Prem smiled over his shoulder as he headed off.

"No problem, Parker Sahib," I mimicked. "Whose ass is on the line here, Prem?" Muttering obscenities, I hurried along behind him. "Prem, if the shit hits the fan, I want you right here with me. You are going to do all of the explaining."

"No problem, Parker Sahib."

The trail gently undulated as it followed the river course. Falling in with the local traffic, we matched their quick pace for almost two hours without a pause. The trail remained crowded, but gradually I realized that almost everyone moved in our direction, away from Gum Gadhi. I was certainly the object of their curiosity, but in a friendly, nonaggressive way. They nodded and smiled, I smiled back.

Towards midday, we came upon a medieval village straddling the trail. Lumsa consisted of a series of dilapidated, flat-roofed, two-story structures, many of which leaned at dangerous angles. In the small, dusty central square, I stopped to change a roll of film. Several silvery black water buffalo tethered to stakes eyed me skittishly. Dung, decomposing animal carcasses and piles of unidentifiable organic debris created a nauseating stench in the midday sun. A glassy-eyed villager dressed in blackened homespun stared at me with benign curiosity from a doorway. Clouds of flies and the stench urged me onward.

Just beyond Lumsa, the trail dropped two hundred feet to the riverbed. Here the gorge opened, and we set out across fields to the river's edge. Tired from having started our day so early, we took an extended lunch break, snoozing under makeshift shelters that protected us from the searing sun.

Later, sitting by a small bridge spanning a side stream, I saw that the trail was now deserted. Only then did I understand Prem's cavalier attitude that morning, for the traffic we had encountered was just the normal early-morning traffic heading from Gum Gadhi towards Mugu and the Tibetan frontier. These ruddy-faced Tibetans were little threat to us. Given their dislike of authority, they had no reason to turn us in, and it might be just like them to protect us. Certainly we were never in any danger, and Prem knew this. I forgave him. After all, he had said "No problem, Parker Sahib."

At four we rose and walked several slow miles through afternoon heat into the early evening. We set camp along the river, and I turned in early after another meal of rice and *sisnu*.

At one-thirty I awoke, cursing myself for not having brought a piss bottle with me as I had in eastern Nepal. Finally, I struggled out of my warm sleeping bag, unzipped the tent door and stepped a few feet into the cool night. The skies remained clear; directly overhead, the Milky Way streaked the sky. A crescent moon rose over the ridges to the south. How many times had I watched that moon wax and wane in these last months? I had never imagined that I would become so attuned to its cycles. But then, I had never before lived outdoors for months at a time, away from the obscuring glow of artificial light. Here the moon took on new meaning, new importance for me. At its fullest, I could write in my journal by its light. In its absence, we stumbled and fell along the trail. By the rising full moon of December, I had met Clara.

Every afternoon I waited. Clara and her friend Sera would come up to the fourth floor, then climb the stairs to the rooftop to smoke cigarettes and talk. A low wall, three feet high, hid them from the prying eyes of the other Nepalese who worked in the hotel. Sometimes I followed them up to the roof and there Clara and I talked. From the beginning she made it obvious she wished to keep our meetings and conversations a secret.

I learned that although she was Nepalese, she came from Darjeeling and was raised as a Catholic, hence her Christian name. Accustomed to wearing skirts and blouses at her convent school, she and the other Darjeeling girls who lived in Kathmandu continued to wear western clothes. She spoke clear, precise English and appeared sophisticated and westernized.

Perhaps that's what led me to ask her out. Looking back now, it seemed such a naive thing to do. Because we had little privacy to talk, we fell into the practice of communicating by passing notes.

One afternoon as we sat hidden by the wall, I surreptitiously passed her a note.

Dear Clara,

    I would be most pleased if you could accompany me for dinner this evening.

Parker

She read the note and then smiled at me in such a beautiful way I thought she might say yes. With hindsight, I could see that she probably smiled because she felt it was a sweet thing for me to suggest—but such a naive boy! She thought for a moment after reading the note, then scribbled a reply.

Dear Parker,

    I would more than anything like to go to dinner with you, but I cannot. Please, you must understand, there are many things you do not know and my life does not always go the way I would like, so full of complications. But I thank you anyway.

Clara

I crawled back into my sleeping bag and pulled the drawstring close around my head. "I will miss you," she had said. I missed her.

CHAPTER FIVE

▲

Mugu Karnali Gorge

Wednesday, March 7, 1984

At dawn, we quietly disassembled the tents and packed them away before other travelers appeared along the trail. I wanted to attract as little attention as possible. We walked steadily until ten-thirty, when the sun began to beat down on us. Once again, we rested and cooled ourselves with a five-hour midday break.

Grass fires dotted the steep slopes on the opposite side of the river. Set intentionally, they burned the dry grasses but left the huge pine trees unharmed.

Later we passed through an area burned some weeks previously, and I guessed at the reason for it. Fresh green shoots pushed through the tufts of burned grass, perfect fodder for the many cows, yaks, goats and sheep that grazed on the slopes. The only detrimental effect was that the flames destroyed the small saplings, preventing new forest growth. Only the large trees escaped unharmed.

The "only" detrimental effect—destroying the young trees—might, as in other parts of Nepal, ultimately prove catastrophic. Here the population pressure wasn't as great as in eastern Nepal, where entire forests had been axed to supply firewood and make way for fields. In addition, the intensive pressures of trekking in Sagarmatha National Park in the Everest region has led to massive deforestation with subsequent problems of landslides and loss of fertile topsoil. Here, in remote western Nepal, we alone would not threaten the supply of wood, but what if others followed us? The native population's needs, even in these remote valleys, could easily lead to environmental degradation. Was I, one lone Westerner, starting an outsider problem here too? Trekking in this part of Nepal was years away, but very likely it would come; bringing in some tourist money, true, but environmentally possibly doing more harm than good. Would the countries from which the trekkers came, mine included, help with foreign aid, family planning, medical delivery systems? Too many questions, no answers.

After our lunch break, we walked quickly, following the increasingly spectacular Mugu Karnali Gorge. As we moved upstream, the gorge narrowed, the slopes steepened. The view offered an occasional glimpse of the himal in the distance.

Towards midafternoon I came to a high stone bench built at just the right height for resting a load if one backed onto it. No need to take off your load or set it on the ground, less energy expended. Five Tibetans, three men and two women, whom I had followed for the past hour, stopped too. Since passing Gum Gadhi I had relaxed and for the first time looked closely at our fellow travelers.

Virtually everyone carried something. The loads ranged from twelve-foot lengths of iron pipe to month-old pieces of meat wedged into the bottom of homespun bags. They dripped blood and fat and each trailed a cloud of flies. Even though we were at 7,000 feet, it was hot at midday and we could smell these loads from many yards away.

These Tibetans had deep olive complexions, high cheekbones, and eyes with a deeper fold than that found on the lowland Nepalese. The three men wore gray wool *chubas*, the traditional oversized Tibetan topcoat, and homespun wool trousers. Two sported dark-colored hats. Each man had earrings of a different design.

The first had a gold hoop, three inches across, pierced through his right ear and soldered closed. The second man had rings in both ears, five-inch-long pieces of hide on which hung a piece of turquoise flanked by two strips of smooth orange-pink coral. He had wrapped both around his ears, the stones facing forward, but as I watched, one came loose and flopped down to his shoulder. Laughing, he deftly twisted it back into place. The oldest man's earlobes were distended by the weight of heavy silver hoops set with oval pieces of turquoise in a flared section that faced forward. Around his neck hung a heavy necklace alternating turquoise with coral beads.

Turning to look at the women, I immediately sensed their strength and self-confidence. Unlike some Nepalese women, they looked directly into my eyes. The younger of the two had cheeks so rosy that if it were not for the dirt, I would have sworn she wore makeup. The other woman did wear a strange type of cosmetic, oblong patches of dark green henna spread on her chin, forehead and cheeks. Sleeveless black dresses with multicolored aprons of dark red, charcoal gray and light tan topped the most incongruous aspect of their outfits, blue and green Chinese sneakers. They draped a piece of wool, the same color pattern as their aprons, over their heads. I had become used to seeing nose jewelry on Nepalese women, but the Tibetan women had none. Six-inch hoops of silver dangled from their ears. Both wore magnificent necklaces of alternating coral and turquoise; the roughly polished hunks of turquoise varied from pea-size to apricot-size.

I tried to take photographs, especially of the women, but they turned shy, giggling and covering their mouths when they caught me pointing the camera their way. Always struggling to take candid shots, I felt awkward and intrusive. But I knew I would regret it later if I didn't at least try for a photographic record of these people.

These Tibetan Bhuddists had their spiritual home in Lhasa. Soon after the Chinese takeover of Tibet in 1959, however, the Dalai Lama had fled to India, taking with him the spiritual center of Tibetan Buddhism. The result now is a religion and cultural heritage in disarray, fragmented by both political boundaries and Chinese oppression. Confronted already with tourists in Nepal and with the impending influx of tourists into Tibet, I wondered how long the nomadic culture of these Tibetans would survive in the face of the encroachment of western influences.

Late in the afternoon, another grimy Tibetan came running after us, shouting loudly. Even as he approached, the pungent smell of his unwashed body enveloped us. *Oh no, another government official!* For several minutes, Prem and I tried to ignore him, until we realized he was only trying to tell us his house lay just ahead. He invited us in for *chang*. The ninety-degree afternoon made the idea of a cool sitdown appealing. So we crossed a cantilevered wooden bridge and walked to his house, a one-story stone-and-mud building. He led us into a large gloomy room with a crude fireplace, yak skins on the floor and drying meat strips hanging from the beams. Smiling, with two prominent gold teeth, his wife served us thick, cool *chang*. Only after a couple of glasses did we realize why the man had been so anxious to have us come to his house. He charged forty rupees per pitcher!

Noticing a pile of potatoes, we bargained with the Tibetan for two *paathis'* worth, about ten pounds. We paid him for the *chang* and potatoes, then walked back outside into the blinding sunlight.

A man dressed in a green sweater and pants crossed the bridge with a purposeful stride and marched up the path in our direction. I spotted him first and recognized him immediately as police. Tall and spindly, with his army sweater a size too small, he carried a small baton. The slanting sun disoriented me momentarily, and I felt a cold sweat on my forehead. Dizzy, flushed from the *chang*, I felt oddly detached from the scene. Certain that he would confront me, I tried frantically to formulate a plan of escape, a lie, a strategy. But before my addled brain could engage gears, he passed not more than a foot away, ignoring me completely, and walked into the house.

With my head still swirling I jammed my Chinese cap down tightly. Seizing the opportunity, Prem and I jogged across the bridge and collected our porters. We walked for another hour before setting our camp near the village of Dhungedhara at just over 8,000 feet.

That evening I still felt lightheaded and nauseated, although I couldn't determine why. I lay awake in my sleeping bag for a long time. Serious doubts began to erode my confidence. Before leaving Kathmandu for the west, I had mentally prepared myself for the possibility of physical adversity. Steep passes, snow and ice, long, hard up-and-down climbs, storms, concerns about food. But I hadn't seriously considered engaging in a game of dodge-'em with the police and military. Perhaps naively, I had assumed that our paperwork from Kathmandu would get us by. A little fudging here and there, a bribe or two . . . I had learned the tricks of getting by in Asia—I thought. Now I knew I had grossly underestimated the true remoteness of western Nepal. I drifted off to sleep about one o'clock, but woke up at three-thirty with a fever, exploding bowels and paralyzing cramps.

Poisoned. By the *chang*, by the gnawing doubts, by my own anxieties. I reached for the Lomotil and the local opium-laced cough syrup. They eased my pain, but I was up four more times, squatting in the cool, still night. I hadn't been weaned in this part of the world where legs become accustomed to this position and by the last time I could no longer squat. With leaden legs and heavy eyes, I watched the eastern sky turn gray and then pink with the coming dawn.

Mercifully, we slept late. At eight, Akaal Bahadur brought me bed tea. Having become dehydrated during the night, I accepted it gratefully, downing the steaming sweet liquid in a few gulps. I dragged myself up and into the already hot sun, my legs trembled under me, my eyelids heavy from the drugs and lack of sleep. Prem and Puraba had also become sick during the night and I offered them Lomotil, which they accepted with thanks.

We weren't as quick off the mark that morning, but moving proved easier than remaining still. Not long after we left camp we passed through a large *chorten* built over the trail. The *chorten* (*stupa* in Sanskrit) is the quintessential symbol of Buddhism. The square base faces the four cardinal directions and represents the earth element. Above the base a circular mound is surmounted by a spire, representing the fire element. On the most elaborate *chortens*, a crescent, representing the air element, and a ball of flame, representing the ethereal element, sit atop the spire. Funerary monuments of important *lamas*, or monks, *chortens* vary greatly in size and style. But they can be found on the outskirts of villages and their appearance alerted us to human habitation. I looked up from the inside of this particularly elaborate *chorten* to see the entire twelve-foot-high ceiling and half the walls painted with intricate religious artwork, exquisitely detailed, colorful scenes and figures.

Two miles on, we came to the convergence of two rivers, the Mugu Khola and the Langu Khola, also known as the Dolpo Chu, from Dolpo. They merged at this point to become the Mugu Karnali. Each khola had cut a gorge several thousand feet deep, and we could see a trail following each, precarious silver threads winding high along the near-vertical walls. A half day's walk to the north, the trail following the Mugu Khola passed through the village of Mugu, then crossed the frontier into Tibet. This, the main trading route between Tibet and western Nepal and India, had accounted for virtually all of the traffic we had seen since leaving Gum Gadhi.

The other route, following the Langu Khola due east towards Dolpo, marked our destination. We estimated our immediate target, the village of Dalphu, to be less than two days' walk.

We stopped just where the kholas merged for our first meal, Prem, Puraba and I eating only plain rice. Puraba, who never complained, and Shera Punzo, who complained all the time, both indicated that we were in for a long uphill climb from here to Dalphu. It *was* steep. For two hours we ascended steadily until we reached a ridge 2,000 feet above the Langu Khola. From there we looked down three hundred feet to the village of Kimri. Although the terrain we had followed along the Mugu Karnali Gorge was rugged, several thousand feet deep, what faced us now was even steeper, deeper and rockier.

Across the river, the village of Tika perched above a 2,000-foot buttress which dropped sheer to the river below. Nestled in its aerie, the village lay beneath slopes that rose in rocky crags and spires for several thousand feet before disappearing from view. It was a formidable location for a village and I wondered what sort of people could inhabit such a place. Did its inaccessibility affect them in some strange ways? Or did it perhaps make them feel safe from the marauding bands of invaders so prevalent in the past?

We continued ascending to Kartik and camped next to a *gompa* (monastery) just above the village.

We left early the next morning to begin the most difficult day of trail-hiking I had yet experienced. Although Dalphu was only five miles from Kartik, the undulating, rocky, near-vertical terrain turned this distance into eleven miles of tortuous, treacherous travel. Cumulatively, we ascended and descended 10,000 feet before reaching Dalphu, although it was only 1,000 feet higher than Kartik.

The trail was a feat of engineering that did credit to the

villagers who maintained it. In places, stone retaining walls one hundred feet high buttressed the two-foot-wide path along near-vertical cliffs. In high winds and during the monsoon season, the landslides along the trail made it impassable and Dalphu remained isolated for months at a time. I found it remarkable that trails existed at all in some of these remote areas of Nepal. But without a trail there could be no village, and these tenuous tracks served as lifelines to the outside world.

Late in the morning we came to an active slide and I wondered how we could possibly continue. The slide, a forty-yard highway of rock and earth pulled by gravity towards the riverbed below, started 2,000 feet above us and continued 2,500 feet down to the *khola* below. Looking up, we could see specks that with terrifying speed grew into near boulders as they hurtled down and then crashed past. I looked into the faces of Prem and the others and they looked wordlessly back at me, Prem impassive, Puraba fingering his prayer beads, Shera Punzo ready to turn back. We all knew what we had to do, and feared it.

"Okay," I said to Prem. "One at a time and run like hell. I'll go first." I moved to the head of the party under a protective overhang.

Prem stepped back several yards to get a view of the slide above. "Parker Sahib, I will tell you when to go."

I crouched against the wall as several rocks bounced by, trailing growing amounts of debris with them. During a lull, I heard Prem's signal and darted out. Moving as quickly as I could through the loose dirt, scrabbling, balancing on moving earth, I surprised myself by reaching the other side without incident.

Gasping from the effort, I turned to watch a large rock smash and obliterate my footprints just twenty feet behind me.

Akaal Bahadur came next, then Jeet Bahadur, Puraba,

Shera Punzo and finally Prem. Miraculously, within half an hour we all stood safely on the far side.

The trails did not simply contour the terrain on one level. The steep slopes formed by streams originating in snow-fields thousands of feet above made this impossible. Thus, we would descend 1,500 feet into a side canyon only to climb 2,000 feet out on the far side, gaining only 500 feet in altitude and only a third or half a mile in distance, but actually walking two miles. All with the knowledge that the precious 500 feet of altitude would soon be lost in our descent into the next side canyon.

The final climb to Dalphu was the highest and steepest, and we took it slowly. As we labored, I was surprised by the chatter of female voices behind me. Turning, I saw an adolescent girl and her grandmother rapidly gaining on us. Local inhabitants routinely used these trails and took the perilous slide crossings in stride.

We stopped to rest and as they came abreast of us, I saw large silver-hooped earrings stretching the old woman's ear-lobes to eight inches. Around her neck were strung large, rounded hunks of amber and coral. And at the bottom of the necklace hung an intricately decorated silver amulet box, roughly three-by-four-by-one-and-a-half inches. I tried to take her photograph, but she protested, shaking her head vigorously. This didn't surprise me, for I had received a similar response from older people in other parts of Nepal. *But maybe the young girl.* For a moment she seemed willing to pose, then laughed and turned away before I could focus.

Shortly after a rest stop, we came to an unusually level, muddy place on the trail. Casually I glanced down at Prem's bootprint in the soft mud. Then I did a double take. There, only an inch from the boot mark, I saw a paw print three inches across. It had to be the track of a snow leopard. Comparing the relative freshness of the two sets of prints—that of the cat and Prem's boot—I speculated that the snow leopard had passed within the hour. Excitedly I searched the slope above me, but saw nothing except a pair of brilliant blue snowcocks.

We crested the last ridge and looked out on the terraced fields of Dalphu, barren and dusty after five months without rain. Boys and girls tending goats in the fields stopped and stared as we walked past. A line of *chortens* split the trail, and in deference to Buddhist tradition we dutifully kept them to our right as we approached the upper reaches of the village proper.

Puraba led us to the uppermost building. The rest of the village lay below us, a primitive apartment complex of two-story dwellings, eight or ten in a row. Several tiers of these buildings comprised the village.

From above, the clean, light-tan rooftops stretched for several hundred feet down the slope, prayer flags on long poles above each house fluttering in the breeze. On the rooftops, children played, lambs brayed, women spun wool and men conversed in small groups surrounded by grain spread to dry in the sun. Once they spotted us, more villagers gathered on the roofs to talk and stare openly at us. They seemed friendly and genuinely curious.

From the rooftop, Puraba led us down a ladder into the main room of the house. The only light in the semidark interior came from a small partially covered roof hole, which served also as a crude chimney. A middle-aged woman placed her hands together in greeting and then motioned for us to sit. Acrid smoke from the open fire stung my eyes, and I quickly moved to my designated place on the coarse wooden floor next to the hearth.

Chang appeared in silver-lined wooden bowls. It was pale yellow and almost clear, in contrast to the milky white of most *changs*, with a slight carbonation and an aftertaste very similar to the mass-produced American beers. Made of barley, it was the closest thing to an ice-cold Michelob that I had tasted since leaving home.

By the time I finished the customary third bowl, my eyes

had adjusted to the dim light. The room measured approximately fifteen feet square, with a fireplace abutting the wall opposite the doorway, next to which stood a small Buddhist altar. On the altar I saw a photograph of the Dalai Lama, small brass cups containing oil and water burning with a primitive wick, assorted hand-held prayer wheels and Tibetan scriptures. Crude wooden chests, decorated with regularly spaced splotches of whitewash, lined another wall. In the far corner, a ring of flour surrounded a hand-powered grinding wheel, and a sack of unground barley rested nearby.

An incredible clutter of bric-a-brac, both old and new, lay randomly strewn about. Huge copper urns containing water or perhaps barley fermenting for *chang*, yak skins piled in a heap, a small box of worn plastic shoes and galoshes for children, mats for bedding, plastic jerry cans, assorted bowls and plates made of brass or silver, shredded pieces of old blankets, torn and discarded clothing, foam sleeping pads. All were covered with a layer of soot, the result of burning pinewood so laden with oils that a large splinter could be lit and used as a candle.

"Parker Sahib." Prem leaned towards me. "This man is the *pradhan panch*, the—how do you say—mayor of Dalphu. He knows all the foreigners who come here."

"Have other foreigners been here recently?"

"Yes. Now there are three or four who are studying the snow leopard. They have a camp not far from here, four hours' walk. They work for the National Geographic."

Perhaps that's where the *pradhan panch* had gotten his shoes. I eyed his pair of Nike Gore-Tex Approach shoes identical to the pair I was wearing.

"Two weeks ago," Prem said, "one man received a snow-leopard bite. The snow leopard was sleeping. Put asleep by the man."

"Tranquilized."

"Yes. He was afraid the snow leopard would give him rabies. So he went to Jumla quickly so that he could go to Kathmandu."

"That was the guy we just missed in Jumla, Rodney Jackson. The Youngkins told me about him. Well, maybe we can visit their camp. Four hours, you say?"

"Only four hours' walk, Parker Sahib."

"Well, not tonight. I've emptied too many bowls of *chang*. Time for bed."

We staggered up the log ladder to the roof where our tents had been pitched. Trail-weary and *chang*-filled, we had no trouble falling asleep.

Next morning, we faced a big decision. Where were we going next? Our plan had been to follow the Langu Khola east into Dolpo along what we called the high route, past the village of Phapagaon fifteen day's travel to the east. From there, we hoped to go either south towards Shey Gompa and eventually southeast over several unknown high passes towards the Barbung Khola, or to continue eastward on the high route along the Tibetan frontier towards Charkabhotgaon, another fifteen to twenty days beyond Phapagaon. Either way, it would be a long, tough and treacherous journey.

Thus far, for all the difficulties and risks, we had really encountered only the normal problems of serious trekking. But we had been warned repeatedly by the locals that the routes we now planned were impossible this time of year, that it would be suicide to head into Dolpo by this route. On the other hand, I didn't believe much of what they said, knowing the locals' inordinate and irrational fear of the weather and terrain. In fact, we learned that some of the people near Jumla had become afraid of *us* because we had braved the Marbu Lekh in a storm. Actually, if it hadn't been for J.B.'s ankle, we could have done it even more easily and faster, because under normal circumstances it was a straightforward crossing.

To get a clearer view of the land ahead, Prem and I walked east about a mile and a half beyond Dalphu. On an outcropping perched 1,500 feet above the Langu Khola, we stopped and sat silently side by side, staring at the formidable terrain.

As I contemplated this twisted jumble of mountains, the sheer walls of snow and rock along our intended path, I realized that nothing in my past years of trekking and climbing had prepared me for the scene of geological devastation that lay before us. The fears, the doubts, the worst-scenario nightmares—they were no longer abstractions in some hazy future time. They were here.

Neither of us wanted to admit his fears to the other, so Prem and I sat for a long time, saying nothing. Because we could carry only limited supplies of food, we both knew that once we got a certain distance away from Dalphu, we would reach a point of no return. From that point we would either make it through or die somewhere amidst the mountains of Dolpo. It wasn't just a matter of food. It was still winter, and we could run into bitter weather. Storms, blizzards could trap us for days while we consumed precious food supplies. Or we could lose our way, fall off the trail, be overcome by snow too deep to traverse. Injuries and illness could plague us, and there would be no helicopter rescues in these areas. Ahead we might face slow starvation, agonizing injury or, merciful by comparison, a quick fall to our deaths.

My head reeled as I tried to think through all the possibilities. What to do? Take the chance and go on into the unknown or turn around and retrace our steps?

Finally, Prem spoke. Though soft, his voice cut firmly through the atmosphere of doubt. "Parker Sahib, I think we should do it. Jeet Bahadur, Akaal Bahadur, you and me. We have come a very long way. Too far to simply go back. We must try."

"Do you know the risks? The food we will have to carry, the mountains we will have to cross, the trails?"

Prem closed his eyes and nodded slowly, thoughtfully. Then he waited as I pondered the decision I would have to make, because in the end it was *my* decision. Actually, I had already decided for myself, but hesitated to make such a weighty decision for the others. I turned to Prem. "We will depend on Akaal Bahadur and Jeet Bahadur to help us get through. It's not just you and me. We have to talk to them. See if they understand the risks. We must get their okay, too."

He nodded again.

Back in Dalphu, we ate boiled potatoes, carefully peeled and dipped in fiery *achar* (chili sauce) and crushed Tibetan rock salt. After our meal, Prem, Akaal Bahadur, Jeet Bahadur and I walked a short way up the slope behind Dalphu, out of earshot of the villagers.

Prem explained to Akaal Bahadur and Jeet Bahadur what we had discussed earlier. I understood roughly half the interchange, but I heard the excitement in their voices. The two porters' eyes sparkled and they smiled animatedly. The thrill of adventure had captured them.

"Parker Sahib, they say they will go. They are strong, they can carry our food, they can carry very heavy loads. They will go anywhere you go," Prem said. The porters' enthusiasm was contagious and I smiled at their eagerness.

Then in my best broken Nepali I spoke to all three of them, mustering the most serious tone I could. "Now things will be different. This is not like the other treks. This isn't like being with J.B. Sahib and me in eastern Nepal. This isn't like going from Surkhet to Jumla. We, the four of us, are together. We are equals. No sahib, no *sirdar*, no porters. Do you understand?"

They all nodded gravely.

"If you want to go back now, you must choose. I will not stop you, this is your choice."

Again they nodded, matching the solemn expression on my face. I knew they would come with me for they trusted me. And I trusted them with my life. But I also knew that the cultural differences would not disappear. I could see in their eyes that although I said we were equals, and they agreed, it was not and never could be so. I would always be sahib to them; nothing I could say or do would change this.

We returned to our tents to work out the logistics. We figured we needed to carry food for twenty-five days minimum, and potatoes were the only food available. When we computed one and a half pounds of food per person per day, times four people, it came to 150 pounds extra weight. This meant three extra porters to carry our food. But since they ate too, we would need still another porter just to carry potatoes for the three porters. Four more porters, with one possibly returning to Dalphu when we had eaten one load of food. The others would have to come all the way to Kathmandu with us, which meant paying their transportation costs home.

I checked our money supply, which was dangerously low, since J.B.'s plane ticket had taken a large bite out of our treasury. After counting carefully, I determined that we could afford to offer forty rupees per day for each porter.

We approached the *pradhan panch* with our request to hire porters. He scowled and shook his head grimly. It would be difficult for him to help us just now.

Prem raised his eyebrow and smiled sideways at me. Then turned back to the *pradhan panch* with a serious expression. A finder's fee could be arranged if he was successful in helping us. That lit up the mayor's face, and he immediately left to visit the other households in the village.

An hour and a half later, he returned and spoke to Prem.

"He says it is impossible, Parker Sahib. No one will go with us. Not even if we pay them eighty rupees per day. They say it is impossible to go our way."

"Maybe we can find porters in Wangri. Puraba and Shera Punzo live there. Maybe they can help us. Besides, we still haven't asked Puraba if he wants to go with us. I'd like him to. Not Shera Punzo, though. He's too young and weak."

"Tomorrow we should go to Wangri," Prem said.

I agreed, as the village was only on the other side of the gorge and should take us just a few hours to reach.

"Parker Sahib, the *pradhan panch* wants to sell us more *chang*."

I couldn't resist, and eventually bought six bottles of the delicious golden beer, which we shared with Akaal Bahadur and Jeet Bahadur.

CHAPTER SIX

▲

DALPHU

Monday, March 12, 1984

SNOW FELL DURING THE NIGHT BUT WITH LITTLE ACCUMULAtion. By morning the storm had blown through, leaving the temperature in the twenties.

Before leaving for Wangri, Prem approached me. "Parker Sahib," he said with a sigh. "Shera Punzo wants to leave the kerosene and stove here at the *pradhan panch*'s house so he doesn't have to carry it. He says we can come back for it later. I think this is a good idea."

I agreed, then looked around at the small pile of gear to be left behind. "What's this?" I picked up several packets of noodles. "Why are we leaving these behind? They don't weigh anything."

"Shera Punzo!" Prem called to the boy sharply.

"Lazy kid," I muttered.

Akaal Bahadur turned and sneered at Shera Punzo, making another snide remark in Nepali on the inadequacies of our youngest porter. Shera Punzo's almost constant complaining and shirking had come to a head.

"First it was funny," I said. "All that whining about needing more food and more clothes. Now it's just damn tiresome."

"And he complains about how much money he makes!"

Prem said. "He is making forty rupees per day. This is more than he has made ever in his life."

"We're only paying Akaal Bahadur and Jeet Bahadur twenty-five rupees per day." (These being standard Kathmandu wages.) "We've got to get rid of Shera Punzo soon."

"Yes, Parker Sahib. At Wangri we can find other porters, much better ones."

"Certainly ones that eat less. Have you seen how much rice he eats?"

Prem laughed. It had been a recurring joke, the enormous amounts Shera Punzo could consume at one sitting. I carried more weight, but he ate more food. "No problem, Parker Sahib. Soon he will go."

The trip to Wangri, less than two miles across the canyon, took us four grueling hours. First we dropped to the Langu Khola, then puffed up the steep face on the far side.

Crumbling *chortens* guarded the trail as we neared the village. Three small girls, dressed in rags, appeared out of the underbrush a hundred feet above to watch us. Puraba shouted and waved as a small boy ran down to greet him. Puraba hadn't seen his children since leaving for Jumla last November.

The village came into view above us, a maze of interconnected multilevel dwellings, denser than in Dalphu but in every other way similar, cluttered with log ladders, prayer flags on long wooden poles and the necessities and debris of daily life. Puraba led us into the village and up to the roof of his house, situated in the middle of a dozen connected dwellings that formed a row fifty yards long.

Within ten minutes, we had attracted a crowd of more than forty children and adults. I sensed their excitement. Few foreigners made it this far, and Prem, Akaal Bahadur and Jeet Bahadur were just as foreign here as I. I squatted down to the level of the children and started kidding with them, making faces and teasing. Soon the children were laughing and the adults smiling.

"*Ausadhi?*" ("Medicine?") someone asked.

"*Ausadhi chhainna*" ("I don't have any medicine"), I answered, denying yet another request for the coveted western commodity.

"Where are you from?"

"Kathmandu," Prem answered. A few nodded their heads, but just as many looked puzzled. "They don't know where Kathmandu is, Parker Sahib. What would happen if we tried to tell them you were from America?"

"Kathmandu is far enough away."

"Yes, to them I am a foreigner, too. They think it is strange that I wear western clothes. They do not know where Darjeeling is. It is as far away as America."

"Japanese, Japanese," someone identified us.

This wasn't the first time I had been called Japanese. Caucasians automatically were called Japanese by many in the Himalayas. This seemed odd, because of all the foreigners who traveled the Himalayas, the Japanese, being Asian, looked most like the indigenous people.

"Parker Sahib," Prem called me away from the crowd of children. "Come this way."

We climbed down the ubiquitous log ladder, steps hewn in a single log split in two, and into Puraba's dark and smoky home. Once again, we were served golden barley *chang*. Each time we drained our silver-lined bowls, Puraba attentively refilled them. We drank several large bottles' worth to avoid offending Puraba or his grandmother, who ran his household for him. The old woman was in her eighties and had severe conjunctivitis. She, too, asked for medicine, but again I couldn't provide it. The smoky atmosphere in the house did nothing to ease her condition. Although in almost constant pain, she was cheerful and cordial to us.

After three hours of drinking *chang*, we stumbled up the log ladder to the roof, had a quick dinner and turned in.

We planned to rest the next day in Wangri. We would spend time learning more about the possible routes ahead, finding porters, washing and, if possible, resting a little. Another clear, cold morning dawned. I huddled in my sleeping bag until eight-thirty when the sun climbed above the towering 8,000-foot rock face a half mile away, across the side canyon on which Wangri perched at 11,000 feet.

At ten o'clock, Prem, Akaal Bahadur and I went further up the side canyon to scout a possible route over the Khapre La to the south in the event we couldn't find porters to carry for us east into Dolpo. We stopped by the stream that flowed down into the village, built a fire and left Akaal Bahadur to wash clothes. Prem and I continued up the canyon past several *chortens*.

Crossing the jumbled remains of two avalanches, we ascended through a birch and pine forest. A route marked on our maps continued up this trail and over the 17,000-foot Khapre La. After two miles, we stopped and looked towards the snow-covered peaks.

"Well, Prem. What do you think? Is it possible?"

"Yes, Parker Sahib. I think it is possible. Maybe it will be good for seeing all the mountains."

I glanced at Prem by my side and smiled affectionately. Without question Prem could have earned a better living doing something else, but he enjoyed this life: trekking, guiding, being in the open air, in the mountains. I could empathize with that.

We bent over the map. "Look, if we go this way," I traced the dotted line with my finger, "we'll be able to see the Sisne, the Kanjiroba, the Patrasi and the Jagdula Himals. It should be beautiful."

"From here we cannot see this pass, but I think it will be possible," Prem said. "Even though there is snow, we can do it."

I turned and looked once again at the steep, snow-blanketed slope above. "If we can't go east, let's give it a try."

Excitedly, we hurried back down the trail. Halfway back to the village, I saw them. Stopping abruptly, I motioned

Prem to do the same. In front of us on the trail was a set of fresh snow leopard tracks, made in the sun-softened mud since we had passed this spot on our way up the canyon.

The mysterious and shy snow leopard (*Panthera unica*) inhabits only these remotest mountain areas of the Himalayas. They prey primarily on the bharal (blue sheep) although with the destruction of habitat and human depletion of their natural prey they have more recently turned to domestic animals for food. This threat to livestock has led to extensive hunting by local villagers, and a precipitous drop in their numbers. Because their spotted coats give them superb camouflage and their reclusive habits keep them out of sight, it was unlikely we would actually see one of these big cats. Counted among the endangered species, even a glimpse of one of these rare and beautiful animals would have made my day.

Hardly daring to breathe, we followed the tracks downhill for twenty-five yards until they veered off into the brush along the trail. Intently, hopefully, we scanned the sparse forest and open meadows above us. We stood there, eyes searching for several minutes, but nothing broke the stillness of the cobalt blue sky and midday sun. Far above us, a pair of lammergeiers spiraled upwards in ever higher circles.

Disappointed, we returned to the stream where Akaal Bahadur waited. We washed ourselves—thoroughly—for the first time in the ten days since leaving Jumla.

Back in Wangri, I spent the afternoon relaxing in the sun on the roof and writing in my journal. Puraba's grandmother came up a log ladder, sat and smiled toothlessly at me. Not far away, a woman wove cloth from homespun wool yarn. Attached to one end of her ten-foot-long loom was a dowel to which was tied fifty pieces of yarn. The woman sat at the other end in a harness, keeping an even tension on the loom. She passed a large ball of yarn between the two layers of stretched yarn and went through a complex series of maneuvers I couldn't follow. Her expert fingers moved quickly and deftly. Fascinated, I watched her repeat this procedure over and over as a piece of cloth slowly emerged.

She seemed to be the only one busy, however. A few men sat about. Some children played. Otherwise, nothing seemed to be happening.

What an idle lifestyle, I thought to myself. These people grew their barley, made *chang*, cooked their simple food. The women made cloth, but so few household chores occupied them. Without schools, the children played on the rooftops or in the terraced fields. They were filthy, their hands, ankles and necks blackened and encrusted with dirt. I knew that if they washed, their skin would be light brown.

Laughing to myself, I looked at my own hands; they had accumulated a layer of grime just since that morning's wash.

Life was hard in Wangri, and what seemed laziness to me was perhaps to them a rest from difficult travel between villages or spurts of intense work in the fields. During the last several days I was also beginning to feel the dulling effects of several weeks of spartan diet. I could only imagine what effects a lifetime of malnutrition could have on one's mental and physical capabilities. And malnutrition was just one of the factors that trapped them in a vicious cycle of poverty and poor health. *You must judge them by their own standards, Parker.*

Late in the afternoon we had more *chang*, then dinner. After dinner, a man in his late forties joined the group around our campfire on the dirt roof of Puraba's house. He asked a few questions, then launched into a tirade. I caught a few words, but couldn't understand much else. When he paused for a moment, Prem translated for me.

"He is angry, Parker Sahib, about the foreigners. He says that some foreigners are here without the proper papers. Even those who have permits, he doesn't like. The foreigners who study the snow leopards, he says they should not be here."

"Why does he say that? What are his reasons? What are they doing here that he doesn't like?"

Ever loyal, Akaal Bahadur and Jeet Bahadur stood and began arguing with the man. Forceful gestures showed their anger and intense passions.

"He does not say why, Parker Sahib. He only says that the foreigners are stupid and ignorant."

The argument went on for almost an hour. Prem was unable to elicit any concrete answers from him. Finally the angry man stood up, shouted a few sentences, turned on his heel and faded into the night. I looked inquiringly at Prem.

"He says that he is going to Gum Gadhi tomorrow to talk to officials about a new bridge. He gave you a threat. He said he would teach you a lesson."

Puraba tried to ease the situation, telling Prem that the man, a former village official, was just blustering, trying to show off, to prove he still held some authority. But he also gave Prem more ominous news, which Prem related to me.

"Shera Punzo has been boasting. He told all the village people that we passed Gum Gadhi at night. And he has told them that we wish to travel to Dolpo."

"That useless little jerk," I said. "We told Puraba and Shera Punzo to keep quiet about that."

"He is too young, that boy," Prem said. "He wants to tell everyone how much money he makes, and how he cheated the police at Gum Gadhi."

Uncharacteristically, the anger rose inside of me and my hands clenched, yearning for Shera Punzo's throat. "Come to my tent, everybody."

Prem, Akaal Bahadur, Jeet Bahadur and I piled inside my tent. Prem was furious and I heard muttered curses under his breath.

"I think, Parker Sahib, that it is not possible to get porters here to go east into Dolpo. I think they are afraid of the mountains and also of demons."

"You're right, Prem. I don't think we can get anyone to go with us over Khapre La either."

"But if we can go over Khapre La, it will save many days," Prem countered.

"Without extra porters, we can't do it. We'll just have to go back through Gum Gadhi to Jumla."

"We don't like to do this, Parker Sahib. To go back."

"I don't like it either, but we can't afford to take any chances that the man was bluffing. We'll just have to head back towards Gum Gadhi as fast as we can to get there before he does. And we'll have to pass it again at night."

We went to bed unhappy, discouraged, angry. I couldn't get comfortable and didn't feel like sleep.

"Damn," I said, suddenly sitting upright. "And we'll have to go back to Dalphu to get our kerosene and stove. Shera Punzo left them there so he wouldn't have to carry them."

Our hopes of doing the high route, of going deep into the wilds of Dolpo, had been dashed. We now found ourselves at a dead end, unable for lack of porters to go east into Dolpo or south over Khapre La. My anger burned hot. I hadn't realized until now how much I wanted to take this high route through Dolpo. It was the most difficult, the furthest out, the purest line through the Himalayas. Ultimately, style was important to me.

Now I couldn't do that. And at least in part because some juvenile wanted to boast to anyone who would listen. All the frustrations of the trip—being unable to bus further west than Surkhet, J.B.'s injury, the porter problems, being alone, the need to avoid local authorities, periodic illness—built one atop the other, eroded my strength and will. Nothing, it seemed, happened as intended. The Himalayas continually forced us to alter our plans, to play it by ear, to take one thing at a time, one day at a time. Perhaps this was the lesson.

But now I didn't feel philosophical. Lying awake, the demons of frustration and doubt tormented me, taunted me, hunted for my weak spots. They would not leave me.

The entire village turned out for our departure the next morning, including Puraba's grandmother. Her bent figure appeared on the furthest roof in the village, standing with hands pressed together, tongue sticking out in the traditional Tibetan greeting. As we descended to the Langu Khola, I turned back several times, and each time I saw her standing there, watching us through half-seeing eyes.

We reached Dalphu at one o'clock and headed to the mayor's house to drink more of his golden *chang*. He greeted us from his rooftop and spoke excitedly. Prem translated.

"Yesterday two people from the snow leopard camp came here to drink *chang*."

"The *pradhan panch*'s *chang* is the best in the region, obviously."

"But they drank too much and when they wanted to go home, they were too drunk. They fell many times. So they returned and last night they slept here. But they left this morning."

"That's a shame. I'm disappointed to have missed them. And now we're not even going to have time to visit their camp. I'm sure they could have used the company. I know I could."

Before leaving the next morning, we sold our ten liters of kerosene to the mayor. We were getting desperate for money, and we could do without the weight. Prem convinced me that firewood would be readily available along the route ahead. I neglected to press him too hard on this point, but I wondered how he could be so confident about it. Besides, we weren't sure where we were going after retracing our steps back towards Jumla.

The backtracking had struck a sour chord in all of us. Kathmandu was over thirty days away, a depressingly long time to contemplate. All that work, day by day, trekking through canyons, over passes. Wangri had been a dead end for us; from here on out our journey seemed as though it would be anticlimactic.

Our first hurdle in getting to Kartik was retracing our steps up and down 10,000 feet and crossing the same slide areas we had crossed before. The day's intense sun reflected from the exposed rock, burning our faces as we struggled through contour after contour into the side canyons.

Then we came to the slide area we had traversed days earlier. We glanced uphill apprehensively. Akaal Bahadur, having looked up and seen nothing coming, launched himself across the danger zone. Then, as though it had been waiting, a football-size rock hurtled down right at his head. His bulky load proved both hindrance and salvation. It kept him from dodging, but pulling his head in like a turtle, he swiftly turned his load toward the hillside. The rock seemed almost vengeful as it bounced off the basket and smashed into Akaal Bahadur's arm, tearing through his shirt and wounding him. He barely hesitated as he scurried swiftly to safety. After the rest of us crossed, we stopped long enough for me to bandage Akaal Bahadur's shoulder. And then we moved on.

We reached Kartik at dusk, tired and thirsty. Once again we pitched our tents on the roof of a house. I was grateful for the absence of tourists. In Khumbu and other places visited by many trekkers, householders charge for camping. They also sell firewood, sometimes asking sixty or eighty rupees for enough to cook a meal. Here we were given wood, and only sometimes would people ask for a rupee or two.

Trekking groups in eastern Nepal must by law use kerosene or other cooking fuel, not wood, to help prevent deforestation. Unfortunately, there was no such rule for the porters that accompany treks, and there are sometimes twice or three times as many porters as trekkers, plus camp staff. The porters use wood to cook their meals, so the deforestation continues, even in supposedly protected areas.

* * *

In our desire to travel quickly, we covered the distance to Gum Gadhi in two days, one and a half days faster than our outward journey. When we camped just short of Gum Gadhi, the porters thought it time for a celebration because Shera Punzo and Puraba would be leaving us soon. Shera Punzo saw the celebration as a farewell in his honor, but the rest of us would be celebrating for a different reason.

In a small village nearby, Prem bargained for three chickens, alive and squawking, and five bottles of *chang* for our feast. When it came time to slaughter the birds, Jeet Bahadur asked Puraba to do the honors.

Puraba recoiled in horror. As a devout Buddhist, he couldn't possibly kill anything. Akaal Bahadur turned to Shera Punzo. He, too, backed off, shaking his head. Disgusted with what he considered Buddhist squeamishness, Jeet Bahadur grabbed a knife in one hand and a chicken in the other. Pinning the squawking animal to a rock, he sawed through its neck, blood squirting everywhere, the chicken flapping in desperation.

"*Om mani padme humji, om mani padme humji,*" Puraba chanted as loudly as he could over the horrendous noises made by the dying chickens. Over and over, until all three chickens were slaughtered, Puraba kept up his monologue of prayer.

The thought of killing may have been abhorrent to Puraba and Shera Punzo, but when it came time to eat the birds, they were first in line. They apparently reasoned that although killing animals was disgusting, as long as someone else did it there was no sense in letting good meat go to waste.

I drank too much *chang* and sneaked off to bed at nine, leaving the party still going strong. I planned to be up with Prem in six hours to make a nighttime passage through Gum Gadhi. The others would follow at daylight. I tried not to dwell on Shera Punzo's loose tongue, which forced us to go at night yet once again. I wasn't willing to risk the chance that the man from Wangri hadn't tipped off the police.

Prem and I moved out quickly in the chilled darkness, just after 3:00 A.M. We walked rapidly along the flat trail as it paralleled the Mugu Karnali River and made the five miles to Gum Gadhi in an hour. The cold, hard light of the full moon was our guide. Once again I was amazed at the brilliance of the moon so far away from city lights. Our eyes adjusted easily and we could see every rock, every undulation in the trail.

Below Gum Gadhi we left the Mugu Karnali and followed the tributary Lumsa Khola. At the confluence, Prem led the way across on a small wooden bridge. Just as I stepped onto the bridge, my foot broke through the boards, trapping my leg at midcalf.

As I tried to free my leg, my knee twisted and pain shot up my leg. "Prem," I called. I saw his receding figure move on across the bridge. "Prem," I yelled again. But the roar of the river drowned my calls and Prem kept going, the dark shadows swallowing him up.

Taking a deep breath, I tried to work my leg out, but intense pain stopped me. The wood pressured my calf and shin; my knee throbbed. I grabbed for the post at the end of the bridge. Using it as leverage, and gritting my teeth, I twisted and pulled and finally yanked my leg out of the hole.

With my leg free, I let go of the end post. That's when I saw that my hand had been resting on a crude carving of a female holding her labia open with her hands. A *dhauliya* figure found everywhere in this region, she protected the villages from evil of all kinds. These figures had survived from ancient animistic religious beliefs. Under different circumstances, I might have thought it either funny or grotesque, but now I just slumped against the post and tried to catch my breath.

Realizing that I wasn't behind him, Prem returned to look for me. He was relieved that I hadn't slipped off the trail or into the river, and he helped me clean up my scrapes. My knee throbbed. I tested it and then gingerly stood. At least I could still walk.

The moon set over the ridges to the west just at dawn. Soon the sun rose to greet and warm us. A steep and tiring ascent brought us to our prearranged stopping place. By eight-thirty we had covered twelve miles. We stopped and spent the day in the open loft of a trailside teahouse. We munched on our high-altitude rations and slept.

We camped near the teahouse that night and discussed a change in plans. Instead of heading directly back to Jumla, we decided to head further east towards Dunai in the Dolpo district. This would avoid the police checkpost in Jumla and also save a few days' travel time.

The next morning it was time to pay off Shera Punzo. Customarily we would have paid him his salary plus a tip— *baksheesh*—but considering his laziness and the trouble he had caused us, Shera Punzo would not get a rupee more than agreed upon in Jumla weeks ago. We called Puraba and Shera Punzo into our tent.

I had Prem translate my sentiments to Shera Punzo. "You are lazy. You have gossiped when you were told not to, you have carried less than anyone else, including me. You have asked for more food and clothing. We will pay you what we have agreed upon, 640 rupees, less your advances and no more. You will get no *baksheesh* because you don't deserve it. Do you understand?"

Shera Punzo looked nonplussed. He turned and whined to Prem. "Parker Sahib," Prem said incredulously. "This boy says he wants some money for *chang*!"

I clenched my fist and shook it in Shera Punzo's face. "Get out of here now. Get out of this campsite and don't look back."

He needed no translation and left immediately.

Puraba, looking alarmed at this outburst, was calmed by Prem. We made it clear to Puraba that we were dissatisfied only with Shera Punzo and not with him. He had been a good porter and a faithful friend and this was appreciated. Although we asked him to go with us to Kathmandu, he declined, saying he would leave us in a few days.

By nine o'clock we were on our way again. The next three days would take us through an area without villages, and we were running low on food. By midafternoon we reached the last village in which we could possibly buy supplies, Mandu.

From a distance, it was a beautiful village surrounded by lush green fields and trees in full bloom, their pink and white blossoms scattering in the wind. But when we entered the village what seemed idyllic from a distance proved squalid at close range. We smelled no perfume of delicate blossoms, but rather the stench of dirt and feces that lay everywhere amidst thousands of buzzing flies. We turned into a central courtyard, dusty and full of debris.

A woman, a huge goiter swelling her neck, pounded millet into dust amidst the filth. The children stared at us. Their clothes, if they wore any at all, were rags.

The bloated bellies of the children, their thin reddish hair and scabrous scalps were signs of malnutrition. Two small girls sat side by side on a pile of pine needles. I set down my pack and took out my camera, thinking they would make a nice composition. The girl on the left raised one arm to rub her eye, but she had no hand. I lowered my camera and stared at the end of her arm—a a dirt-blackened stump. Leprosy had left no vestige of a hand. Now her limb was useless except as a wand to wave at the numerous flies that gathered around her. Averting my eyes from the child, I looked at the girl on the right. She sat with dulled eyes, oblivious to her surroundings, perhaps mentally retarded or just malnourished. It was no longer a nice composition, but rather a grim record as I took their picture, two children of Mandu sitting side by side on the bed of pine needles.

Prem had been trying for fifteen minutes to buy some

food. "Parker Sahib, they say they have no food. I think this is true."

"Keep trying, Prem. We need something else for the next three days, even if it's only some millet, anything."

Finally he found someone who would sell us a few potatoes and enough millet dust for two or three days. He also came to me with another request.

"Parker Sahib, could we buy some *ganja* (marijuana) for the porters? This woman has some. It costs only two rupees."

I followed Prem and the woman into the ground floor of a dwelling which smelled worse than the courtyard outside. The woman bent down and scraped a pile of debris up off the floor and filled a small plastic bag with a horrible mixture of sticks, chicken shit and marijuana leftovers. I thought that if it kept the porters happy, then I was happy. There was about a half ounce of the vile-looking stuff and I wondered how long it would last.

Leaving Mandu, we followed a newly constructed trail up Riyan Lekh, ascending through a lush pine and hemlock forest. We made camp above 10,000 feet in a small open area sheltered by towering pines several hundred years old. The loam underfoot cushioned each step, muffling the sounds of setting camp. The Nepalese called this the "jungle," and it had an ominous connotation to them. Danger and bandits, lions and tigers and bears.

Their fears had a degree of validity. Bandits and plunderers, particularly the Tibetan nomads, did roam these forests. But we faced far less chance of a confrontation now than in the past. And the same for attacks by leopards and bears. Few such large mammals remained in the Himalayas. But at dusk the forest came alive. Animals reclaimed the land through which we trespassed. Flying squirrels floated from tree to tree above us in an eerie, silent aerial display. Just beyond the light of our campfire, we felt the presence of unseen eyes, heard the hooting of owls and the barking of the deer.

The forest and its animals lifted my depression somewhat, but I couldn't entirely shake the melancholy with which Mandu had filled me. Amidst those lush fields and groves of fruit trees, roaring streams and lofty pines, such disease and famine. The United Mission workers in Jumla had told me the problem was not lack of water or arable land, but education. Now I knew they were right, for I had seen it that day. The people of Mandu knew nothing of basic hygiene or effective farming practices. And the lack of education made it almost impossible to effect meaningful change.

The missionaries had told me the story of a Peace Corps volunteer who had brought vegetables into the area a few years ago. He had taught the people how to grow them, and also how to prepare seeds for the following year. Just before the harvest, however, his father became ill and he returned to the U.S. When he returned to Nepal a month later, the people had harvested and eaten all the vegetables, saving nothing for seed. When he asked them why, they replied that it was too much trouble. They had lived without vegetables for many years, and could do so again. Such attitudes would take many years to change. Could one Peace Corps volunteer really expect to do much in a year or two?

I thought of my home town, Darien, Connecticut, an enclave surrounded by a neat white picket fence. Republican ladies having teas, good little boys and girls going to school, people opening their pretty shops in town or riding off to the city every day to well-paying jobs. We knew no poverty in our world, no prejudice against our neighbors—against whom in our homogeneous society could we show prejudice? We all led healthy lives, got our teeth straightened and enjoyed every opportunity to realize our full potential. I thought of the contrast between my older sister, Betsy, born mentally retarded, and the children of Mandu. Unlike them, Betsy had attended school and had a small army of trained professionals working with her, guiding her and helping her to become a productive member of society. She had received the best medical care available and now, in adulthood, is, I believe, happy. Those children of Mandu who perhaps shared her disability would not be so lucky. Without food and proper medical care, it seemed unlikely that they would even live to adulthood. Now they simply sat and stared blankly at a bleak future.

I fell asleep that night, troubled by what I had seen. But my last thoughts were of more immediate problems: we had only a two-day supply of food left. We had to continue to make good time to reach the place called Chaurgaon to resupply, or . . .

Prem

Jeet Bahadur

Akaal Bahadur

Pema

J. B. Gross, immediately after his injury on Marbu Lekh.

The captivating village of Dillikot on the north side of Marbu Lekh.

Ascending Marbu Lekh, looking south over rugged hill country towards the plains of India.

The great stupa of Bodnath, Kathmandu Valley, by night.

Reaching the pass on Marbu Lekh at 12,300 feet.

Village below Dillikot,
near the Tila River.

The author with children of
Dalphu.

A girl from the village of
Dalphu.

Prem and the porters along
the Barbung Khola east of
Tarakot.

Lama Dorje and his children in the village of Tarengaon. Dressed in tattered homespun, they pose in front of their house. A carved stone mask is embedded in the wall.

Eroded terrain looking east of the Barbung Khola beyond Tarengaon.

A remarkable gompa at Daragaon, built directly into the crumpled sedimentary layers.

Ascending above Daragaon, at 17,000 feet, looking west at the mountains of Dolpo.

Does the river flow north or south? Frozen river encountered after descending from the first pass east of Daragaon.

Descending off the second pass east of Daragaon. Frozen rivers, snow-capped mountains, crumbling cliffs of burnt umber and gray.

Three boys in the village of Sangdak.

Descending through the Cha Lungpa Gorge, Akaal Bahadur helps Jeet Bahadur along a crumbling face of rock and dirt.

Leaving Sangdak, looking back at the ocher-colored buildings, with the Sangdak Pass beyond.

We reached the Kali Gandaki watershed and looked south towards the Annapurnas. Tilicho and Nilgiri form a sheer 10,000-foot wall of rock and hanging glaciers.

CHAPTER SEVEN

▲

THE UNMISTAKABLE AROMA OF MARIJUANA WOKE ME IN THE morning. *That's it. We won't get anywhere for the next two weeks, not till all that stuff is gone.*

Akaal Bahadur and Jeet Bahadur giggled, happy as school-boys with a forbidden treat. Out on the trail, however, they were high-spirited and nothing more. When we came to difficult sections, I feared they would stumble. But quietly and deliberately, they took their time and carefully negoti-ated even the most intricate passages.

Our gradually ascending path lay through still more pine-canopied forest. Groves of ten-foot-high bamboo grew be-neath the canopy. Then, just after lunch, the trail petered out at the crest of Riyan Lekh. Prem and I sat down with the map.

"Look." I pointed at the map. "If we head southeast this way, we should intersect with this trail."

"Yes, Parker Sahib, if this map is right."

"We'll have to trust it." I looked out ahead at the pro-posed route. "We'll just have to bushwhack, that's all."

Ridges separated a series of verdant, forested bowls. But snow, ice and mud covered the north sides of each ridge, making conditions even more difficult for the porters with their bulky loads. And slowing our progress even more, the porters stopped for frequent smokes, rolling their marijuana cigarettes with oily birchbark instead of paper.

Near evening, we came to a small khola. While trying to cross it on a log, I fell in. *No harm done, just a little wet.* But as I shook out my pack, pulling things out to dry, I found a roll of film I had finished but had neglected to put back into its watertight plastic canister. Ruined. Wet through. I checked the others. All dry, except one with its snap top lid slightly ajar. As I pulled the top off, water trickled out. Another roll lost. It was always effort enough to prod myself, *Parker, take out your camera, take that picture.* Now I had lost two rolls of film. I sighed, and wondered what images I would never see again.

We had a one-day supply of food left.

Next morning, fifteen minutes after breaking camp, we crossed a faint path that ultimately ran into the trail on the map leading to the village of Chaurgaon. We lunched beside the Sinja Khola, the same river we had camped beside many miles downstream the day after leaving Jumla seventeen days before. We followed the gently undulating trail through the jungle for several hours, until we broke out into a high meadow. A long, broad valley stretched for twenty miles below us and off to the southeast. Chaurgaon, our destination, lay at the near side of the valley, about four miles away, and to the east rose the 22,000-foot peaks of the Patrasi Himal. Snow-covered Hinchuli Patan, 19,750 feet, loomed to the south.

The trail descended gently for two miles through lush conifer forest. At a split in the trail, we stopped. One path, directly in front of us, headed towards Chaurgaon. I started down the trail but fifty yards on turned at Puraba's shout from behind. He signaled that we should follow the path leading off to the right, towards Jumla.

"We can't go that way," I shouted back at the others. "We

don't want to go towards Jumla. We want to go to Chaurgaon." They didn't move, so I backtracked to the fork.

"Parker Sahib," Prem said apologetically. "We told Puraba that we would go to the village of Chaubesi, near the village where he has another house. It is not the same place as Chaurgaon."

It was a long, two-hour walk along a stream called the Chaubesi Khola. We arrived at the village at three-thirty, tired and hungry.

That evening, while drinking *rakshi* with some of the locals, I learned that Chaubesi was also known as Luma or Lum, which I located on our map. Once again I cursed the map makers of Kathmandu and wondered if we might be better off with no map. Distances and names were often inaccurate, trails and villages appeared in the wrong places, contour lines bore little resemblance to reality.

The next day was a rest day in Chaubesi/Lum. Early in the morning, Akaal Bahadur and Jeet Bahadur set off to Jumla to restock our rice, sugar and spice supplies. Replacement batteries for our Chinese flashlights completed the shopping list. The men were also to look for another porter.

Puraba left us that morning heading for Larpa, a village an hour's walk away. There he had another house where his wife waited for him. We paid Puraba 690 rupees and said our thanks.

"Tapaai asa maanchhe" ("You are a good man"), I told him in Nepali.

He grinned his appreciation, then swiftly moved out on the trail. I watched him go. *A gentle, hardworking man.* I would miss him.

At eight that evening, Akaal Bahadur and Jeet Bahadur returned from Jumla. They had found the necessary food supplies, but no additional porter. For their extra effort, I bought them a bottle of *rakshi* and we made sure they had a hearty meal. They had earned it.

Early the next morning, Prem and Akaal Bahadur set out

through the village in search of a porter. They returned at eleven o'clock empty-handed.

"Parker Sahib," Prem said. "No one wants to go with us because they are afraid to walk back to their village alone. But we have told everyone. We will wait for a time and see."

A few minutes later, a man in his late twenties dressed in black jodhpurs, dusty suitcoat and black *topee* arrived at our camp. He was willing to travel with us the entire way to Pokhara if we could guarantee his safe return.

"Tell him, Prem, that we will fly him to Jumla."

"Yes. He will go if he can fly in an airplane," Prem announced happily. "He has never been in an airplane."

And so we hired Auri Bahadur Raut, a Chetri.

Within the hour we were once again on the trail, following the open river valley to the southeast. A few miles from Chaubesi/Lum, we crossed the trail that came from Wangri over Khapre La.

"Look, Prem." I pointed up the trail towards Khapre La. "There's the trail. Just think of how many days it would have taken us from Wangri if we had come this way. Three, maybe four. But it took us ten."

"If we had been able to hire porters in Wangri . . ."

"All that way. All for the lack of two decent porters. Don't remind me. I'll get mad all over again."

The next day, the thirty-ninth since leaving Surkhet, we camped near the village of Chautri where Prem convinced a villager to sell us a chicken. As soon as the squawking bird arrived in camp, the butchering took place. Akaal Bahadur and Jeet Bahadur cleaned the chicken thoroughly and divided the pieces into three different dishes.

The first course included the heart, lungs, liver, kidneys, brain and intestines. Fiery red chilies made a mouth-burning but tasty stew. For the second course we had the legs fried. The final course consisted of all the rest of the chicken, hacked with a *kukri* into small pieces, bones and all, and made into a curry. We wasted nothing.

I bit into the stringy chicken as deep as I could get my teeth. Then I sucked every bit of meat off the bones. Amused, I thought of all the meat I had left on bones over the years, good food that went wasted into garbage cans.

The next day we continued heading southeast, then turned south to struggle up the steep but short Mauri Lekh. The north-facing slope presented a quagmire of snow and mud melting in the afternoon sun. I hacked a functional walking stick from the underbrush for myself and gave my ice axe to Jeet Bahadur.

We sat and rested near a *chorten* that guarded the crest of the ridge. Prayer flags snapped briskly in the rising afternoon winds. *"Om mani padme hum"* ("Hail to the jewel in the lotus") hurtled endlessly, a perpetual muffled prayer that hastened before the breeze across Dolpo, Mugu and on into Tibet. The glaciered peaks of the Kanjiroba Himal played a power game of hide-and-seek with the rapidly building storm clouds. A few heavy drops of rain and hail spattered on the surrounding rocks, and the distant reports of thunder spurred us to retreat several hundred feet down to the tree-line.

The mighty Bheri Khola, 9,000 feet deep, lay two ridges away, although the river's course was visible for many miles. Following the descending trail until almost dusk, we arrived at the village of Chaurikot, where we set camp for the night.

Early in the morning, we followed a wide trail hugging the steep river valley. Two thousand feet below, the seething waters swept by. The morning was still and clear, and by nine we felt the full heat of the sun. Beside a tumbling stream at the edge of the trail, we stopped for a meal. Before eating, I slid off my pack and dug out a bar of soap. I stripped to the waist, hanging my shirt over a bush to dry the sweat. Then, luxuriating in the cold, clean water, I washed my head and scrubbed my upper body for the first time in five days.

By noon, the winds had risen and the daily build-up of

thick, bilious cumulus clouds over the Himal to the north and east had begun. Above us eagles and falcons soared with the thermals to thousands of feet over our heads, then in single mad downwind dashes covered what might take us a day or more to do on foot. Before we finished, a half dozen Tibetans with their monstrous full-blooded yaks stopped to share our stream. As we set out again, swirling dust devils played around our feet.

Far below, another trail wended its way along the river's edge. Destination: Jarjakot, six days to the southwest. I stopped, contemplating this fragile path. Auri Bahadur had traveled this way many times, and he had told us about the flat, easy trail along the river's edge. From Jarjakot, the route led due east through Dhorpatan, then Beni and Baglung.

"That's it, Prem," I said. "The last chance to go the easy way."

"O Parker Sahib, it would be too hot."

"Yes, and too boring. If we had been able to go to the north, through Phapagaon . . ."

"So which way do we go?"

"This way." I waved with a broad, vague gesture towards the east.

Prem gave me one of his crooked smiles and nodded with understanding. Though we had not discussed it, we both knew we would go on through Dolpo with little food, no guide and our all-but-useless map.

Prem and I quickened the pace, hoping to outrace the coming storm. The trail descended gently through the open fields of the Buddhist village of Rimi and on towards Kaigaon and Hurikot on the edge of the Bheri Khola. Luckily, the rains held off until we reached the valley floor and the shelter of a crudely constructed building beside the trail. I quickly ducked under the porch and was leaning against an upright post when Prem arrived just a minute later. He looked up and translated the sign above our heads: "Kaigaon Secondary School, Dolpo District." My surprise at finding a school here was overshadowed by the realization that we had slipped into the most restricted area of Nepal; we had entered Dolpo.

Heavy rain splashed against the earth as the porters arrived some twenty minutes after us, completely drenched. We dashed over a wooden bridge and found shelter for the night in the empty front room of a small abandoned house. In a rough hearth dug into the dirt floor, we built a fire, brewed tea and were enjoying the warmth when Akaal Bahadur rose, pulled a tent from his *doko* and left the smoky room.

"Akaal Bahadur, where are you going?" I asked as he disappeared in the rain.

"He is putting up the tent, Parker Sahib," Prem answered for him.

"But it's pouring out there!"

"It is too smoky in here. He will put the tent up for you and for me to sleep in."

Exasperated, I went to the door and looked out. Through the obscuring downpour I saw Akaal Bahadur struggling alone with the tent. He could put it up by himself, he had done it many times before. But I had to stop myself from going out into the rain to help him. I knew I wasn't wanted, my offer of help would be refused. So I just watched as Akaal Bahadur erected the tent, then dug a small trench around the edges to deflect the runoff.

"Prem, I've said this before. We can't be sahib and porter, we can't be master and servant. Not here."

"But Akaal Bahadur wants to do this, it is his job."

"Where I come from, we all share. I don't always have to have bed tea, or the best place around the fire, or the best portions of food."

Prem looked at me. His eyes—gentle, silent, pleading— tried to tell me that here things were different.

"Look how wet he is," I started to protest again.

Prem reached over and touched my arm. "You must forgive us, Parker Sahib, for it is our way."

Defeated, I slumped down on the small carpet we had placed next to the fire. His reply had been so simple and so complete. It was their way. How could I pretend to alter anything so fundamental?

Five minutes later Akaal Bahadur returned, dripping wet. I started to get up, to offer him my warm place by the fire. But the weight of centuries, of their way, pushed me back to my appointed place. He smiled at me. Despite the mud clinging to his feet, the rain-slick hair plastered to his face, his worn clothes soaked completely through, nothing could detract from the man's dignity. He had completed his task; I had not shamed him by interfering. Joining us by the fire, he stretched out his hands to warm them.

Within an hour we were set upon by a dozen villagers, all wanting to know in that Asian way where we had come from and where we intended to go.

"*License chhaa?*" ("Do you have a permit?")

"*Ho, license chhaa*" ("Yes, we have a permit"), we answered again and again.

We offered *chang* to every visitor and the villagers soon became our friends. They repeatedly informed us that we needed special permission to be here or to continue further into Dolpo. We were consistently evasive in our replies, but equally insistent that we had trekking permits. We must have finally convinced them that all the necessary documents were in order, for the awkward questions stopped.

Late in the afternoon, the steady rains changed to snow and hail, and three inches blanketed the ground by sundown. Several pitchers of thick *chang* took the edge off our discomfort.

After a meal of rice and potatoes, we sat around the fire in the small, smoky room and rehashed the events of the last two days. Prem commented on the wild appearance of the group of Tibetans from Lhasa, the ones who had shared our lunch spot earlier in the day.

Through the *chang* haze, pictures began to flash through my mind, an eerie late-night slide show. I saw myself barechested, washing by the stream. Then a slow zoom focused on my necklace lying on a rock where I had put it after taking it off to wash. That picture now made me grab at my chest. My necklace! Aghast, I realized that I had left it at the edge of the stream. Hung on the chain was a silver good-luck scarab from Susan and, much worse if lost, a military-style dog tag with my name, nationality, social security number and blood type.

"Prem. I left my necklace by the stream. I have to go back to get it. I don't know how I could have been so stupid to leave it there. I'll get up early so we won't lose any time."

Prem turned to Akaal Bahadur and said a few words.

"Akaal Bahadur will go with you, Parker Sahib," Prem said.

"We will go at three o'clock," I said to Akaal Bahadur as I made my way outside to my tent.

Snow still fell gently as I ducked inside. Setting my watch, I fell asleep instantly.

My wristwatch alarm resonated from underneath my makeshift pillow through to my head, giving me a painful reminder of last night's *chang*. Unzipping the tent a few inches I peered at the star-filled sky. The storm had passed, leaving in the still night four inches of frozen snow. I dressed quickly, stuffed my pockets with the few remaining snacks from our British high-altitude rations and went to awaken Akaal Bahadur.

Within minutes we were off in the predawn darkness, silent except for our steady breathing and the crunching of snow underfoot. Without packs we moved rapidly and soon I fell behind Akaal Bahadur. Breathing in labored gasps, I strained to maintain his pace as he skipped effortlessly up the trail. We had been on trek for forty days and I believed I was in excellent condition. But a lifetime of porter's labor had given Akaal Bahadur fitness far surpassing mine. If he chose, he could have left me floundering within three hundred yards.

He danced, I struggled up the gently ascending trail for three miles before stopping for a break. As I gulped down draughts of air, he lit a cigarette as if to taunt me further. As soon as he had it glowing, he set off once again at the same blistering pace.

The eastern sky lightened and the stars disappeared one by one. We passed through two small villages, eerily silent at that early hour. But then, as though given a signal, roosters at farmhouses scattered along the mountainside greeted the new day in crowing unison.

We covered the seven miles to our previous lunch spot in an hour and a half, and my hopes were high that the foul weather had dissuaded anyone from lingering along the stream's edge. Once there, I went immediately to the rock where I had carefully placed the necklace. Nothing. It was gone. We cut leafy branches and swept away the accumulated snow from the ground. Nothing.

Angry, tired and embarrassed at having dragged Akaal Bahadur all this way for nothing, I brushed the snow off a small rock and sat at the stream's edge. Swollen now from the rains of the day before, the stream carried bits of decaying leaves, twigs and shards of schist, sweeping them towards the Bheri River far below. Could my necklace be traveling on this same course? Could it be tumbling, rolling, catapulting down to the Bheri and beyond, to the mighty, sacred Ganges?

More likely, it had found a new home around a Tibetan's neck. The Khampa traders we had encountered here the day before were heading to Lhasa. That it might find a home in this forbidden city was of some solace, for it might see places I could only hope to visit one day.

We snacked on fig cookies and the last few pieces of chocolate from the rations kit before beginning our return to Kaigaon. The sun was now upon us, turning the snow under our feet to mud as we dashed along. It took less than an hour for our return journey. Prem had our first meal ready for us, and we ate quickly. Akaal Bahadur and I were on the trail with the others by ten-thirty, having already walked fourteen miles.

Our route ascended to a ridgeline just south of Kaigaon. Sloppy with mud, the track switchbacked up through broad open fields interspersed with cool shaded stands of hemlock and birch. Our presence startled into flight a huge flock of sparrowlike birds. They flew as one, changing directions in midflight several times before settling among the moss-laden oaks. As we stopped to rest from the midday sun, I roused them back into flight with a well-hurled rock and watched them wheel, spin and turn as one again and again. I looked for the leader, the headman of the tribe that dictated the erratic but unified movement of this large flock of birds. Within a few minutes, though, I realized that I searched in vain, for with each change of direction the lead bird became the last and the last became the newly followed leader.

Another half hour of walking brought us to a hogback. Across a deeply forested valley, the snow-covered peaks blocked our view to the south. A fresh breeze soothed us and dried our sweat into salty streaks on our faces. As we rested on the ridgecrest, a local Chetri villager stopped to talk.

"He gives us a warning, Parker Sahib," said Prem. "He says that the land ahead has Khampas. These men are from Tibet, from the east. They are nomads, they follow their sheep and goats and yaks."

"Like the Tibetans we saw yesterday?"

"The same. He says we should be careful, not to trust them because they will steal from us. He says we should be careful in the night, that we should not camp next to them."

"Sounds like a good idea to me," I said, and started to leave.

Prem remained engaged in a heated discussion with the Chetri. I could catch little except Prem's repeated firm, "No!"

Then I caught the gist of the conversation. "Shoes, socks, boots, sugar or cigarettes" were his demands. I laughed. For what? Just for telling us to watch out for thieving Tibetans?

Coincidentally, just then three Tibetans, one astride a beautiful white Tibetan horse, approached us from up the trail. They smiled broadly, their perfectly white, even teeth offset by one gold tooth each. When they stopped abreast of us, the sickly sweet, pungent smell of those who never wash came with them. They spoke to us in broken Nepali.

"Where are you going?"

"Where are *you* going?" Prem turned the question.

After a few desultory comments their attention settled on our porters' *dokos*, chock-full of interesting and enticing new objects. While Akaal Bahadur, Jeet Bahadur and Auri Bahadur sat under the nearby trees, puffing *beedies*, cheap cigarettes, and unaware of what was happening, Tibetan hands greedily delved into our baskets. Exclaiming with wide-eyed wonder about utensils, knives, sugar, plastic storage bottles and rice, they fingered every object. "How much for this, and for this?" they asked, holding each object aloft.

Inexplicably, just then Prem hoisted his pack and began heading up the trail, leaving me to deal with the rapidly deteriorating situation.

"Not for sale!" I shouted in Nepali, stepping forward and showing them my ice axe gripped in my hand. "Akaal Bahadur, Jeet Bahadur. *Jaau!*" ("Let's go!") I used my best angry-sahib voice in a desperate attempt to get their attention.

Looking up from their smokes, the porters now realized the danger and jumped to their feet. Snatching items from out of the grasping hands of the Tibetans, they repacked and secured their loads.

"How much for this?" came the last bargaining demand from one of the nomads.

"Thirty-five rupees, last price," I said forcefully as I reached for the empty leaky kerosene container in his hands.

"Thirty-two rupees."

"No, thirty-five rupees." I pulled the container away from him.

This last demand was answered by the Tibetans with hard, leering smiles.

"*Jaau, jaau,*" I urged the porters. "Pick up your loads and let's go."

I took up the rear with my ice axe still held determinedly and in obvious view. Before a bend in the trail, I turned to see the Tibetans still staring after us as we followed the trail out of their sight.

In the high mountain forest, the late afternoon sun cast a golden light onto the green of hemlock trees. As I climbed up towards 12,000 feet, the air cooled. The trail contoured along the hillside, slipping into four heavily wooded side canyons before again emerging.

Beside a rushing stream in the deepest recess of one of these side canyons, I stopped to catch my breath. I sat on the trunk of a huge, downed hemlock, resting the weight of my pack on the stub of a broken branch. The stream emerged from a dense forest and above me I could see its source, a vast, treeless alpine meadow that formed the northern ridge of the valley. To the southeast, this ridge met the 15,000-foot, snow-covered peaks across the valley. A deep notch marked the Balangra Pass, a natural gateway to Tibrikot, Dunai and the forbidden interior of Dolpo.

Stampeding hooves jolted my attention from the view. Whirling, I saw two enormous yaks rushing down the stream bed—right at me! In a panic, I jumped from my seat and leapt aside just before the yaks thundered by, their huge shaggy bulks passing directly over the spot where I had been seated. I think now that if I had stayed put, they would have veered off to another course. But at that moment my heart pounded with adrenaline. I wondered what had frightened them as they hit the trail below me.

"*Namaste.*"

Startled, I swung around. I looked into the gold-toothed smile of a man about my age, but many inches taller and broader. He wore a patched and dirty Tibetan *chuba*, and a long Tibetan knife with a silver handle and sheath hung from his hip next to a small silver-and-leather purse. His oily black hair, braided with red yarn and wound around his head, framed his high-cheekboned face.

He laughed at my discomfort at being surprised, but then his throaty laughter subsided into a chilling smile. In broken Nepali he asked where I came from. And then, without waiting for a reply, "*Kahaa jane ho?*" ("Where are you going?")

Another question followed, frightening in its transparency, "Are you alone?"

It was asked hopefully. Alone, I was vulnerable. I thought about the Chetri's warning and the stories of other foreigners who had been murdered for their money, their cameras, their boots.

"No," I answered in Nepali. "I have a guide ahead and many porters behind me."

He looked both directions along the trail and, seeing no one, smiled at me again. I'm not sure he believed me.

He pointed to his mouth. "*Ausadhi?*" ("Medicine?")

"*Ausadhi chaainna.*" ("No medicine.")

He moved past me and strode slowly up the steep trail. With his hands clasped behind his back and shoulders hunched, he walked in the splay-footed duck walk so characteristic of the Tibetan nomads. He motioned me to follow, indicating that he had friends further up the trail.

Wonderful, more of them. Pretending that my twenty-kilo pack was too heavy, I slackened my pace, hoping my new-found companion would go on ahead.

Looking up, I spotted Prem several hundred yards ahead and above me in an open pasture. I swung my arms wildly, frantically indicating he should wait for me. I continued slowly, but my guide stopped every few yards to let me catch up. Another Tibetan emerged from the bushes beside the trail. He was equally as tall and wide, although much older and stooped. He fell in directly behind me and so close that I could smell his fetid breath and unwashed body.

I stopped several times and wheezed in an exaggerated manner, indicating with my hand to the Tibetan that he should go on ahead and not wait for me. He spoke in broken Nepali, saying that he was in no hurry, he would wait for me. I sat on a rotten log and with slow deliberation hacked at it with my ice axe.

Prem was waiting for me on a grassy knoll. He smiled as I dropped down beside him, heaving a sigh of relief. Behind me came the two Tibetans with three yaks and a calf in tow. They were camped a few hundred yards ahead amidst an ancient moss-covered scree field, and they urged us to join them for the night.

Prem declined politely, saying that we were headed for the pass and hoped to cross before sundown—an obvious lie since it was now almost 5:00 P.M. and a good two hours to the pass. And our porters were still another half hour behind us. Nevertheless, we walked quickly past the Tibetans' camp and on up the trail. Prem walked on even faster as he began his daily search for firewood, water, a place to camp for the night. I let him go.

It was here, as I walked on alone, that I met a young Tibetan mother and her child. I stopped in a silent grove of ancient trees and watched a red panda bounding along the trail.

The sight of the lovely and innocent mother nursing her gift of new life, of the rare red panda surrounded by the moss-laden trees—all juxtaposed with the massive and eternal mountains, dramatized the fleeting, transient nature of life. My environment had never before moved me to such thoughts, such powerfully felt emotion. As I sat there, tears slid down my cheeks.

Two tremendous lammergeiers cruised the steep slope, the wind rustling their feathers as they passed less than sixty feet over my head. Wingtip to wingtip, the bearded vultures flew in unison, one a perfect shadow of the other as they searched hopefully along the slope. They thermaled upward, ascending rapidly in a tight spiral. I followed their moves, watching intently for several minutes until they were 2,000 feet above the ridgeline. I blinked twice, and the two specks were lost in the blue afternoon sky.

As the giant birds disappeared, I heard the familiar Tamang folk songs I had enjoyed so many times before in eastern Nepal in October and November. Then I saw the porters appear from out of a side valley half a mile away. Akaal Bahadur and Jeet Bahadur, prodigious vocalists, sometimes sang for hours on end as they carried their loads up and down the valleys of Nepal. Now I heard Auri Bahadur chime in on a song.

The wind increased, and as the sun dropped behind a snow-covered *lekh*, the temperature dropped towards freezing. Hurrying up the trail, I found Prem at a splendid campsite a mile below the head of the pass. Beneath an ancient oak tree bedecked with hanging moss, a small fire already burned. When the porters arrived, they quickly dropped their loads, pitched the tents and scurried to gather firewood.

After a meal of rice and *tarkaari* (curried vegetables), I slipped into my sleeping bag. It had been a long day full of inspiring contrasts. By the light of the fire coming through the open tent flaps, I inspected the map and the next few days' route. Tibrikot, Dunai, Tarakot. Police. Military. The next week promised to be interesting. And long.

Our spirits were high, however. Tomorrow we would cross the Balangra Pass and head further into Dolpo. The challenge excited us all. The sheer sport of it had Akaal Bahadur in his highest spirits of our journey to the west. His boisterous attitude infected all of us, and smiles circled the campfire that night. *Let's just do it well, fellows, because I for one have no desire to see the interior of a Nepalese jail.*

Sinking into the warmth of my sleeping bag, I thought again of the Tibetan mother and her child. She seemed so at peace with herself, her surroundings. She didn't fight the natural forces of her world, she lived with them. After all these months trekking, I was beginning to see some of the rewards of this way of life. I had noticed time and again that my Nepalese companions looked at so many things differently. Time was not measured in minutes and quarters of hours that someone paid for. They did not see themselves as masters of their fate, controlling their lives, directing its course towards carefully planned goals. Theirs was life without the hurry, the status-seeking, the sheer cussedness of western existence. I began to think about the possibility of not going back, ever. Of staying here, of being part of this world where people seemed so much more content with themselves.

CHAPTER EIGHT

▲

WE CRESTED THE BALANGRA PASS AT 12,700 FEET BEFORE 9:00
A.M. Without stopping, I tossed a few stones on the summit
cairn and began the long descent along the tributary gorge
of the Balansuro Khola towards the deep canyon of the
Thuli Bheri River, still ten miles to the southeast. Somewhere near their confluence lay the village of Tibrikot and a
police checkpost. A day's walk further east along the Thuli
Bheri, the village of Dunai, with both police and military
garrisons, stood in our way. My trekking permit did not
mention Dunai, and once again, I wanted to avoid contact
with anyone in an official capacity and bypass the
checkposts.

Not since our passage of Gum Gadhi at night had I felt so
tense about my high visibility as a foreigner.

As we passed before the entrance to a government yak
farm and agricultural project, I shielded myself with Akaal
Bahadur's load. Soon after, we stopped to rest and eat, and I
secluded myself behind a stone wall.

Again I looked at my creased and dirty trekking map. It
showed the trail continuing along the northeast side of the
Balansuro gorge to the Thuli Bheri, where it passed through
Tibrikot. Perhaps by crossing over to the other side of the

gorge and following along the south side of the Balansuro until it reached the Thuli Bheri we could bypass Tibrikot. My map showed no trail on the south side, only a village called Huma. But where there was a village, there had to be a trail.

For two hours we kept to the north side of the gorge. Gradually it opened into a valley, the treeless slopes having long ago lost their forests to the human demand for fuel, fodder and tillable fields. Several miles ahead we saw three villages, which on our map were called Pahad, Para and Liku.

Reaching a breezy promontory with a view of the entire valley and the brooding canyon of the Thuli Bheri in the distance, we again stopped to rest.

"Prem, we need to know exactly where Tibrikot lies and which trail we can take to avoid it. What do you think about crossing to the other side of the river? My map says that there is a village. Maybe we can reach the Thuli Bheri from there and miss Tibrikot."

"Perhaps this is so. But we should find out from the local people."

Prem turned to the porters and instructed them to scatter and see what they could find out about the routes and checkposts. Akaal Bahadur soon returned with a grizzled man and simpleminded son. Standing on the promontory, the man pointed to the tiny white speck of a building barely discernible in the middle of Liku village, several miles ahead.

"Parker Sahib, this man says that white house is a police checkpost. We cannot see Tibrikot, it is beyond Liku where the rivers meet." Prem asked the man a few more questions.

Jeet Bahadur and Auri Bahadur returned, having asked three or four people and receiving as many different answers. From these stories we wove together the common threads of information we thought most likely to be true. Yes, they said, we could reach the Thuli Bheri and bypass Tibrikot by following a trail on the south slope of the valley.

Filled with the false confidence that this information provided, we descended and crossed the Balansuro, at this point a lively stream with many water-powered mill houses. By late afternoon we had reached the village of Huma. We stopped to buy a few potatoes and to ask our way.

Prem reported to me. "Parker Sahib, I am sorry. These people say we cannot go this way to the Thuli Bheri. Ahead there are steep cliffs."

"Then why were we told otherwise just two hours ago? So where does the trail go?"

"The trail goes down to the river, to the Balansuro, then it goes up on the other side. To Tibrikot."

"So the terrain is funneling us right towards Tibrikot. There doesn't seem to be any way out."

Reluctantly we followed the contouring trail out of Huma as we descended once again towards the Balansuro. An hour later we stopped for our second meal. I conferred again with Prem.

"Look, if we bushwhack down the slope here," I pointed down eight hundred feet to the Balansuro, "we can follow the river to the Thuli Bheri. That way we should pass below Tibrikot, which the villagers told us sits several hundred feet above the river."

Prem thought for a minute. "But Parker Sahib, there is no moon, it will be very dark and we have almost no batteries. And the locals say there is no trail following the river."

"Prem, you know there are always trails along rivers. People go there to get water, to wash clothes, and to shit. And I'm sure we can find some way to get down there."

We waited until the last lingering twilight, just after eight o'clock. What looked from above to be an easy way turned into a steep, loose scree slope. Prem was right; without the moon, movement was treacherous. For more than two hours we slipped, slid and blundered our way down until we reached the riverbed. As I had figured, a faint trail followed the river bank. We moved steadily for an hour through the blackness as the roar of the Thuli Bheri grew steadily louder.

Just before the confluence, we came to another bridge embellished with erotic sculptures, and crossed the Balansuro for the last time. We rounded a corner and the roar of the roiling Thuli Bheri overwhelmed us. The water charged over immense boulders and plunged through piles of debris, the din so loud we had to shout into each other's ears just to be heard.

Stopping to rest, we sat directly in the trail, our backs supported by the cliffs behind us. Our feet dangled over the edge just above the sheer one-hundred-foot drop to the river. No one attempted to speak above the roar of the river, that tremendous display of power, the demonstration of the immense forces of nature all around us. The red glow of the porters' *beedies* brightened and dimmed as they inhaled.

As we rose to continue, Prem came close to me and yelled in my ear. "Parker Sahib, we are very lucky that we passed Tibrikot so easily. Now we should be safe until we reach Dunai."

"I'm sure that getting through Dunai will be easy too," I shouted back. "Let's go, but still no flashlights, we're too close to Tibrikot."

We had become adept at this night travel, even in the blackest times, as now without moon or flashlights. After months together on the trail, we had also come to know one another's movements well. Little needed to be said, as we knew almost instinctively what the others were thinking and what to do. Auri Bahadur, our newest porter, seemed to fit in easily. He was quiet but with an inner toughness that meshed with the others. I was sure he hadn't the faintest clue what he was getting himself into when he signed on with us. But he appeared unflappable and readily went along with our nighttime sojourns.

From our resting spot, the trail switchbacked steeply up the face of the river gorge. Loose rocks and gravel churned

up by yak caravans made for a slow, dusty ascent. The roar
of the river slowly diminished. After several hundred feet, a
ghostly apparition loomed out of the night, a newly erected
chorten that split the trail.

We stopped beside it to rest while Prem went ahead to
check the trail, which appeared to level off. He returned
before the porters had extinguished their *beedies* and silently
signaled us to move on.

In a low, tense voice, he whispered to all of us. "Keep
together, very close. Very, very quiet."

Not until we had passed the second house along the trail
did I realize the cause of his concern. For it was then that the
dogs began to bark. First, off in the distance, then closer as
they moved towards us from several directions. We moved
quickly, close together in single file, with Prem in the lead,
then me, Jeet Bahadur, Auri Bahadur and Akaal Bahadur
bringing up the rear.

More houses and crude structures lined the trail. A village.
But which one could be so close to Tibrikot?

Ahead, the trail split; one path maintained a flat course,
the other headed further up the hillside. Prem veered and
took the upper trail. For a hundred feet we climbed, but
soon realized that this path led only to a large Hindu temple.
Communicating with hand signals, we rapidly reversed direction and went back to the fork.

The level trail that we had avoided the first time led directly into the center of the village. Prem waved for absolute
silence. The dogs that we had shaken off when taking the
upper trail now caught our scent again and began barking
with renewed vigor. Ice axes at the ready, we moved deeper
into the center of the village with a pack of a dozen dogs
surrounding us.

Some were knee-high mongrels. The larger ones, huge
beasts of mastiff stock, gave us more hesitation as their deep,
gruff growls echoed among the moving shadows of the

night. Hearing the mounting frenzy behind me, I turned, thinking to help Akaal Bahadur fend them off.

With little warning, a black mastiff attacked. Wielding his ice axe with wicked accuracy, Akaal Bahadur sidestepped and slammed its flat blade down against the dog's skull, inches before the animal could sink his teeth into Akaal Bahadur's leg.

The dog yelped, then fell to the ground, stunned. Slowly it slunk back into the night. Instead of putting the pack on guard, Akaal Bahadur's defense seemed to incite the others, and they moved in closer, increasing their barks to a furious cacophony. Quickly I stepped to Akaal Bahadur's side and we both walked backwards, protecting ourselves with readied ice axes. As we moved through the village their number slowly diminished until we were left confronting only two malnourished mongrels.

At an airy whistle from Prem, Akaal Bahadur and I turned and followed the others, trotting slowly towards the far side of the village. Ahead, a thirty-foot-long enclosed archway spanned the trail. Long benches lined either wall, a table partially blocked the far end.

Following the trail that passed directly beneath the structure, I paused briefly halfway through, thinking this must be some kind of *gompa* or covered *chorten*. A shallow drainage ditch crossed the trail and in the dark I stumbled momentarily. Akaal Bahadur heard my staggering step and turned to me. Grabbing my arm, he whispered urgently, *"Chitto, Sahib!"* ("Hurry, sir!")

We ran. As quickly as our loads permitted we raced down the trail for a hundred yards. Then slowing, Akaal Bahadur turned to me, a broad grin splitting his face.

"Chaulki, Sahib, chaulki" ("A checkpost, sir"), he said excitedly, pointing back to the covered structure.

I looked back at the faint outlines of the police checkpost. With a shiver, I realized that we had literally passed through the very thing we had desperately sought to avoid, the checkpost in the village of Tibrikot.

We continued to run as best we could and caught up with Prem and the other porters several hundred yards down the trail. They had hidden among some boulders.

I found Prem leaning back against a rock. Sweat streaked his face. He shook his head gently back and forth. "Parker Sahib, we were very lucky. The police must have been sleeping. But the dogs made so much noise. Maybe the police will get up and come after us." He peered nervously back along the trail.

"You're right. We should walk all night. Put as much distance between us and Tibrikot as we can. Let's go. And no lights, it's still too risky."

We hoisted our loads and continued along the trail, contouring high above the Thuli Bheri River.

Stunned by our mistake of entering directly into the village when we thought we had passed it, disturbed by the attack of the village dogs and shaken by the encounter with the police checkpost, I walked quickly despite the dark. My one thought was to get away, leave this place behind as soon as possible.

For long stretches the trail clung precariously to the vertical face, hundreds of feet above the rumbling torrent that we could hear in the darkness below. Because we had no lights, the going was tricky. To traverse the stretches more quickly and safely, we kept close together, each placing an outstretched hand on the load of the person ahead. In this manner, we moved like a snake winding its way along the trail.

We walked all night, stopping only twice for short breaks. In the warm and humid night sweat soaked my clothes, stung my eyes. Only during our brief stops did I begin to dry out. I was tired and hungry, but still I felt a growing exhilaration at having passed the checkpost and now traveling at night further into Dolpo.

With Tibrikot behind us, I also sensed the porters' excitement. Akaal Bahadur laughed a satisfied throaty chortle as he retold the story of urging Sahib to hurry up and get out of the police *chaulki*. Their mood recalled the childhood thrills of going to horror movies or sneaking around haunted houses on Halloween. It was a game to them.

The trail gradually descended to the riverbed, and just before dawn we crossed a bridge spanning the Thuli Bheri. Soon we began to see others on the trail—Tibetan porters carrying heavy loads, travelers on horseback.

"Prem, it's time to stop," I said. "Too many people."

"Yes, Parker Sahib. We must find a safe place to eat and sleep. But where?" We looked up at the near-vertical canyon walls.

"We'll just have to keep looking for a flat place somewhere off the trail."

For two miles we continued on the narrow trail. From around a bend, two figures on horseback appeared several hundred yards up the trail and heading our way. I spotted the telltale khaki green of their uniforms.

"Parker Sahib," Prem intoned warningly.

"I see them." Quickly we ducked behind some boulders at the trail's edge.

As we crouched behind our screen, waiting for the men to pass, I leaned towards Prem. "Now. We have to get off this trail *now*."

He nodded, then cocked his head, straining to catch a sound over the roar of the river.

I heard it too, the unmistakable sound of an airplane. I knew an airport existed at Dunai, but within this narrow, precipitous canyon it seemed inconceivable that an airplane could find a place to fly.

Within a minute, from the direction of Dunai, a single-engine Pilatus Porter came into view. It flew three hundred feet above the river, following the contours of the deep canyon. It passed almost overhead and then, still constrained by the canyon walls, disappeared out of sight around a bend in the river.

The khaki-clad horsemen passed. I scanned the cliffs above and from our hiding spot could just make out a small ledge three hundred feet above the trail. A breathless scramble up the steep, loose scree brought us to a flat spot covered with large thorny bushes. We cleared out the small brush as best we could, then laid out our gear in the open spaces underneath the larger bushes. I fell back on my bedroll, exhausted after twenty-four hours without sleep.

A quick meal of rice and potatoes satisfied our immediate hunger pangs, and by eleven o'clock we were all spread out among the bushes, resting or sleeping. Finally out of sight of the trail, I relaxed and tried to sleep, but large, noisy flies buzzed around my face and arms. "Too tired to sleep"—the phrase seemed apropos.

Late in the afternoon, we ate another large meal, then waited until eight. Prem and I figured it should take a couple of hours to reach Dunai, but it made no sense to expose ourselves to the late afternoon traffic. Because of the narrow canyon, there was no place else to hide. Not until after dark did we abandon our hiding spot and descend to the trail.

By ten-thirty we reached what we assumed was the outskirts of Dunai. Prem motioned us off the trail and we hid in some bushes.

For two hours we crouched waiting, listening . . . Silence. At twelve-thirty Prem rose and we followed suit, bunched closely together. Without a word we headed off into the night. Prem and I had discussed earlier in the day a way to bypass Dunai altogether. If we could find a path leading towards the river, we might find a bridge and cross to the opposite side.

We walked for fifteen minutes until we reached the outskirts of the town.

Suddenly the path veered away from the river and crossed

a large flat area. For ten minutes we continued, but then stopped.

Prem spoke with Akaal Bahadur, then turned to me. "Parker Sahib, this trail is too big. We should look for a small trail near the river and away from the *chaulki*."

Just then Akaal Bahadur turned on his flashlight and shone it across the flat expanse of ground between us and the river. Panning the light across the open space, he paused to illuminate a two-story building. Seconds later he doused the light, swearing colorfully in Nepali.

The flat space was the airport and the building was the flight tower! There was a collective intake of breath at the realization that we were so close to this official installation, and we quickly moved on.

A dog's incessant barking emerged and echoed from a farmhouse behind us as we followed the trail ever closer to the center of Dunai. I was beginning to hate dogs. The trail, which until now had been loose gravel and dirt, suddenly became a raised slate path five feet wide. Buildings appeared ahead, and with them came the dogs.

In ones and twos, then in larger groups, they appeared. They barked, setting each other off. Two stalked us from behind, grizzled mongrels in the shadowy darkness.

"Parker Sahib," Prem whispered, breaking the self-imposed silence. "What to do?"

I approached him, our heads together as we talked softly, trying not to rouse the ire of the fiends circling our feet. "You go ahead," I said. "Akaal Bahadur and I will follow. Then Jeet Bahadur and Auri Bahadur. You can talk to the police or anyone who stops you. I can hide behind Akaal Bahadur's *doko*."

"Okay, Parker Sahib. If someone stops me, I will talk very loudly so you will know to hide. We must go quickly."

Akaal Bahadur and I waited until Prem was out of sight, then stepped out into the trail. Soon the raised trail became lined on either side with barbed wire fencing. Behind it we saw the outlines of several long, low buildings. A hundred yards further on we came to two opposing archways that led to the buildings. Signs, large and freshly painted in red and white, identified the compounds as police and military barracks. The trail had funneled us into the largest police and military garrisons in the region.

I walked behind Akaal Bahadur, peering right and left, alert for lights or any signs of movement. The barracks remained dark.

We left the garrison behind and entered the village proper. Small, shuttered houses and shops lined the street, and apparently each harbored a dog. Akaal Bahadur walked ahead, ice axe ready. A small pack followed us, lunging periodically. I kept them at bay to the rear, but my ice axe seemed merely to infuriate rather than drive them off.

"Sahib," whispered Akaal Bahadur over his shoulder. *"Chaulki."*

Looking around Akaal Bahadur's *doko*, I saw a small building ahead. A light flashed and the figure of a man emerged.

I immediately stepped off the trail and hid behind a boulder. Akaal Bahadur held his ground on the trail, fending off the growling, snarling dogs that surrounded him. The man, using a flashlight to guide his way, crossed the trail and disappeared down an embankment on the far side.

For two minutes I waited in the shadows. Then, feeling safer, I emerged and rejoined Akaal Bahadur on the trail. Just as we reached the *chaulki*, however, the man reappeared and aimed the beam of his flashlight directly at us.

With the quickness of hyperalert senses, I shielded myself on the far side of Akaal Bahadur's *doko*. Grabbing the flaps of my Chinese hat with both hands, I pulled it low over my brow. Without hesitation, we walked past him and into the cover of darkness.

"Chitto, chitto," I urged Akaal Bahadur. We broke into a half trot and soon left the dogs and most of the village behind us.

A hundred yards beyond the *chaulki* we found Prem waiting near a small shed. We stopped, breathing heavily, sweat-soaked in the warm night.

"Prem, did you see anyone?"

"No, Parker Sahib, no one."

"Well, we did. And he saw us." I told him what had happened. Just as I finished, Jeet Bahadur and Auri Bahadur appeared and the five of us moved out onto the trail. We jogged silently, intent on putting as much distance as we could between us and Dunai.

I looked back. Two flashes of light bobbed along the trail. Someone was coming after us.

Akaal Bahadur took my arm roughly and pushed me ahead of him. "*Chitto*, Sahib, *chitto*," he urged, his voice tight.

I ran. After a hundred yards I glanced behind me, but saw only the swaying bulk of Akaal Bahadur's *doko*. My breath came more easily. We continued, but again fear caused me to look back.

They came, two yellow bouncing lights still behind us.

With a burst of speed I ran to catch Prem.

I saw Prem's swiftly moving figure ahead but hesitated to call out his name. I lunged and grabbed his arm.

"Prem," I said. "They are coming!"

Prem stopped and turned to face me. We had only seconds to make a decision. We had no time to even ask the question, "What should we do?"

"Run," he said.

"I'll find someplace to hide and wait for you."

"We will talk with them," he assured me. "Go!"

I dashed ahead, looking for a hiding place. The trail, which once again followed the river, was bounded to the left by a sheer fifty-foot drop to the river, to the right by raised fields. A small lean-to came into view and I scrambled behind it. One last glance told me I was just in time as the two lights reached Prem, now waiting with the porters.

From my vantage point I listened carefully and heard the

low murmur of conversation. Struggling to keep my breath even and soft, I monitored the encounter between the authorities and my Nepalese staff. What were they saying?

After three minutes I saw the two lights heading back towards Dunai. Waiting another cautious minute, I reemerged and walked silently back towards Prem and the porters.

I found them sitting by a house, not talking, their silence ominous. At the sound of my footsteps, Prem turned.

Jumping up he grabbed me by the shoulders and pushed me down the trail. "They are coming!"

Looking behind me I saw lights approaching. Not more than thirty seconds, I judged, and they would be on me. This time I saw four dim beams weaving in the darkness. By the pale yellow light I saw that each man carried a long object in his other hand. They had rifles.

Run.

That primitive reaction prompted by adrenaline gave me strength.

Run. And I ran into the cover of darkness. My eyes were accustomed to the absence of light, I could feel the trail under my feet, hear the roar of the river to my left and sense the closeness of the crude retaining wall to my right.

Run. My mind focused on the flight, to put distance between me and those rifles, and to look for a place to hide.

I ran for several agonizing minutes. My pack jolted and swung wildly with every step. My eyes searched the blackness for an escape.

Finally I glimpsed a tiny break in the retaining wall. With a heave, I pulled myself over it and fell silently into a muddy field. Lying flat on my stomach and pressing myself into the freshly plowed earth, I struggled to catch my breath.

My heart pounded. *Be quiet. Be calm. Deep regular breaths.* I willed myself silent.

As soon as the sounds of my gasping breath died away, I peered over the wall. I saw no one coming, but the darkness could have hidden a person. And the river below bellowed its presence, masking any silent footfall. I took off my light-colored jacket but put my Chinese hat back on. Removing my pack I rummaged for my water bottle and downed half the quart of water I carried.

I took stock of my situation. I had no food, little water, no flashlight and spoke poor Nepali. I did have 3,000 rupees in cash. If Prem and the others were taken by the police, I would be alone, a foreigner in forbidden Dolpo.

Going alone further east into Dolpo, I knew, would be foolhardy and possibly suicidal. Even if I survived the elements I might be murdered just for the boots I wore. But I was on the wrong side of Dunai to get back to Jumla. What should I do?

The only reasonable course was to wait. Wait until sunrise at least. If Prem and the porters did not show up by then, I would try to make my way past Dunai and return to Jumla. Passing Dunai, especially during the day, would be difficult. Most likely I would be caught and thrown in jail.

I found a place just off the trail to sit, and waited. Visibility was less than thirty feet and the noise from the river muffled any footsteps. Although I wanted enough warning to hide if someone approached, I didn't want Prem and the porters to pass me by. If they went ahead, I would be on my own. I looked at my watch. One-fifteen.

The sounds of the river engulfed me. It was alive with the crunch and boom of rocks as the waters powerfully pushed and ground the boulders downstream. Nature creating another feature on the landscape, carrying the land before it like a giant bulldozer.

I was covered with sweat. I resisted drinking all of my water, even though my mouth was dry. Where were Prem and the porters?

At 2:10 A.M., silhouettes moved out of the darkness towards me. I leapt back over the retaining wall and lay flat. Seconds later they passed, and I made out the tops of our porters' loads. Were they alone? It was too dark for me to see, but I couldn't take the chance of letting them pass me by. I had to stop them. I crawled to the edge of the wall and leaned out over the trail.

"Prem."

"Come, we are going," came his cryptic reply.

Still concerned that they were not alone, I waited until they had passed me, then hopped back onto the trail and followed fifty yards behind.

Twice, the last person in line stopped to wait for me, but each time I, too, stopped until the group moved on. It was impossible to count how many they were, and I was afraid one or two policemen accompanied them.

After an hour I closed in and grabbed Jeet Bahadur from behind, pulling him off the trail. "Everything okay?"

"No problem, Sahib."

A half hour later we stopped to rest and I heard their story.

"There were four men, police. They had guns," Prem said.

"Yes, I saw them," I said. "I ran, but they didn't follow me, did they?"

"No, they did not see you. They talked to us there by the small house. I told them we worked for a sahib who took an airplane from Jumla just two days ago. That we walked all day and all night to go back to Pokhara. I said we tried to save our sahib money by going very fast. They didn't believe me."

"No wonder. What porter goes fast to save a foreigner money?"

Prem chuckled and continued. "So they made us untie our loads. And they counted the bowls and spoons to see how many people in our party. We have all given them the wrong names. I was Bira Bahadur Rai." He laughed again.

"So what happened?"

"Nothing. What can they do? We are Nepalese, we do

not need any permits. No problem, Parker Sahib. They let us go. They didn't want to, but they let us go."

We walked along the Thuli Bheri until three-thirty, then pulled off the trail. Not bothering with tents, we threw our bedrolls out underneath a large conifer tree and fell asleep.

CHAPTER NINE

▲

A HAND PRESSED FIRMLY DOWN ON MY HEAD AND WOKE ME FROM a deep slumber.

"Do not move," Prem whispered.

Pulling my head inside my sleeping bag, I heard the jingle of harness bells, then the sound of hooves approaching.

"*Namaste*," Prem called out.

"*Namaste. Kahaa jaane ho?*" ("Where are you going?") A man's voice, warm, unthreatening. I relaxed. Prem spoke to him for several minutes, then the sound of bells and hooves receded.

"It is okay now, Parker Sahib."

Rising up on one elbow, I saw three *lamas* astride sturdy Tibetan ponies twenty yards down the trail. Their flowing red robes and brightly colored saddlebags shone resplendently in the midmorning sun.

"Parker Sahib," Prem said. "The *lamas* have said that the crops were very bad this year, and that there is little food in the villages ahead."

"What about Tarakot?"

"We have two days of food left, we can easily get to Tarakot. But the *lamas* said that even there it may be difficult to find more."

After a cup of tea and some cold potatoes, we got quickly underway, walking along the increasingly spectacular gorge of the Thuli Bheri River. Hazy morning sunlight silvered the sheer rock walls, which rose on both sides of us for thousands of feet before disappearing from view. In such rugged terrain the only conceivable place for a trail was here, just beside the river.

By late morning, the sunlight had descended the walls of the gorge to the riverbed. The temperature soared. The sun soon baked our brains and sent us in search of cover. We stopped for a meal, then hid in the cool alcoves of some boulders that we shared with menacing black spiders. In the sultry afternoon heat I dozed and caught up on my journal. With the pace of events during the last few days, I hadn't had much chance to record what had happened.

I wrote about the day before the Balangra Pass, meeting the Tibetans, seeing the young mother with her child, the panda, and my emotional response to that inspiring day. Now, lazing in the heat, having been cheated out of a good many nights' sleep, I wondered what in the hell I was doing here. Where were the mountains I'd come to see? I was avoiding not only the police, but the local people, most of whom wished me no harm. This wasn't what I'd come to do. I consoled myself with the thought that in just one more day we would be past all these checkposts and into the high mountains just north of Dhaulagiri. Then we could relax, enjoy ourselves, take it easy. . . .

Also our nocturnal schedule of late had left me sluggish and not thinking clearly. Perhaps our diet of rice and potatoes, which did not provide me with enough calories and nutrients, had dulled my mind. There seemed little chance, however, that our diet would improve as we traveled further into Dolpo. Only a small portion of the wheel of yak cheese remained, and our buffalo salami also was almost finished. Both had by now petrified so that they required extended cooking just to make them edible. In the mornings, we had taken to breaking off a small chunk of the yak cheese which we sucked throughout the morning as it slowly softened. Both our cheese and salami would soon be gone, and with them our only source of protein.

This was not to suggest that my diet lacked taste. During the past few weeks, my fare had changed in a manner that more than counterbalanced its increasing monotony. Before Jumla, J.B. and I had eaten the same food as the porters, with one exception—chilies, or in Nepali *korsani*. Prem and the porters seemed addicted to them. When Prem prepared the food, he would serve J.B. and me and then add the chilies to their portion. Time and again, I had watched Prem eat half a dozen large chilies with a meal. Then, with swollen lips and tearing eyes, he would lament. "O Parker Sahib, I eat too many *korsani*. I must stop." But at the next meal, the story would be the same; he could not lay off the chilies. Prem and the porters lost their appetite and had little desire to eat without them. For them, running out of *korsani* and running out of rice were equally grim prospects.

Just before Tibrikot, we had passed a man carrying an entire basket of bright-red dried chilies. Our progress halted for almost an hour while Prem and Jeet Bahadur bargained for a large sack. Though that was only days ago, those chilies were already half gone. Since Jumla and J.B.'s departure, the Nepalese had me far outnumbered. They figured that Parker Sahib would eat whatever they cooked. And they cooked with chilies. I remembered their smiles as they served me those first few meals, then waited for my reaction. My lips tingled, my tongue burned, my face flushed, but I said nothing. The food got hotter by increments until finally it was wholly to their liking, the equivalent of five or six dried *korsani* per serving, ground up so they could not be removed. Now I feared I, too, was addicted, which seemed to have been their intent all along. Sneaky bastards.

* * *

Because of the heat and traffic on the trail, including police, we waited until eight-thirty when the western sky held only the faintest trace of gray light. We left our hiding spot and followed the trail, which recrossed the river several times before climbing hundreds of feet up the canyon walls.

We walked until twelve-thirty, when dogs barking in the distance gave us a hint in the dark night that the village of Laban was close by. We had planned to stop near it for the night and the next day obtain information about the route ahead. Our sketchy information indicated that the last police checkpost along this route through Dolpo lay somewhere ahead of us in the village of Tarakot. Tarakot, capital of the former kingdom of Tichu Rong, was known also by the locals as *Dzong* (Fort), for it once held the fort that controlled this medieval kingdom.

In the dark we stumbled about, searching for a flat area large enough for all of us to sleep. We looked through dense thickets of thorny scrub, to no avail. Then, hacking our way through heavy brush, we climbed a steep run-off gully and found a near-level area. We cleared a spot right in the middle, then squeezed five of us in a space big enough for only three. After several minutes of flailing arms and legs, we found the only mutually agreeable position, stacked front to back like a set of spoons. Exhausted, I slept soundly.

Just after dawn two Magar men and a girl spotted us from above. In the Nepalese manner, they came to snoop, to find out who we were and where we were going. Prem shook me awake and warned me of their approach. I pulled my sleeping bag over my head, then listened as best I could to the conversation.

First they asked why we were sleeping here when their farmhouse was only two hundred yards above us. Answer: We couldn't have seen it in the dark. Where were we going? Answer: None of your business.

Prem, of course, didn't give these answers but said just enough to keep them talking as he listened to everything they could tell us about the route. These farmers hung on to chit-chat for an agonizing sixty minutes as my bladder nearly burst. Smothered in my sleeping bag, even I couldn't stand the rank odor of my unwashed body. *As bad as a Tibetan.*

As soon as they left, we took up our loads and got under way. Once more we headed down to the river and crossed it on a cantilevered bridge, the large posts on either side of which were decorated with erotic carvings. Many of the Magars who live in this area called Tichu Rong speak Tibetan and practice a form of Tibetan Buddhism, although they are ethnically related to people who live further south in the lower valleys of Nepal. They migrated north, adopting Tibetan ways, but hold themselves aloof from the ethnic Tibetans found in other parts of Dolpo.

At a rest stop, Prem and I discussed our strategy for the next few days.

"These Magars have said that the Jang La going south from Tarakot is not passable because of snow," he said.

"We didn't want to go that way anyway," I answered.

"They said that we can go this way." He pointed along the Thuli Bheri. "We can follow the river all the way to Mustang."

"But our map doesn't show any route that way."

Prem looked at me quizzically. "Maybe the map is wrong."

"You're right. It's been wrong before. I have this feeling that some Kathmandu bureaucrat who once came this way twenty years ago sat there in his office, probably half-crocked, and said, 'Oh, I remember the trail went this way.' And so that's what he put on the map. I'm pretty sure of one thing though, we're going to have to cross a mountain barrier somewhere up ahead."

I took the map and spread it out. The printing had begun to fade in the sunlight and flecks of curried vegetables stained it. I traced the thick line of the Barbung Khola as it wound around the Dhaulagiri Massif, then followed a route

east over the mountains to the Kali Gandaki River. "Look,"
I pointed. "Once down to the Kali Gandaki we can go over
the Thorung La to Manang and then on towards Kathmandu. But that's weeks away . . . what did the farmers say
about the checkpost at Tarakot?"

"They said there was no checkpost," Prem answered.

"How can they say that? They must know that's not
true!" I fumed in frustration. Why was it so hard to get
accurate information? Why did people lie to us? The mountains and rivers threw physical barriers in our path, but the
helpless feeling at the lack of information created a mental
frustration that weighed at least as heavily upon us.

Just before noon we stopped just below the village of
Tarakot. Sitting three hundred feet above the river plain, we
saw the roofs of a few buildings standing out against the
deep blue sky. White prayer flags on long poles rippled in
the breeze.

As we started to prepare a meal, a Tibetan approached us
from the east. Prem hailed him and offered a cup of tea,
hoping to learn of the route ahead. After a short exchange,
Prem hurried to my side.

"Parker Sahib, this man says there is a checkpost just
above us." Prem pointed to one of the buildings. "We can
see it. He says the police look for people from the roof with
binoculars."

I looked up and, sure enough, on the roof I saw the silhou-
ette of a person. Sliding down behind some rocks, I reached
for my binoculars and carefully focused on the building.

A man watched the trail.

I pulled back. Despite the heat, I jammed my Chinese hat
down on my head as far as I could. Lifting the binoculars
again, I took another peek. The man watched but seemed to
pay no particular attention to us.

"Parker Sahib," Prem said. "Let me look."

Prem scanned the village and the trail ahead.

"What do you think, Prem?" Sweat trickled down my face.

"They do not see us."

"So we should be thankful for small favors," I mumbled. "Let's put some miles between us and this place."

"But first we need food, and Tarakot is perhaps the only place between here and the Kali Gandaki."

"Let's get out of this spot, away to a more secluded place. Then we can send the porters into the village to buy food."

"Yes, Parker Sahib. But let us go one by one. Maybe the police will look for a group."

"Auri Bahadur," I called softly. "*Chuba dinos.*" ("Give me your coat.") I mimed putting on his Tibetan coat.

Auri Bahadur looked puzzled for a moment, then, with a grin, nodded. I wanted to borrow his Tibetan *chuba* as a disguise. He untied his *doko* and extracted it.

Now with my Chinese hat, green canvas pack and the black Tibetan *chuba*, I attempted to pass as a local, hoping my foreign aura didn't extend as far as the checkpost.

Prem went first. I waited until he was out of sight, then followed. The three porters brought up the rear. For nearly a third of a mile the trail crossed a flat expanse directly below the village and within sight of the checkpost.

I walked rapidly with my head down, silently cursing our bad luck, or our stupidity, at not passing this checkpost at night as we had the others. I remembered the remarks of the police chief in Jumla and Prem's assessment of these remote outposts of the Nepalese government. Although the medieval fortress no longer stood on the hillside, the modern equivalent of the king of Tichu Rong probably lurked in the buildings above.

I found Prem a mile down the trail. He had stopped at a small stream amidst some boulders far enough off the trail to hide us for the day. Once the porters arrived, we set camp and cooked a meal.

Then Prem and I sat down with Akaal Bahadur and Auri

Bahadur. They were to go into town to buy food, matches, batteries for our Chinese flashlights and to obtain information. To keep from attracting undue attention, they left thirty minutes apart.

Early in the afternoon I drifted out of camp to a place near the stream. As soon as I was out of sight of Prem and Jeet Bahadur, I slipped out of my pants and began to wash away the grime and filth from weeks of wear. This work normally was done by the porters, but I figured that Jeet Bahadur could use the rest. I could wash my own clothes this once.

I wet them in the icy stream and then rubbed in the soap. Just as I began to pound them on a flat rock, Jeet Bahadur silently appeared.

"Sahib," he said, squatting on his haunches beside me.

"Yes," I answered cautiously, perhaps feeling a little guilty for being found out. A sahib washing his own clothes.

He told me that Prem wanted to see me, he had something important to talk about. I looked at Jeet Bahadur and he steadily returned the gaze. Silently, I left my task and went to look for Prem. It was a lie and I knew it, for Prem had nothing important to say that couldn't wait. But I couldn't do anything about it. I had already offended Jeet Bahadur by trying to wash my own clothes; to insist on continuing would have been an insult.

Some tasks I was permitted to do. Akaal Bahadur and I usually set the tents, which was easier with two people anyway. Maybe because they were western tents, the porters made an exception. Also, I usually got away with collecting firewood. I frequently arrived at our camping spot before the porters and hurriedly collected enough wood to last the evening, sparing the porters that one task. It was a small enough contribution.

But I know that I frequently offended them by undervaluing the status given me by birth, by taking on tasks not meant for me. In trying to change our daily routine, I tried to change history, to negate thousands of years of the caste system, plus hundreds of years of British occupation in the Indian subcontinent.

Their social structure was so different from mine; would I ever understand the cultural gaps, let alone bridge them? And should I even attempt to do so? The only answer that came to me now was that I should give up gracefully, to allow Jeet Bahadur to finish his task unobserved, not embarrassed by the bumbling sahib, who didn't always know his place. This was the best I could do. Complaining to Prem would do no good. He had lectured me before. *Parker*, I told myself, *don't impose your values on them. Leave it*.

Akaal Bahadur and Auri Bahadur had been gone for several hours. Worried, Prem had just asked Jeet Bahadur to go find them when they appeared out of the surrounding boulders. They had been delayed by their inability to find food and matches. I had fallen into a river just past Mandu, ruining several packets of matches and seriously depleting our supplies. I had also lost my plastic lighter, something that upset Prem a great deal more than me. One of the cheap, sealed-plastic disposables made in Hong Kong and Bangkok, it had been refilled in Kathmandu by someone who drilled a hole in the bottom. Stories of these unstable lighters exploding in users' faces, or even in someone's pocket, made me nervous about having one and I was relieved to have lost it. Matches, even the warped, undependable Nepalese ones, were preferable to me. But in Tarakot those had been in short supply as well, and Akaal Bahadur and Auri Bahadur paid eight rupees per packet. They bought fifteen kilos of rice, a sack of potatoes and, of course, *korsani*, the addictive chilies. Twenty packets of *beedies* were my bonus to Prem and the porters. They found no batteries.

Canvasing the bazaar for information, they had received conflicting reports about the route ahead. Locals confirmed that the Jang La to the south was buried in deep snow. They heard several different stories, however, about the route east along the Thuli Bheri. Some said the trails were impassable;

others said we could reach Jomoson in only a few days' time. It was exasperating.

"Prem. What is the truth?"

"I do not know, Parker Sahib."

We looked at each other. Once again our constant obstacle—lack of information.

"How long will our rice last?"

Prem checked our supplies. "We bought fifteen kilos today, plus a little left from before. If we eat two kilos every meal, we have eight meals of rice."

I laughed: almost a pound of *uncooked* rice per person. Much more when cooked. It never failed to astonish me how much rice a small Nepalese could eat. I had never heard a porter say he was full, although Prem occasionally refused more food. *My* problem was an inability to consume such vast quantities of rice and potatoes, which meant I was slowly wasting away, starving for lack of a large enough stomach. I hitched my belt two notches tighter these days, an indication of how much weight I had lost. Jeet Bahadur had also grown perceptibly thinner, and I urged him to eat more rice, hoping I didn't look as gaunt as he.

"What else do we have?" I asked.

"Some potatoes. And *korsani*!" Prem laughed.

The next day the porters began singing again and that lifted my spirits. I hadn't realized how much I missed their songs. In eastern Nepal they had sung almost nonstop as they carried their loads along the trail. In western Nepal the singing had stopped suddenly above Jumla. I realized that the tension over the authorities had been weighing on all of us. Now with the checkpost at Tarakot behind us, we all felt lighter, unburdened.

By now I knew many of Akaal Bahadur and Jeet Bahadur's favorite songs by heart and I sang along with them—quietly, so they wouldn't hear. Like the Tamang people, their songs were boisterous and full of life. I didn't know what the

Tamang words meant, but the melodies seemed somehow appropriate to these mountains. With each song, my mood lightened.

The air, free of dust and moisture, allowed spectacularly clear views down the canyon and above to the mountains. The cloudless blue sky, the glaciered peaks, the deep thrust of the canyon—all seemed closer. Late in the morning we passed a tributary that rushed out of a chasm from the north, its water tumbling into the Thuli Bheri. The Tarap Khola drained a large valley of the same name in the interior of Dolpo to the east of Shey Gompa and Crystal Mountain. Once past this confluence, the river we followed changed its name to the Barbung Khola. And it was this Barbung Khola to which we now seemed tied. Possibly we would make a pilgrimage to its source on our way to cross the mountain barrier between Dolpo and the Kali Gandaki watershed.

In the afternoon, while walking alone, I rounded a large boulder in the trail. Deep in thought, I didn't see the group of people sitting there until I ran into them. I had to place my hands on the shoulders of two of them to avoid tripping. Embarrassed, I mumbled an almost incoherent "*Namaste.*"

Then I looked at the group of six Tibetans around a small fire just at the trailside—six of the scariest people I had ever seen. I put my hands together with a bow and took two steps to keep moving along the trail.

"*Namaste,*" came the thickly accented reply from one who stepped into the trail directly in front of me.

I looked up and up. He was easily six foot three, and another two inches were added by the thick black hair wound around his head. His girth, accentuated by his oversized sheepskin *chuba*, was the greatest I had seen in a Tibetan. His right arm hung out, leaving his shoulder and torso bare. Around his waist a leather belt held a satchel and a long, silver-handled sword. The ubiquitous multicolored, yak-soled Tibetan boots adorned his feet.

I smelled his foul breath and unwashed body. He smiled

and I saw that half of his teeth were gone and one of the few remaining was capped in gold. Instinctively, I took a step backwards.

I almost fell over the large aluminum box that two of the others now opened. Jammed inside were cigarettes, tobacco, chilies, chocolate, coral, yak rope and other bric-a-brac I couldn't identify.

In halting Nepali, the tall Tibetan asked, "You want to buy something?"

"No. I have very little money."

With a chilling, twisted leer, he asked another question. "Where is your house?"

"America."

"Ahhhhhh," came a chorus from around the fire.

"Where are you going?"

"Jomoson." It was the best I could think of quickly, as I felt the hairs on the back of my neck stand up. Two more rose to their feet.

"How much for your boots?" Three frightening Tibetans now surrounded me, asking a question I had answered at least three dozen times before in my travels. They stared at my feet, assessing the potential value of my footgear.

"Not for sale. They are the only pair I have."

I continued smiling all this while, as the Tibetans smiled back. Despite my outward calm, my heart pounded and jumbled chaos raced through my mind. They were Khampas—nomads, drifters, ex-CIA allies against the Chinese. Feared for centuries in Tibet for their lawless ways, they had drifted into Nepal, seeking a livelihood. They had continued in their old professions as bandits, businessmen and mercenaries. I remembered the stories about the murdered French couple and Peace Corps volunteer.

"Who are your friends?" came the next question. I knew what these bizarre words meant. They wanted to know if I was alone, just as had the Khampas I'd encountered before the Balangra Pass.

"Many porters coming behind and a guide," I answered, hoping fervently that one of the aforementioned would suddenly appear around the boulder. Unfortunately I was feeling strong that day and had marched out ahead of the others. I guessed that Prem and the porters were twenty minutes back. *At least I have my ice axe. Get out of here. Move.*

"Namaste," I said, walking around the towering Tibetan, who still stood resolutely in front of me, and hurrying on down the hill.

I continued at a bruising pace for half a mile. Then I became worried about Prem and the porters, how they might fare with the Tibetans. I climbed fifty feet up and off the trail to a spot where I could see but not easily be seen and waited.

How confident I had been getting! How presumptuous to think that just because we had passed the police checkposts all of our problems were over! So many had warned us of precipitous trails and high mountain passes covered in snow. But it was not the wilderness I had feared that day. It was the wildness of men whose cultural values differed so much from my own.

Fifteen minutes later Prem appeared along with Akaal Bahadur. I slipped back onto the trail.

"Prem, did you meet the Khampas?"

"Yes, Parker Sahib."

"Na ramro maanchheho." ("Not good men.") Akaal Bahadur shook his head.

Prem seemed as shaken as I, and related their conversation. "First they wanted us to buy things from them. Then they wanted to buy our pots and containers. They wanted to look in Akaal Bahadur's *doko*. Then, Parker Sahib, they wanted us to camp with them."

"Na ramro maanchheho," Akaal Bahadur commented again.

"Camp with them!" Prem was indignant. "But I told them we would go on until dark."

"Which way are they going?" I asked.

"I do not know," Prem answered.

"Real smart of us, forget to ask them the same questions they asked us. Everybody in Nepal asks 'Where are you going?' except us! Let's keep a sharp eye to our rear."

Jeet Bahadur and Auri Bahadur arrived ten minutes later. Closer together, we walked steadily for two hours, hoping to put distance between us and the fearsome Tibetans.

We set camp well off the trail and immediately next to the river, which was smaller now and not so foreboding since becoming the Barbung Khola above its confluence with the Tarap Khola. As soon as we set camp, we sent Auri Bahadur back along the trail to keep an eye out for our "friends."

We cooked and ate our second rice meal of the day, and this favorite food lifted the porters' spirits considerably. I thought that Prem had done this intentionally to lighten their mood. As we sat around our small fire, the earth shuddered for a second, then suddenly jolted. Startled, we looked at each other. An earthquake. I had never felt one before, but it was an unmistakable tremor. "Earthquake," I said.

The porters laughed and told me the Nepali word for it. We heard the sharp reports of falling rock above, but far away and no danger to us. Over quickly and no harm done.

As I crawled into my tent, I mulled over the words of the Magar farmers of Tarakot. Five days to Jomoson, they had said. Seeing how little we had covered so far, I found this assessment preposterous. Now I was no longer so confident.

CHAPTER TEN

▲

BARBUNG KHOLA GORGE

Sunday, April 1, 1984

THE GORGE NARROWED. BEYOND THE DIRT, ROCKS AND GLACIAL debris we saw a wooden bridge spanning the Barbung Khola. But the trail traversed for sixty feet along a vertical rock wall a hundred feet in the air. A trail had been created along the sheer face with long poles bracing two tree trunks that spanned the gap, a rough scaffold. The trunks were one and a half feet wide, and below them was nothing but air.

We approached this section cautiously. No one spoke. Prem and I went first, facing forward with our slender packs, but the porters with their bulky loads had to face the wall as they inched along, six inches at a step. We crossed safely, one at a time, but I fervently hoped we would meet no more trails like this one. It slowed us down—worse, it scared the hell out of us all.

Beyond the bridge we tramped down through loose rock and dirt to the riverbed, a torrent tumbling through huge boulders. In the warm sun I stripped to the waist and washed my head and upper body in the icy water.

Beyond this narrow gorge the valley opened up into a broad flood plain, the river meandering haphazardly through it. We kept to the north side of the river, threading through scattered stands of towering conifers and ancient deodar cedar.

The trail passed through a tremendous walk-through *chorten* in partial ruin. Although the near entrance was blocked with rubble, the opposite side remained open. Cautiously I crawled through scattered debris to get inside. Shafts of sunlight shone through the shattered roof and illuminated the interior. High above the collapsed entrance, four painted figures sat serenely, streaked by the rare rainwaters that entered freely through the ruptured roof.

The whole structure stood twenty-five feet high, and the guts of it had spilled out so I could see the tons of various sized rock that had been used to construct it. Large wooden crossbeams and joists formed a framework for a carefully constructed outer dry wall of rock. Although spiritually it meant little to me, I was unsettled to see the *chorten* in ruin. Perhaps an earthquake had done the damage. If so, it had yet to be mended, and in the meantime the harsh climate was tearing it apart. I could not help but feel that I was observing a culture and religion in decline.

Late afternoon sun illuminated the squat stone houses of the village of Khakotgaon, a medieval fortress that clung to the base of the cliffs along the north wall of the gorge. Curious villagers came out on the roofs to stare down at us, foreigners from far away. Prem asked to buy food and we purchased four eggs, ten kilos of potatoes and three kilos of *tsampa* (roasted barley flour).

A young man stepped in front of me with a broad smile. His western dress and facial features identified him as another outsider.

"Good to see you. I need English," he said slowly and with a heavy Nepali accent.

Taking this to mean that he wanted to speak English with me, I attempted a conversation. Unfortunately, we didn't seem to speak the same variety of that language and we lapsed into Nepali. I learned that he was a schoolteacher from the *terai* sent here to establish a school. He had served fourteen months of his "sentence," with ten months to go before he could leave.

He leaned close to me. "Very lonely. Not good people," he whispered.

Beyond the village, a series of *chortens* spaced two hundred yards apart stretched out across the barren plain. Further ahead on the south side of the river, a side canyon rose 13,000 feet in one continuous upsurge to the northern ramparts of the 24,000-foot Churen Himal. So vast was the vertical rise that the scene looked surreal, like a painting. In the flame-colored late afternoon light it seemed the most beautiful mountain I had ever seen. We stopped by a small *chorten* to rest.

As we sat, a man and a lame boy approached and rested thirty feet from us. After a minute, the man spoke to Prem in passable Nepali, although he looked and dressed like a Tibetan—more aristocratic version, though, than the Tibetan Khampas we had met the day before. His black hair was interwoven with red wool and wound around his head. He wore a monk's robe.

Still nervous after our encounter with the Khampas the day before, Prem talked only briefly with him. The sun dipped below the mountains to the southwest and the temperature plunged. Saying a hurried goodbye to the man and his boy, we moved on to find a place to camp a mile from Khakotgaon.

As we set camp, I asked Prem about the man.

"He says his name is Lama Dorje, Parker Sahib. He lives in the village of Tarengaon, one or two days' walk. He wanted to camp with us."

"I don't like that idea, Prem. Not after yesterday."

"But Parker Sahib, they are only two, we are five. Maybe they think of the Khampas too."

"Maybe. What did you find out in Khakotgaon about the route?"

"They told me about a trail over the Mukut Himal. It is shorter, but very high and may have deep snow. One man said '*Mukut baato mateeeeeeee*'—Mukut trail is high. His voice was very high like the trail."

"I think it must be close to twenty thousand feet. I don't like the idea of taking the porters that high this time of year."

"In Tarakot they told us that the Mukut baato was not possible."

"Tarakot seems pretty far away now. I'm not sure they knew what they were talking about."

The next day we passed behind the Dhaulagiri Massif and entered a barren desert terrain almost totally devoid of vegetation. In the cool morning we followed the Barbung Khola. The trail alternated between hugging the river and climbing the steep slopes on either side. A few times it traversed slide areas several hundred feet above the river—active slides that cascaded rock and dirt in intermittent barrages across the trail and down to the cold waters of the river.

At one fifty-yard-wide slide, I stopped to take a picture of one of the porters as he crossed carefully but quickly. Then I changed film. The camera jammed. Cursing, I fiddled with it for several minutes, spooling in a new roll. By the time I had finished, I was alone; the others had gone ahead.

Remembering that we had promised to keep together, I wanted to catch up and hurriedly stepped out onto the edge of the slide. As lightly and as quickly as I could, I tiptoed through the loose rock, creating mini-slides with every step. Stopping would have meant sliding with the debris. Halfway across, a large rock, five feet in diameter and partially embedded in the slope, gave me the idea to pause briefly. I stepped onto the rock. It moved. I lost my balance and fell backwards. From beneath my feet, the boulder disappeared down the slope. I swung my ice axe over my head and with a gratifying *clunk* I felt it dig into the earth. An instinctive movement, it had checked my fall, but I realized the axe might not hold, that the whole mountainside could follow the large rock down to the river bed.

My body hung over the void left by the boulder. For sickening seconds I swung, suspended from above by my ice axe stuck into conglomerate that threatened to rip apart at any moment. Over my shoulder I saw debris raining down on either side of me, picking up speed as it slipped down the slope. A growing cloud of dust rose from the avalanche of earth around me. Breathing shallowly, I tested my ice axe. It still held, nothing over my head moved. The ground immediately surrounding me seemed stable. I dropped into the small depression created two feet below me by the missing boulder. *Quick, before it starts moving.* With three jerks, I worked my ice axe free, then looked across the remaining twenty-five yards to the trail. I saw sandy soil that wasn't moving. With no time to waste working out a strategy, thinking of what to do, I just went with fast, light steps, straining to reach the trail. Behind me the mountainside continued to move, gathering speed, noise and dust.

Stable ground under my feet! I stopped. My lungs sucked for air. *Calm down.* I looked back. The leading edge of the landslide had just reached the canyon floor. I had not noticed the noise in my attempt to reach the trail again. But now it filled the air, a roaring freight train accompanied by a thick and rising cloud of fine dust.

Impervious to sound while on the slope, I now felt weak, especially my knees. I sat down and threw myself backwards as the blood rushed from my head. For several minutes I lay lightheaded and out of breath.

Finally my breath returned more or less to normal and I sat up, propping myself against a rock on the uphill slope. Still feeling weak, I looked once more at the hillside. Only thin tendrils of sand now spilled over the small rocks towards the river below. Leaning forward, I could just see the terminus of the slide area at the river's edge. Dust obscured the tons of rock and dirt that had just fallen.

Dark clouds scudded across the sky, adding to the forbidding view of the barren and lifeless mountain terrain of inner Dolpo to the north. After our confrontation with the Tibetans we should have hung together, but now I was alone. It was too easy for the last person in line to fall behind without being noticed. What would have happened if I had fallen into the landslide? I could have been entombed forever in this vast desert and no one would have known what happened. My epitaph would have been a simple "Lost in the Himalayas of western Nepal."

I did not want to be alone now. Cinching the shoulder straps on my pack, I headed out rapidly along the trail, jogging as best I could. A half mile ahead I saw the last porter round a promontory and then disappear from view. Determined not to stop until I had caught up with them, I picked up my pace. A half hour later I found them resting beside a small bridge spanning a narrow section of the frigid waters of the Barbung Khola. I approached and sat on a wall without saying anything, breathing heavily. Glad only to be in their presence again, I had no words.

For the first time on this trip, I felt totally vulnerable. Even with the fear of the police, the military and the Khampas, I was always quickly able to revive feelings of confidence, assuredness, strength. I knew I would make it through western Nepal alive. But I felt deeply shaken by this brush with death.

It had been so close! If my ice axe had not held, if I hadn't found the bit of solid footing, I would have been hurled down to the river, a fragile human body crushed in the midst of tons of dirt and rock, buried in a crude tomb. I shuddered as I envisioned the helpless plunge, the pain, the fine dust covering my face, cutting off light and air and then suffocating me. But strangely, sitting there under the dark gray sky, I came to feel something else—something new to me. I realized how attuned I had become to the earth, the mountains, the rivers, the sky and snow, even the landsliding rocks. Although they had almost killed me, I didn't view the earth as menacing.

Not believing in an afterlife, I had no reason to fear death, that moment when I would no longer exist. Although I had fought with an animal's instinct to preserve my life, it was not so much a passionate wish to avoid death as to avoid the act of dying. These thoughts troubled me, for they seemed somehow negative, and because I now realized that death itself need hold no fear for me.

But if death meant little to me, what would it mean to the other people in my life? What effect would my death have on my parents? I remembered my father at the airport on the day I left. Not a man to shed tears, he felt an anguish that I now understood. My mother, so quietly accepting of whatever it was that I wanted to do—what would it mean to her? I was their only son, they would be devastated if they lost me. And Clara? What did I mean to her? How would the news of my death affect her?

I said nothing as I sat, breathing heavily, lost in my contemplation of death. Then I heard the voice of a stranger. Turning, I saw that we were not alone. Prem was talking to Lama Dorje and his son. Where had they come from? How did they get here? Not having seen them since the day before, I felt disconcerted at their sudden appearance. I listened to the conversation, catching bits and pieces of what was said.

After fifteen minutes, Prem came and sat with me. "Parker Sahib, Lama Dorje says we can stay with him. In his house in Tarengaon. It is three hours' walk."

"Can we trust him, Prem?"

"Yes, Parker Sahib. I think so."

"Good. Will he sell us food?"

"Yes. He will sell us food—and *chang*!"

"Then tell him we will stay at his house, Prem."

Lama Dorje smiled broadly when Prem relayed the news to him. As it was already three in the afternoon, we set off quickly. We crossed a new wooden bridge and headed up the north side of the Barbung Khola. Pulverized rock covered this slope and soon the dust caked our clothing and faces, clogged our noses. Before long, Lama Dorje veered onto a shortcut up and over a *lekh*, leaving the trail behind. Struggling up through the loose soil, with each step up we sank down again.

We passed two long *mani* walls, each containing hundreds of stones carved in Tibetan script with the mantra, *"Om mani padme hum."* Fifty yards away sat the ruins of buildings, almost invisible against the desert mountainside. Above them I could trace the faintest outline of abandoned terraced fields. Prem asked Lama Dorje about this deserted place.

"Lama Dorje says that it was a large *gompa* and village," Prem said. "He says that when he was a small boy, they had big festivals here. Many *lamas* came from Nepal and Tibet. But then they had a fire. And many of the *lamas* left. Then the Khampas came. They burned houses and stole food. And then there was no more water. Nothing would grow, the people left."

"How long ago did all this happen?"

"He does not know."

"What was the name of this village and *gompa*?"

"Sorry, Parker Sahib. He does not remember."

I looked again and made out the faint traces of more buildings above. An eerie feeling overcame me as I remembered the Mani Rimdu festival at Thyangboche Monastery in eastern Nepal last November. *Lamas* had gathered from Nepal, Bhutan, Sikkim and India. From their scattered villages, hundreds of Sherpas flowed into the monastery in long lines. Early in the morning I had been awakened by the sound of the horns, twelve-foot-long brass *thugchen*. They boomed across the valley and, joined by the beat of drums and the ringing of six-foot gongs, created a lilting sensation, transporting me backwards in time. The masked dances had been alternately stately and wild. *Lamas* wore painted masks of deities, wrathful devil-faced gods that Buddhists believed they would meet after their death. Dozens of dancers in brilliant multihued silk costumes appeared before the crowds, moving with the music of conch shells, reed oboes, horns, cymbals and bells. I asked but never found an answer to my question about the meaning of all I had seen, the sounds and sights of the elemental, timeless legends of all cultures. That was what it must have been like here thirty years ago or more, when Lama Dorje was a young boy. I thought that if I closed my eyes, I might hear the *thugchen*'s deep bass call.

The top of the *lekh* stood at 13,000 feet. While the loose ground had left us panting on the way up, going down was pure joy. In just ten minutes, great bounding steps cushioned by the soft soil brought us back to the main trail eight hundred feet below. We hit the trail and headed east towards Tarengaon, following the Barbung Khola again, this time six hundred feet above the rushing waters. Dusk approached, and the sky turned a darker gray as the previously intermittent cloud cover consolidated into a blanket of drab slate.

A forest of *chortens* appeared. Hundreds, more than I had ever seen in one place before, straddled and blocked the trail. The path meandered among them on its way to Tarengaon. Many arched over the trail and one particularly large one caught my eye. Several tiers rose one above the other, and as I stepped inside I saw the hollow vaulted interior. On the ceiling were sixteen panels, each a two-foot-square *thangka*, a religious painting on cloth. Of mediocre quality, they were nevertheless adorned with generous amounts of gold and silver paint. One of the corner panels was missing, the canvas crudely ripped from the ceiling. That disappointed me; vandalism—particularly of religious artifacts— should have been unknown in this remote backwater.

We rounded a bend and the village of Tarengaon came into view, nestled in a large hollow in the mountainside. At first glance I missed the village altogether. The squat stone structures huddled together along the upper third of the hollow and blended in with the drab tan and gray shades of the surrounding mountains.

Whereas Tarakot and Khakotgaon looked medieval, Tarengaon was biblical, a Jericho in miniature. A dozen fortresslike houses were scattered over a few acres of parched land. On each flat roof was piled carefully hoarded *daura* (firewood), which at this altitude was little more than dried scrub. Except for a few tattered and dirty prayer flags moving in the wind above the larger houses, there was no sign of life. Fallow terraced fields stretched for a hundred yards below the houses. Below the fields, the slope fell away sharply to the abyss of the Barbung Khola.

As we approached the village, our feet kicked up clouds of dust from the parched soil. It seemed impossible that the meager rains that would arrive in June and July could bring life to this dust, but the proof that they did was this village.

We followed Lama Dorje as he wound his way towards the topmost house, his place of distinction as the nominal head of Tarengaon and the local dispenser of justice. As we neared his house he bellowed a few words in Tibetan and two small children, barefoot and filthy, with runny noses and dressed in tattered homespun, appeared on the roof. Above and to the left of the door, a carved stone mask was embedded in the wall, a religious icon to ward off evil spirits. Directly above the door, suspended from a wooden peg, hung a slate *mani* stone, intricately chiseled with Tibetan script.

Lama Dorje led us through a low wood-framed doorway and we found ourselves groping in the dark for the hewn log ladder that led to the upper floor. The porters remained below, stowing the loads away safely while Prem and I climbed to the upper level. The darkened main floor received light only from a single small window and from the flickering fire at the hearth burning in the center of the far wall. We ducked low to avoid the choking smoke. Lama Dorje beckoned us to sit next to him on small Tibetan rugs near the hearth.

His wife appeared from a small side room with three silver-lined wooden bowls and two bottles. A large metal ornament was perched on her head. Two pieces of flat brass, the ends rolled into thin cylinders, formed a peaked roof. Pieces of coral and turquoise dangled by sinew off the front and back. I had seen these strange headpieces only one other place, at Bodnath in the wintertime when Tibetans gathered from the far reaches of the Himalayas.

Lama Dorje poured us each a bowl of golden *chang*. Then, lighting a small piece of incense, he made an offering to the altar behind him. Using the smoking incense he traced a circle around a photograph of the Dalai Lama three times, then dipping two fingers into his bowl of *chang*, he flicked drops first to one side then the other. Turning back to us, he urged us to drink. Cool and refreshing, the *chang* reminded us of the drink we had found in Dalphu.

As soon as we drained our bowls and set them down, Lama Dorje's wife refilled them. Five minutes later, under their watchful eyes, we had downed our three polite bowlfuls.

Prem began bargaining for food. Quickly Lama Dorje agreed upon a price and summoned his wife. We were not sure what we had bargained for, but our entire group would be fed. To show our gratitude, Prem gave her a sizable chunk of our remaining petrified yak cheese, which she accepted with a great show of thanks.

Prem summoned the porters from below and together we sat around the fire. By now word had spread that a group of foreigners had arrived and villagers began to trickle in. An hour after we arrived I counted eighteen people in the room. Some sat but most stood, staring curiously at us. Our hostess served the food she had prepared, a hard *chapatti*-like flat bread and potatoes with fiery *achar* (chili). More *chang* appeared, and with the drink the villagers' tongues loosened.

As the center of attention, we had to submit to innumerable questions, asked through Lama Dorje. They were unable to distinguish my foreignness from that of Prem and the porters; to them we were all strangers from Kathmandu. Only a few of the men from the village—none of the women —had traveled as far as Kathmandu. Because the land was so barren, many men turned to trading for livelihood, traveling as far as Jumla in the west, Jomoson in the east and Tibet to the north. Lama Dorje indicated, though, that travel and trade into Tibet had decreased considerably in the last twenty years, making it more difficult for the villagers to turn a profit. Few traveled any further south than Jumla or Jomoson because they were afraid, and rightly so, of *aulo* (malaria), the lowland disease.

Suddenly Prem turned to me with a question from Lama Dorje. "Parker Sahib, Lama Dorje wants to know. Do you have any hashish?"

I stopped for a moment to think about how to answer this one. I *had* brought some hashish from Kathmandu which I was saving as a treat for the porters. "Yes. Tell him, Prem, that I have some hashish."

When Lama Dorje heard this he asked if we could smoke some. I found a small chunk and handed it to him. He looked at it closely, turning it over in his fingers, smelling it like a fine cigar. He commented that it was very fine hashish.

"It's from Afghanistan," I said. Prem translated but Lama Dorje had no idea where Afghanistan was.

He produced a *chillum*, a small pipe, which he loaded with hash and passed around the room. Within minutes everyone was high and, emboldened by the drug, many who had held back in the shadows moved forward, pressing questions on us.

Where were we from? Prem answered that he was a Nepalese, but not from Kathmandu, from further away. How many days walk was it from the sahib's village to Tarengaon? To these people the world was flat, or rather a series of mountains, and every distance was gauged by how many days it took to walk.

I thought, trying to calculate. "One thousand two hundred days' walk," I answered. "And many great lakes to cross."

This answer was met with exclamations of disbelief, but Prem insisted it was true. When the villagers tried to counter this bizarre answer, he still insisted, although I don't think anyone ever truly believed him.

Late in the evening our attention turned to barter. We needed food and these villagers wanted our belongings. The first topic, the most important to them, was our boots. We repeatedly insisted that our boots weren't for sale. Next they focused on our plastic containers, two empty, beat-up cooking oil jugs. A woman appeared from the crowd wanting to buy one, but refused to produce her barter. She indicated she wanted me to accompany her down the stairs.

I rose and followed her in the dark down to our loads stowed below. I picked through my pack and found a flashlight, the only one that still worked among the three we carried. She pointed to the battered green oil container that she wanted. Then, rummaging in her sleeve, she pulled out a rolled-up piece of canvas.

In the beam of my dim flashlight she carefully unrolled the object. It was a *thangka*. Startled, I looked closely at it, the lines of the figure lavishly illuminated in gold and silver. It was the missing panel from the chorten just outside the village. Taken aback, I untied the jug from Akaal Bahadur's basket and gave it to her.

She handed me the *thangka*, but I pushed it away. "No," I indicated to her, "keep it, I don't want it."

She scuttled out the door before I could change my mind and demand payment for the plastic container. How could she do such a thing? How could she desecrate the beautiful *chorten* for an old cooking oil jug? Perhaps the answer lay in a different way of looking at things. Perhaps the *chorten* was not beautiful or sacred to her, merely something she could use, or abuse, to ease her life a bit. This plundering and destruction of the indigenous culture and religion occurred throughout Nepal. Was it an inevitable effect of foreign influence? It was not only the villagers who destroyed the ancient monuments and relics to benefit from them. Profits had been known to line the pockets of some of the highest government officials.

My only solace that night was that the panel had been ripped from the *chorten* before my arrival. At least it was not the direct result of my being there. But if not to me, then to whom did she intend to sell or barter it?

We slept that night curled up on Tibetan rugs next to the hearth. As I drifted off to sleep, I recalled my close encounter with death earlier in the day. What would happen to me if I died here? They could hardly send my body home to be buried in a cemetery in Connecticut. Would I be given a Buddhist burial?

On the way from the Khumbu last December, I had witnessed a funeral that the Tibetans call a "sky burial." A long procession carried the body, flexed into a tight sitting position, from the village of Bhandar to the top of a nearby pass. The last two men in line carried axes. We watched them as they hacked the body to pieces, exposing it to the elements and to the vultures, which would pick the flesh from the bones.

Or perhaps they would burn my body. I thought of the *ghats* (crematory platforms) at Pashupatinath near Kathmandu which poured forth smoke every morning. Was there enough firewood here in Dolpo? The thought of my body burning, not feeling the flames as they consumed my flesh, left me strangely abstracted. Probably if I had been buried in the slide that day, my body would never have been found. A fitting way to go, if that was to be my fate—united with the earth.

CHAPTER ELEVEN

▲

Food. The first business of the day was that of procuring food. For an hour we canvased the village houses and in the end bought potatoes and thirty-eight eggs, enough to last for four days at full rations. Somehow, within that time, we had to make our way across the mountainous barrier that formed the eastern boundary of Dolpo to the Kali Gandaki watershed. The Kali Gandaki river sliced between the towering peaks of Dhaulagiri and Annapurna, creating a gorge nearly four miles deep, the deepest on earth. For us it was our immediate destination, an inhabited region and a source of food and supplies.

We ate our first meal early before setting out, already dipping into our meager supplies. After packing the *dokos*, we sat with Lama Dorje and thanked him for his generous hospitality.

"Prem, yesterday he told us about a way to the Kali Gandaki that was shorter. Ask him to describe this route very carefully for us." I took out a notepad to write down his directions.

Prem, Akaal Bahadur and Jeet Bahadur sat listening carefully while Prem translated for me.

"We will go north for one day. Then east over two passes

to the Kali Gandaki River. It will be maybe four days. He says we could also take the Mukut baato, but this has much snow and is very high."

We stood and I pressed my hands together, thanking Lama Dorje one last time. His genuine friendliness and persistence in pursuing our acquaintance impressed me. He had been a beacon of hospitality, his house a place of refuge, his village a source of sustenance for our small band of wanderers. Although we had met him only three days before, he had assumed a place of importance far outweighing what he had actually done for us.

As the trail ascended out of Tarengaon, we could look down into the deep gorge to the point where the southward flowing Barbung Khola was forced by a 10,000-foot wall of the Dhaulagiri Himal to make an abrupt right turn and flow east to west. Below us we could see a tiny bridge spanning the river and on the far side a thin ribbon of trail heading east towards the Mukut Himal. In passing this trail junction we had forsaken that route in favor of one of two possible routes further north. Prem and I had decided that this evening we would take a hard look at the options and then settle on which of the northern routes to take.

For an hour, we headed east as the winds steadily increased in intensity. At the elbow, just where the river turned, the winds were funneled and deflected by the wall of the Dhaulagiri Himal looming to our right. The northern flanks of Dhaulagiri II, III and IV, each at over 25,000 feet, were only fleetingly visible through dense, snow-laden clouds, dazzling white jewels floating miles above us.

As the winds increased to forty miles per hour, our porters struggled to make headway. The constant roaring blast of air caught and pulled at their bulky loads. Prem and I forced our way ahead, dropped our packs in the lee of a side canyon and went back to help.

We found Akaal Bahadur in the lead, followed by Jeet Bahadur and Auri Bahadur, their eyes mere slits, their clothes pressed tightly against their bodies as they tried desperately to hold their own against the gale. Prem took the lead, I pushed from the rear. In tight single file, pressed against the man in front, we slowly made headway. When we rounded the bend, the wind abated and we stumbled gratefully down the trail. I dashed on ahead and, looking back, saw Prem and the porters, tiny specks silhouetted against the immense barrier of rock and ice to their backs.

Now in the lee of the elbow, we got our first look at the terrain ahead and to the east of the Barbung Khola. Bleak, awesomely rugged peaks lined up one after the other, monstrous hurdles stretching as far as we could see. As we looked at them, we all knew that somewhere up ahead the lack of food would force us to attempt a crossing of these formidable mountains.

Three times we emerged from side canyons to face the fierce winds on the promontories overlooking the river. Each time the porters became immobilized by the wind, unable to move without help from Prem and me. Each time, we lined up and forced our way around the point to the next side canyon. Slowly the path dropped towards the riverbed and the winds diminished. By midafternoon, we had reached the *khola*.

"Parker Sahib," Prem said. "We should go along the river. The trail above is too windy. The porters cannot walk."

"Okay," I said. "But the trail goes back up the mountainside just ahead. I wonder why it does that? Why doesn't it just follow the river?"

I got my answer an hour later when we came to a cliff rising directly out of the water on this west side of the river. We had no alternative but to cross the frigid waters. No doubt about it, trails went where they did in the Himalaya for a good reason. Generations had traveled on foot or horseback with yaks, sheep and goats. They had chosen routes along the path of least resistance. Our choice was to return and face the wind or stay and face the icy waters.

We chose the waters. We stripped off our shoes and socks, rolled up our pants legs as high as possible. The water looked no more than two feet deep, but moved swiftly over smooth rounded stones. And it was cold, as if just that morning it had been part of an icy glacier. We discussed and agreed on a plan of attack. For better balance, we would link arms and wade the river together.

We lined up, linked together and stepped into the water.

"Ahhhhhh," a collective gasp rose from the five of us. In a matter of seconds, our feet went from cold to numb.

We moved quickly, but being linked together made it difficult for us to go at our own pace; we were forced to adopt the timing of the slowest, the one who was currently having the most trouble. The bank was only twenty-five yards away but it seemed like miles as we agonizingly made our way towards it. Steadily, with gasps of pain, we progressed. As we neared the far side, I opened my mouth to express delight at the end of the torture.

"We're almost theeeeeeee . . ." I stepped down. Chilling tendrils of water reached up my legs. Over my thighs. Stopped at my waist. We had hit a depression. Caution and sure footing no longer mattered. With screeches of alarm, defiance and pain, we moved more quickly than I have ever seen five men move.

We crumpled as we hit the far bank, each falling to the ground, immersed in his own private agony. Although it took only a few minutes to cross the river, my feet had turned an ugly blotched purple. I heard gasps and whimpering around me as I sat hunched over my tortured feet, then realized it was myself I heard, crying out loud in pain. But the way to warmth lay in movement and we pulled our socks and shoes on quickly.

With soaked pants we continued along the river bank, hoping for no more river crossings. But just as my pants began to dry out a half hour later, we found ourselves again staring at a vertical wall of rock emerging from the water and blocking our way.

The river was shallower at this point, but, at seventy-five yards, twice as wide. With no questions asked, we sat down and took off our shoes and socks again.

"Parker Sahib," Prem said. "I don't like this. Maybe this time we should go faster."

"Right. Look, if we link arms like we did the last time, but go much faster, as fast as we can, I think we can make it. It's not as deep and if somebody slips, he will have the others to help him. What do you think?"

Prem consulted with the others and we all agreed with this strategy. We stood on the edge of the river, frigid water lapping the stones inches from our exposed feet. Prem counted down for us, *"Ek, dui, tin!"* ("One, two, three!")

"Arghhhhh!" we bellowed together, plunging into the freezing stream.

We splashed energetically, keeping up our momentum until halfway across. But the river exhausted us and then we slowed, agonizing over every step yet again. Although my feet were numb, every protruding rock, every sharp stone pierced through the unfeeling outer layers of flesh to the sensitive ones underneath.

Nearing the far bank, we broke ranks and each of us stumbled onto shore by himself. Just as I hit the bank, I heard a cry and turned. Jeet Bahadur had stumbled only a few feet from the edge, his bulky *doko* pulling him off balance. He floundered for only a few seconds as I watched, unable to even think of reaching out to him. Then he pulled himself to his feet and came to shore. I slumped down on the ground in agony.

I wanted nothing more than to curl up and cry. Involuntary whimpers once more escaped from my lips as I forced myself to reach for my shoes and socks. *They will make you warm, put them on now, Parker.*

Around me the others lay each absorbed in his own personal anguish. Akaal Bahadur lay on the ground, repeating an undecipherable Tamang phrase over and over. Prem hunched over his feet, crying out and clutching his toes in his hands. Jeet Bahadur sat miserably wet, shivering and moaning. While the first river crossing had been painful and a nuisance, this second one had broken us. For fifteen minutes we sat, saying nothing, each concentrating on warming his own frozen toes. Then the clouds parted and the welcome warmth of the sun spread over and around us, a gesture of mercy from the gods.

I looked ahead and spotted a flat sandy area slightly up from the river. "Prem," I called out. "Camp there?" I pointed to the spot.

Slowly Prem raised his head to look to where I pointed, then smiled. "Yes, Parker Sahib. We cannot go any farther today."

We set camp and ate potatoes, *tsampa* and tea. I had no stomach for any of it, but forced myself to swallow the tasteless food. After our meal, the temperature began to drop, so we crowded into one tent to discuss the route options that lay ahead.

Using one of the three remaining candles, I spread out the map and we all perused it. Suggestions and possibilities flew back and forth until we had narrowed them down to two.

The first we called the "long route." This route, which was marked on our map, would take us far to the north, along the Barbung Khola, past the village of Charkabhotgaon, then south, in a large arc, crossing either the Sangdak Pass or the Dhampus Pass to reach the Kali Gandaki. We estimated it would take six days. That would leave us short of rations and would mean that we had to find food in Charkabhotgaon.

The porters favored this option because the route was easy and we would cross only one high pass. But Prem and I hesitated for several reasons. First, we had heard that

Charkabhotgaon was a sparsely inhabited village, and might even be deserted this time of year. Therefore, resupplying with food along this route seemed dubious. Also, we had heard that it was a Khampa stronghold, and that the villagers had in the past not taken kindly to strangers. Based on our past experiences, I was uncertain that we could reach the Sangdak Pass even in six days by this route. If we didn't find food somewhere along the way, we might come close to starving.

The second option was what we termed the "Dorje route," after Lama Dorje who had described it to us. By this route, we would continue north along the river until reaching the village of Daragaon. From there we would turn east, ascending past the village and over a pass. After this, we would descend to a river which flowed north, then follow this river upstream until we crossed either the Sangdak Pass or the Dhampus Pass, we weren't sure which. From our present position to this pass, according to Lama Dorje, would take us two days. The drawback to this plan was that no such trail was marked on our map and, although Lama Dorje was most sincere, experience told us that sincerity did not always mean accuracy. And even given the gross inaccuracies of the map, the distance seemed too great to cover in two days. Although shorter, this route would also take us over two high passes. Given our alternatives, I was more afraid of running out of food than ascending passes. As we all felt the effects of prolonged poor diet combined with a high exercise level, I could not imagine we would fare well at this altitude without food.

Prem and I favored this second option and ultimately won the porters over. Now we were unanimous in our choice of the "Dorje route" which, when translated, meant the Path of Lightning Bolts. A light to guide our way.

That night, lying in my sleeping bag, I felt a sense of relief, knowing which way we would go in the morning. I had worried about this crossing for a long time, how we would reach the Kali Gandaki. The choice seemed appropriate for us, given our food supplies, although I knew it would be far from easy.

The next morning, having abandoned the trail of the previous day, we continued along the riverbed. Within half an hour, we once again found ourselves facing a river crossing. This time we scouted the river, looking for the best place. We chose a twenty-five-yard-wide section with an even depth, and then crossed in silence. With the bright sun warming us, the chore seemed easier.

By late morning, the village of Daragaon came into view, three hundred feet above the river. Squat flat-roofed houses sat among a few scrubby conifers. We stopped for our first meal a mile before reaching the village.

After lunch, we passed young boys tending yaks that grazed near the river. There was no response to us, only unfriendly glares. After we had passed, I turned at the sound of stones hitting the earth behind me. An ominous reception from the first inhabitants of this remote village.

A line of *chortens*, overgrown with weeds, with peeling plaster and faded whitewash, heralded the approach to the village. A remarkable *gompa*, a stone fortress structure of white and red built directly into the cliff, greeted us. The cliff, made of sedimentary layers laid down by the ocean hundreds of millions of years ago, had buckled into a swirling vision of the cataclysmic forces of nature. An astonishing sight, the *gompa* represented a tiny intrusion of man into the overwhelming predominance of raw nature here in Dolpo.

A few yards further on, just before we reached the village, we passed a stream descending from the ridges far above us. A vision of frothing white water flowing over the rocks met our gaze, but no sound emanated from it. No gurgling, babbling, swishing rush of water met us. We walked closer, but the stream didn't move, the water didn't flow. Frozen solid, the water had been caught and trapped in the act of flowing downstream to meet the Barbung Khola. We stopped and looked, not quite believing this frozen apparition. Auri Bahadur poked and chipped at it with his ice axe, but did not find a single flowing drop. A stone causeway had been set on top of the ice and thus we crossed this bizarre frozen stream.

Coming up to the village we saw several people on their roofs. "Prem," I said. "Let's see if we can buy some food here."

Setting down his pack, Prem approached the first small house. Just as he called out, we heard the door slam shut with a heavy *thunk*. Prem knocked and called, but no one answered.

He went to the next house and received the same treatment. Looking up, I could see no one. They had all disappeared inside their houses. Two scraggly mongrels eyed us from atop a wall a few yards away. The entire village had shut its collective door to us.

Below we saw groups of women preparing the fields for planting. Their bent figures seemed to ignore us as surely as the people in the village.

"Parker Sahib, should I ask these women for food?"

"No, Prem. I don't think anyone wants to sell us food. I don't think anyone wants to talk to us. I don't think anyone wants us here at all. Let's go."

Hoisting our loads, we followed the faint trail leading upwards out of the village. As we climbed, we realized we would soon be above the tree line, above any vegetation at all. Having sold the kerosene for our stove to the mayor of Dalphu, we spread out across the slope and collected anything that might burn; twigs, sticks, dried yak dung.

We climbed for two hours. The late afternoon wind blew steadily at our backs as the temperature fell. Behind us the corrugated peaks of Dolpo turned earth shades of ocher, then ethereal shades of pink, orange and finally the night shade of purple as the sun descended.

A small grassy level area became our camping site, a summer yak pasture at 15,600 feet. As we set the tents, a movement caught my eye a hundred yards above us on the slope. I turned to look, but saw nothing and returned to the task of setting camp. A few moments later, I saw it again, a subtle stirring among the rocks. I looked, staring for twenty long seconds at the spot that I thought had moved.

Then they materialized. One, then three, finally twenty sheeplike animals camouflaged against the rocky terrain. I pulled out my binoculars and picked out a male, his head weighed down with huge spiraling horns.

"Prem," I called. "Come and look. A herd of *bharal* (blue sheep)."

"The Tibetans call them *nah*," Prem informed me.

For ten minutes I stood watching as they slowly made their way up and across the slope away from us. With brown legs, dark chests and nearly white underbellies, they blended in well with their surroundings. If their slight movement hadn't caught my eye, I would have missed them, these magnificent wild animals of the Himalayas. In all the wilderness I had crossed in Nepal, I had seen so few wild creatures. The others—bears, wolves, leopards, wild yaks—had been hunted almost out of existence or their habitats destroyed by the pressures of human population. How long would this herd of blue sheep survive here on this mountain slope? Would my descendants be able to return here in twenty or thirty years to see theirs?

Reluctantly, I turned from the sheep and back to the camp chores. The temperature had plunged after the sun dipped below the Himalaya to the south and east. Using the circular cakes of dried yak dung scattered near the camp, Prem soon had a hot fire to cook the evening meal. Yak dung makes a particularly good fuel, burning hot with an even, reddish glow. Luckily, we had a ready fuel source in the pasture. I was not sure what we would do the next day if we were forced to camp still higher. The fuel we collected on the way up from Daragaon would last only through one more meal.

Akaal Bahadur and I went to the nearest frozen river and hacked off several large ice chunks for our evening water. Huddling around the fire we watched our miniature icebergs melt in our largest pot. Into it went two large potatoes and two eggs each, our evening ration. At our altitude of over 15,000 feet, it took more than an hour for the potatoes to soften sufficiently for us to force them down. Tea laced with salt and pepper was a favorite of the porters, and that night we each got a large mugful. I forced that down as well, even though I thought it tasted like the Pacific Ocean.

As soon as we had finished eating, we slipped off to our sleeping bags or, in the case of the porters, blankets. The temperature had fallen into the low teens.

I woke at three-thirty, my bladder aching. I tried to ignore the call of nature, but eventually extracted myself from my warm cocoon. Stumbling over a sleeping Prem's head, I unzipped the tent door and stepped out into the night.

Wind, blowing subzero air from the heights above, hit me with a chilling force. High in the sky, a blazingly white half moon flooded the earth with light. The entire length of the Dhaulagiri Himal spanned the southern horizon, ghostly frozen citadels. To the west in Dolpo, uncounted, unnamed peaks stretched into the distance, reflecting white under the light of the bleak, raw moon. As forbidding a land as I had ever seen, this stained moonscape looked uninhabitable, uncrossable, as cold and as hard as any earthly place. I shuddered against the piercing cold, then remembered my business. I finished quickly, sending my compliments in a great arc down the slope towards Daragaon.

I smiled as I remembered another nighttime foray, the previous November at Thyangboche. We had camped on the field just below the monastery, along with hundreds of other foreigners and locals who had come for the Mani Rimdu festival. There, when I also woke late one night and had to get up, I had witnessed another frozen spectacle. It had been fifteen degrees and a dusting of frost clung to the tents, the trees, the ground, even the yaks scattered in the one hundred acre grounds. The full moon of November, the harbinger of the festival, reflected brilliantly off the frost. To the north-east the summit of Everest rose behind the Nupste-Lhotse face; to the east, Ama Dablam, Kangtega and Tamserku; to the southwest, framing the famous Thyangboche Gompa it-self were the twin peaks of Kwangde. To the west rose the sacred Khumbiyula. The full moon high in the sky, its re-splendent light reflecting off the peaks, convinced me that this must be the most beautiful place on earth.

Awestruck by my surroundings, I had returned to my sleeping bag. Just as I had tucked myself in and stopped shivering, I realized that I had forgotten what I had gone out to do! Groaning in frustration, I pulled on my clothes, hat and boots and crawled out of the tent, refusing to look up until I had finished. Then I stood for another ten minutes with my mouth agape, not quite believing that anything could look quite like that, a 360-degree vision of glistening peaks conceived in an artist's eye. Suddenly, the deep bass rumble of the *thugchens* resonated from within the monas-tery, announcing the beginning of another day of the festi-val.

The frigid winds brought me back to Dolpo. As I stepped back towards my tent, I heard a soft guttural sound. Walking closer to the porters' tent, I made out Jeet Bahadur's moan-ing voice. The cold had penetrated through his lightweight sleeping bag and the too-thin Jeet Bahadur could not with-stand the intensely frigid temperatures. His discomfort fol-lowed me as I returned to my warm sleeping bag.

CHAPTER TWELVE

▲

FOOLISHLY, I HAD LEFT MY WATER BOTTLE OUT INSTEAD OF PUT-
ting it into the bottom of my sleeping bag along with my
boots. In the morning, a solid block of ice was my reward. I
looked at the thermometer. It had dropped to the minimum
on the gauge, minus four degrees Fahrenheit.

That morning, we remained huddled in our bags until the
sun began to wash our tents with warmth. As soon as I got
up, I took all of my clothes and laid them out on my sleeping
bag. Separating everything into two piles, I put aside only
what I could wear at one time. Then, I took the other pile—
a pair of pants, four pairs of socks, a pair of gloves, one
flannel and one wool shirt, a light polypropylene top, a wool
hat and a bunting jacket—and distributed them among the
porters. They made a show of refusal, but I insisted.

"Please take them," I said. "They will keep you warm.
Tonight it may be colder than last night."

At this the porters took the clothes and thanked me. Auri
Bahadur, who up until now had seemed especially impervious to the cold, accepted a shirt, then a pair of socks which
he immediately put over his hands and pulled up his arms as
far as they would go. I knew I had parted with these things
forever. At least I was now on a similar level in terms of

clothing, if not in the way of sleeping gear. The haunting sounds of Jeet Bahadur's shivering would not allow me to act otherwise.

To take advantage of the available fuel, we decided to have our first meal of the day before starting out. Because there was no source of running water, we had to melt our drinking water for the day as well. It was well after ten before we got underway.

We followed the course of a frozen stream upwards through loose scree slopes. The stream became smaller, then just intermittent patches of white ice along a dry course. Finally it petered out altogether at over 17,000 feet, having sublimated into the dry desert atmosphere.

The mountains now appeared totally barren, devoid of any form of life. Not even lichen clung to the talus around us. The shifting loose slopes made our ascent arduous; with each step forward we slid backwards half the gain. A saddle several hundred feet above gave us hope of finding a pass and we pushed on towards this goal without stopping. Our breath wheezed in our chests as we struggled towards the pass. Close together, we came up onto the saddle, but stopped only briefly. Disappointed, we found it to be a false pass and I looked ahead to see yet another saddle still hundreds of feet higher.

"Damn," I said aloud.

"Yiss, Sahib," Akaal Bahadur answered, making it the consensus of us all.

An hour later fierce, cold winds greeted us as we neared the top. Any joy at reaching the pass soon evaporated, however, as we looked out on nothing but vast expanses of frozen rivers and lifeless mountains. Total desolation to the horizon. Our spirits plummeted.

With stiff, cold fingers, I extracted my altimeter from my pack. It read just over 19,000 feet. The porters started off the pass ahead of me; they had started to shiver with cold in the blasting winds despite their new clothes. Lingering, I hastily took a few photographs, then plunged down after them. We descended effortlessly with great bounding strides in the soft earth. Forty minutes and 1500 feet later brought us to another ribbon of ice which we followed down to its confluence with yet another larger frozen river. Auri Bahadur spotted a few yak patties and started a small fire. At 16,500 feet we had tea.

We had now followed the first part of Lama Dorje's instructions, we had crossed a pass high above Daragaon. The next step was to find a north-flowing tributary of the Barbung Khola.

"This must be the river that flows north that Lama Dorje told us about," Prem said.

"It looks like it flows north to me," I answered.

Akaal Bahadur countered this, insisting that the river flowed south.

I looked again. The river was frozen solid. The barren, treeless terrain was disorienting. To our left the river appeared to flow towards us, yet in the distance to our right it also appeared to flow in our direction. My head ached, I had no desire to argue with the river. A deep gnawing hunger stretched to all parts of my body, making me tired, fatigued beyond words. But words there were. An argument quickly arose as to which direction the river actually flowed. Prem, Jeet Bahadur and I felt that it flowed to the north, as Lama Dorje had indicated to us. Akaal Bahadur and Auri Bahadur insisted that it went in the other direction. Words flew about, overheated in the thin, cold air.

Akaal Bahadur jumped up. Pacing back and forth in an imaginary cage, he shouted at us. Agitated, he shook his fist as foul Nepali curses spewed forth. We were fools if we thought that the river flowed north. Couldn't we see with our eyes that it had to flow south? Our brains were less intelligent than a demented yak's and our opinions as worthless as its excrement.

"Sit down and be quiet," Prem told him in Nepali.

"No, I won't. You are all fools."

Prem leapt to his feet and confronted Akaal Bahadur. Chest to chest they stood, arguing with rising voices. Auri Bahadur and I bounded up and placed ourselves between the antagonists, angry shouts ringing in our ears. *Stop this before anarchy breaks out. At all costs, we must stay together. Now more than ever we cannot afford to degenerate into quarreling.*

Disgusted, Akaal Bahadur took his ice axe to the river. Stepping out onto the ice, he began chopping away at it, venting his anger on the white frozen froth.

"He's out of his mind," I said to Prem in English. "What does he think he can prove?"

"You're crazy, Akaal Bahadur," Prem yelled at him. "Parker Sahib thinks so, too. Breaking up the whole river won't do any good."

"Fuck off," Akaal Bahadur answered in Nepali. He threw more curses at us as he continued to flail wildly at the ice, chipping away pieces that flew in the air along with his swearing.

Such erratic behavior unsettled me. This deep, brutal anger was intense, destructive and so out of character. Akaal Bahadur had a fine vocabulary of curses, but they usually accompanied laughter rather than anger. What had caused this radical change in behavior—lack of food, mental fatigue, altitude?

We turned our backs to him, gathering around the teapot, waiting for our water to boil. Twenty minutes later, we heard him.

"*Pani!*" he yelled, throwing his hands into the air. "Look, look," he commanded us.

He stood over a two-foot-deep hole in the ice, sweat standing out on his forehead despite the chill air. His face bore traces of anger, but it also showed triumph. At the bottom of the hole a tiny trickle of water, *pani*, flowed, dripping steadily through the ice. It flowed south.

He was right. This river ran south, not north. Akaal Bahadur gloated. Incongruously, now that we knew which way the river flowed, more confusion entered the picture.

"Maybe we are turned around," Jeet Bahadur suggested. "Maybe this is north and that is south. Maybe this river really does flow north."

"That's crazy," I groaned.

"What ever gave you such a stupid idea?" Prem asked him in Nepali.

"Maybe he's right," Akaal Bahadur joined in. "Everything here is turned around. There are no trees, the mountains all look the same. Maybe this river does flow north."

Auri Bahadur agreed with Akaal Bahadur. I shook my head.

"What's happening here?" I wailed. "Look, I'll get my compass out, that will prove it to you." I dug deep in my pack and produced my magic piece of western technology. We crowded around as the needle swung gently and stopped, pointing to the north, the direction opposite to that of the stream's flow.

"Why should we trust this?" Akaal Bahadur said. "What does this thing do that we cannot do? How do we know what it says is true? Foreigners' machines break, maybe it is broken."

Jeet Bahadur and Auri Bahadur seconded Akaal Bahadur's opinion. I sat stunned. They didn't believe the compass!

Angrily, I snapped at Akaal Bahadur in Nepali. "Now that you have so much ice, put it in the pot. We will have another cup of tea. No one will talk until the tea is ready."

Quietly we sat watching the pot until the bubbles rose and the water steamed, far below 212 degrees. With fresh mugs of tea, we sat close together, ready to voice our opinions. Prem suggested that every one be allowed to speak and that no one interrupt until that person was finished. We all nodded, in agreement at least about this point.

Prem went first. "I believe this river runs south. I know which way is north and Parker Sahib's compass points this way, too. Maybe Lama Dorje is wrong or maybe we have not yet come to his river. Maybe we need to cross another pass. This is what I think we should do. Follow this river north. When we find a good place, we should go up and over the next ridge. There we should find the river that flows north."

None of us had thought of this insightful suggestion, and I realized that it was a good plan.

Jeet Bahadur said he wanted to talk next. "I don't know which way is north or south. But I trust Prem and Sahib. Wherever they go, I will go with them."

Inwardly sighing a cautious breath of relief, I felt the tensions lessen. Now we had three on our side.

Auri Bahadur spoke next. In a quiet assured voice he spoke his mind. "I think we should stay together. It would be dangerous and foolish for us to go two ways. I, too, will go where Prem and Sahib go."

I turned to Akaal Bahadur. The still air held an expectant hush. He pursed his lips and stared at us. I could tell he weighed the consequences of heading off alone. There were no trails, no sign of humans anywhere. We had just had an hour's confrontation and discussion about which way was north and which way was south. How could he think he could find his way alone? Stubborn, angry, but not stupid. "I will go with you. *But*," he growled, still angry, "I am right. We will be lost if we go the way Prem says to go. You will see. I will come with you and you will see."

With Akaal Bahadur's final words ringing in our ears, we finished our tea and quickly got underway. It was now late in the afternoon, the skies were overcast and slate gray. We hurried along the river valley, anxious to cover as much distance as possible before cold and darkness overtook us. Despite our consensus, we felt an uneasiness, an urgency to our journey. To say whether or not we were lost was only a matter of semantics.

We walked until dusk, then dropped our loads as we spread out along the river valley, searching for precious fuel.

Isolated tufts of grass stuck out of the rocky soil, but not in sufficient kind and quantity to cook a meal. Although we still carried a few sticks, we needed something else, preferably yak dung.

Deepening twilight threatened to rob us of the necessary light when Jeet Bahadur called out to us from a third of a mile up the frozen river. We converged on the site, ultimately finding enough fuel for a sizable fire. Gathering as many yak patties as we could, we hurried back to the campsite. We worked with near-desperation in setting the tents and starting the fire. Sharp gusts blew down the river valley, and as the sun set the temperature plunged towards zero. We chopped our ration of potatoes into small pieces to speed the cooking, then added them to the boiling water along with one egg each. None of us had much appetite, and Jeet Bahadur complained of nausea and headache. He had not felt well since early afternoon, but now he groaned in misery. His symptoms resembled those of altitude sickness. This worried me because at 16,700 feet, our campsite was the lowest place for miles around. He asked for medicine but I had nothing for altitude sickness. I gave him some aspirin, but within a few minutes he vomited it up.

As night fell, the sky cleared, an ominous harbinger of a frigid night. Prem and I had heavy sleeping bags, though neither was rated below five degrees. The porters had only an assortment of light sleeping bags, bedrolls and blankets. Before we went to sleep, Prem and I emptied our packs, into which Jeet Bahadur and Auri Bahadur stuffed their feet as short bivvy sacks. They slept huddled together, body heat as important as blankets that night.

Just as I headed for my warm sleeping bag, I felt my bowels complain and quickly headed over a small ridge behind our tents. Before returning, I stopped and looked at the stars. In clarity and abundance, they were the most magnificent display I had ever seen. Hundreds of miles from the nearest city, there was no light, nothing to dilute their brilliance. The Milky Way spilled across the center of the sky, the accumulated glow from billions of stars. For the first time, I noticed the great spiraling arms of our galaxy. With our tents not visible, I felt truly alone, not a trace of human existence anywhere in sight. Now, here, in the remotest place I had ever been, my thoughts turned to my family, my parents, my friends back home. I wondered what they were doing at this moment, whether they thought of me. So incredibly far away in every respect, so many layers removed from me. Kathmandu. How distant that city seemed now! From where I stood, it seemed the center of civilization. Even to the Nepalese of Kathmandu, Dolpo represented a mysterious, far-off place few had ever visited. Huge mountains, a vast portion of the Himalayas, stood between us and Kathmandu.

I remembered that when I left the U.S., a friend had commented that his vision of Kathmandu was of a place at the very ends of the earth. New York City to a frozen river in Dolpo, how far must that be? Was it more than fortuitous that a person could not jump instantly from one to the other, that one had to approach in steps? Almost as if it could damage a person to make that leap too quickly; damaging to the psyche if not to the physical being.

During the months in eastern Nepal and especially here in western Nepal, I had sensed an awakening of a spirit that seemed new to me. Something that had been lying dormant in my life in the West, with its remarkable capacity to buffer our daily lives from the earth, struggled to the surface. I felt a new kinship with the mountains, the water, the wind; the daily cycle of day and night, the monthly cycle of the moon, the yearly cycle of the planet.

By coming halfway around the world, by removing myself in multiple cultural and physical layers from the West, the life, the culture, the view of the world that I had known, I began to see the earth and my relation to it in a new light. I sensed my spirit more closely tied to the earth than I had ever imagined.

Was this perhaps the reason for my coming here, for attempting this traverse of the Himalayas? Could this have been the real reason why I left my family, my job, my friends, my life at home? Was this longing to make a connection between myself and the earth as the cradle of human existence what lay at the root of my dissatisfaction?

I hurried back to my tent. Burying myself in my icy sleeping bag along with my boots and my water bottle, I shivered uncontrollably until my body heat warmed it. Prem lay beside me.

"Parker Sahib, I am worried."

"So am I, Prem. We don't really know where we are, our map may be inaccurate, but we're still farther from Jomoson than Lama Dorje said we should be in three days."

"We have only one day's food left."

"The question is, then, how far to the nearest village, and can we get food there?"

"The nearest village on our map is Sangdak. Lama Dorje said that we must go over two passes. But Parker Sahib, maybe it will take more than one day to reach there. Maybe almost two."

"So what will we do?"

"If we eat less, we can have three meals. Then maybe we can get to Sangdak."

"Cut rations? We haven't got enough to eat as it is. This is a catch-22, Prem. That means that if we don't get enough to eat, we can't go far or fast enough to get to the village where we can find food. Whatever we do, we get screwed." I sighed in resignation. "Okay, cut rations. What else can we do?"

I fell asleep, thinking of the unsettling prospect of running out of food. I pondered the possibility of a yak steak or two, hot, sizzling. Would it be asking too much for them to be tender as well?

*   *   *

The night treated us brutally, reaching into our bedding with icy cold talons, causing us to shiver for long hours. As soon as the sun reached our tents, we got up and moved around. The porters looked tired, lines of fatigue creased their faces, their movements were slow and uncoordinated. We brewed large pots of tea, and once more ate our first meal before setting out. When Prem announced the rationing scheme, the porters nodded in agreement, taking it in stride, although I knew they were hungry. I was; we all were.

We broke camp after collecting what yak dung we could find and stuffing it into our packs. We headed upstream due north for a mile. Finding a small frozen tributary that entered from the mountains directly to the east, we decided to begin our ascent following this stream. Our climb seemed a carbon copy of our ascent of the day before. The same scree slope, the small river of ice dissipating above 18,000 feet, a false pass and more climb.

At 18,500 feet we rested for a time. Looking back we could clearly see the pass we had crossed the day before and our route along the frozen river. Looking upwards, we could not yet see the next pass. With a mighty heave I righted myself and trudged upward on the endless slope. Soon I saw the porters stop and heft curious rocks, round and the size of grapefruit. Jeet Bahadur struck one on another rock, breaking it open. I peered over his shoulder to look at his treasure.

Crystals! The rock had a hollow interior lined with dazzling quartz and purple rhomboid crystals that I could not identify. Each porter stuffed several of these geodes into his load, exclaiming that they would fetch a high price in Kathmandu. My mind reeled with the thought of adding more weight to their *dokos* by loading up on rocks, of all things.

Here we were ascending to over 19,000 feet, half lost and almost without food somewhere in the most remote part of the Himalayas. No trails, our map so inaccurate as to be nearly useless, no sign of another human anywhere, and these men stuffed their loads with rocks! At least it was a sign of their faith. They had no thought of not reaching Kathmandu.

After more than three hours of slow climbing, the crest of what appeared to be a pass loomed above us. The altitude slowed us to a crawl and I locked into a regular rhythm. Step, inhale, step, exhale, for thirty steps. Then, when my pulse thumped alarmingly in my temples, I stopped for ten breaths before continuing. In the thin air we moved, each in his own oxygen-starved world, each at his own pace. Soon we were stretched out for half a mile as we climbed towards the broad saddle that we hoped was the pass. As we neared the top the wind increased and the temperature dropped. The weather pattern of the previous days held; clear morning skies, then increasing winds and overcast by midafternoon. In fact, it had not rained or snowed on us, and as we ascended towards 20,000 feet, even the frozen rivulets had evaporated into the atmosphere.

Ahead of me, I watched Prem and Akaal Bahadur struggle to reach the pass. I stopped, rested heavily on my ice axe and watched their progress. They climbed the loose scree slowly, almost painfully, the wind whipping their clothes. A steep headwall marked the last hundred feet. A nightmare for them, as a step forward was followed by a slide back almost as far. They neared the top, and as the slope leveled out, they sped up and made a final dash to the pass.

They leaned forward, almost doubled over into the fierce wind. Waiting for their reaction, I found myself holding my breath, watching to see what effect the view of the other side might have on them. Two small figures, so familiar to me, their loads resting easily on their backs as if they had grown there. I waited for a sign of what they saw ahead.

With a shake of his body, Akaal Bahadur swung his bulky load back and forth, as if he were saying "No!" Prem dropped to one knee.

With heightened anxiety, I pushed on, reaching the pass ten minutes later alongside Jeet Bahadur. The wind tore at our clothes, roared in our ears. Desperate to descend but anxious to take a photo, I took off my pack. Checking my altimeter, I found it reading 20,200 feet. I now saw for myself the desolate and forbidding view to the east. More of the same, frozen rivers, snow-capped mountains, crumbling cliffs of burnt umber and gray as far as I could see.

With freezing fingers, I took two quick photos, then Jeet Bahadur and I followed Prem and Akaal Bahadur down the far side. They had stopped a mere hundred feet below the top where the wind had slackened considerably. Auri Bahadur soon arrived and we rested together. Closing my eyes, I sucked in deep draughts of the thin air. My rapid heartbeat pounded in my ears. A minute later, I opened my eyes, astonished at what I saw.

Prem sucked at a cigarette, then passed it on to the porters. At 20,000 feet, I was dizzy from the lack of oxygen, and I watched in amazement as the porters puffed at the dregs of this cigarette. I could not imagine smoking at this altitude, but these men had the capacity to smoke just about anything, anywhere. I remembered them in the forest just beyond Mandu, out of cigarettes, out of *beedies*, pulling oily birchbark off the trees to roll and smoke the foul marijuana I had bought for them. My head spun just looking at them now.

Once again, we made quick work of the descent on the vast open slopes, dropping four thousand feet to reach a valley floor within two hours. We found a river, frozen on top, but we could clearly hear the rush of flowing water underneath the top layer of ice. I approached it cautiously, fearful of what I would find. Which way did it flow? Was it north or south? Was this Lama Dorje's river? Or had we lost ourselves again?

It flowed north!

The weather closed in, thick clouds lowered around us, making it seem later than it was. A summer yak corral nearby with readily available fuel tempted us to camp for the night.

I had hoped to continue on towards early evening, our food supplies being so meager. But the route began ascending once more from here, and with the increased altitude came the cold. In the interest of the porters we elected to set camp in the shelter of the corral at 15,500 feet.

Once again we turned in with the setting sun. With more than ten hours until daylight, I lay awake in my sleeping bag. My thoughts turned to Clara.

She was an enigma in many ways. We had met almost every afternoon on the roof of the hotel where we perused the Kathmandu valley and watched the sun set over the majestic Himalayas.

Although she never said anything, I began to suspect that she was involved somehow with the hotel owner, Praven. I saw them leaving the hotel together in his car and, from his manner towards her, surmised the closeness of the relationship. One afternoon I made an oblique remark about it.

She responded, "And what do you think my involvement with him is?"

I looked at her and spoke truthfully, "I think he is keeping you as a mistress."

She seemed pained by the suggestion, but did not answer. I knew it was true. Despite this revelation, every afternoon I waited for her on the roof, and she too kept the unspoken rendezvous. Our mutual attraction was evident to the other foreigners and to her friend Sera. One day Clara appeared late in the afternoon, visibly upset. We talked desultorily for a few minutes.

"Clara. What's wrong?"

Close to tears, she blurted it all out. "You were right, Parker. Praven is keeping me. But it was all right, he said he would marry me. You must understand, our family has obligations to his. His family has helped mine for many many years, even before I was born. He has always been very good to me. He has paid for many things. It is our families, you see.

"But now things are different. He has kept things from me. I didn't understand. Some of his family I never met. Now I have learned that he has betrayed me. The maid told me. She said that of course he could afford to keep three wives. Three wives! He has two wives already and he thought that he could marry me and I would be his third wife! The maid is right, he can afford it. He would just keep me in a separate house, away from the others. He was only waiting until I got pregnant, and then I would have to marry him."

I shook my head; this was a bizarre turn of events. "Clara, I don't understand."

"In Nepal it is okay to have more than one wife if you can provide for them. But how could he think I would do that? I am a Catholic, not a Hindu. How could I marry a man who is already married? How could I have not seen this? How could I be so blind?"

"Clara." I reached out for her. She looked at me through the tears in her eyes, and I sensed her yearning for me as well.

"For me, this is terrible news. I must go now." She rose and walked towards the stairs.

The next day Sera and Clara came to the fourth-floor balcony. Clara looked around anxiously, then whispered, "May we see you in your room?"

"Of course." Quickly the three of us slipped into my room and I closed the door. We talked for a few minutes, then Sera got up and left. As soon as the door closed we were in each other's arms, our lips met and for a long minute we kissed. Finally she gently pushed me back and spoke.

"Parker, I have something to tell you. I have decided to go back to Darjeeling."

Devastated by this news, I tightened my hold on her.

"I cannot stay here with him, he has betrayed me. It is the

only thing I can do, go back and live with my parents. I'm so sorry."

We held each other, but every minute or so she looked towards the window, afraid someone was spying on us through the curtains. Finally she jumped up and headed for the door.

"This is too dangerous, I must go."

I stopped her just behind the door and we kissed again. "Please, Parker, they may be watching. I must go."

"How can I let you go when I may never see you again?"

"Oh, you will see me again." With that she walked out of my room.

The Asian ways of male-female relationships frustrated me. I couldn't understand how she could be kept by a Nepalese but couldn't be seen with me. Praven had two wives already and wanted her as a third. But if I were to take her to dinner, she would have been immediately branded as a prostitute. I didn't fully understand, but I was awakening to the vast chasms that existed between East and West.

Clara left later that afternoon on the night bus to Darjeeling.

Ten days later, I bounded up the stairs to the fourth floor, two at a time. Rounding one of the landings in the gloom with my head down, I plowed into someone coming down the stairs. She let out a quickly stifled scream as we collided. Instinctively I grabbed her to keep from falling and looked up into Clara's face, six inches from mine. She smiled at me and my heart raced. She let my arms linger for a moment around her, then gently she pried them loose, fearful that someone may have seen us.

"I came back," she said.

"So I see."

"I couldn't stay away."

"I'm glad."

Like a magnet I felt drawn to her. I reached out for her again. But she pushed me away and scooted down the stairs with a happy laugh, leaving me gasping for breath, with surprise, and hope. She paused and looked back. "I'll see you later on the roof."

A tantalizing sweet pain, to see her, to talk with her, but unable to be alone with her. I met her on the roof.

"I have come back to Praven. But we are not really together. I came back to see you."

Our clandestine meetings continued. We talked of her life in Darjeeling, going to Catholic schools, how she became involved with Praven. She told me then that his relatives who worked in the hotel had been telling her she should be happy with her lot in life. After all, she was twenty-five and an old maid, unlikely to get married to anyone else, why not just marry the man, be happy with a house and children, not worry about the other wives.

"That may be all right with them. But I don't want to share my husband with anyone. I cannot forgive him for what he has done." She burned with rage and the humiliation of what she saw as betrayal.

I suspected that Praven's relatives who worked at the hotel knew what was going on between us. I received long stares from many of them and I think they probably told Praven of their suspicions. Western friends warned me to leave Clara alone, that it was just bad news, nothing could come of it. I might even get hurt in more ways than one. But I couldn't leave her alone. For two weeks while I waited for our departure to western Nepal, I fell in love—for only the second time in my life.

On our last afternoon, we sat behind the short wall on the roof, saying nothing. She had decided to go back to Darjeeling as soon as I left and wait for me there. Our fingertips touched as we watched the late afternoon sun paint the glaciered peaks to the north golden, then pink. When the eastern sky turned purple she rose from our spot on the roof.

"Goodbye, Parker."

"Goodbye," I said, almost inaudibly.

She stepped quickly down the stairs. I waited for a few minutes, then slipped off the back of the roof onto the narrow rear balcony and crawled in the window to my room.

It had been all so confusing to me. I had just scratched the surface of the vast cultural differences that separated us, choking social customs that made it so difficult for us even to discover if we wanted to be together, let alone explore what we meant to one another. I loved her, of that I was sure. But what of the future?

Now in my sleeping bag in the mountains, the future muddied in my mind with the present. Fatigue overcame me. Lack of food, the altitude, our uncertain situation—could I think clearly about anything now?

CHAPTER THIRTEEN

▲

IT SNOWED DURING THE NIGHT. THREE INCHES OF WHITE POW-
der covered the barren, lifeless terrain, transforming the
landscape to a sparkling and brilliant white. The thermometer read zero, the air was still, with a clarity found only in the
high mountains.

We did not wait until the sun hit the tents to get started
that morning, so anxious were we to make good mileage.
Our food supplies now consisted of a dozen potatoes, four
eggs, chicken bouillon, tea, salt, pepper and one packet of
dried soup that Prem found in the bottom of Jeet Bahadur's
doko. The tea and bouillon would last for several days, but
the other food would make only one meal. We decided to
save the food for later in the day, and so had only a large
mug of salt-and-pepper tea.

We headed upriver towards what we hoped was Lama
Dorje's pass. Just around the first bend, the river forked into
two streams, the larger continuing upstream to the left, the
smaller remaining on a steady course. We discussed which to
follow for several minutes without any of the arguments that
had divided us two days earlier. The porters had defaulted,
leaving the route choice to me and Prem.

Prem and I opted for the larger stream that headed left,

more in the southeast direction that we imagined the pass might take. For two hours we followed as it meandered through rolling hills. Although we continued to gain elevation, the landscape changed from the barren rocky slopes to gently undulating hills covered with stubby brown grass. Abruptly the river bent far to the left, heading due north. For another half hour we followed the rapidly diminishing stream directly towards the Tibetan border. To continue further meant a steep ascent. We admitted our mistake in following it, and made the return trip to the river fork in an hour and a half. But the total time loss stood at four hours. Dejected, frustrated and hungry, we built a fire and cooked our last full meal.

As the potatoes boiled in water hacked from the frozen stream, I contemplated our predicament. The situation was deteriorating. *Critical* was the word that came to mind. Without food, we had to commit ourselves to move with all the speed we could muster until we found some sort of civilization. Sangdak, the only village on our map, lay somewhere ahead, over the pass. At that point, I did not even know which pass we were looking for, whether the Sangdak or the Dhampus. With all the jumbled information we had received, I now began to wonder if they might be one and the same.

If we found Sangdak or some other village, our four-hour delay would have only been an inconvenience. But if we couldn't find food, if we made another mistake in finding the route or encountered bad weather, we would rapidly find ourselves desperate. Until now, I had never considered that we might not make it through. Intellectually, I feared the high passes; emotionally, I dreaded the police. But not until this moment, looking ahead to the unknown, did I seriously consider that we could lose our way and starve.

I pulled Prem aside. "Prem, things are becoming very serious. We must move out of here—fast. Our mistake in following the wrong *khola* has cost us a half day. We can't afford to do that again."

"Yes, Parker Sahib. I know this. We should walk until dark, and maybe later. If we can find our way. We only have one torch left."

"And that's hardly any help, its batteries are almost dead. But we have two candles. And what about the moon?"

"Yes. Maybe the moon will light the way. It is almost full and it will be very bright."

"The moon. I never thought I would rely so much on the moon. But the weather pattern is against us. It's been clear in the mornings, then clouding up in the afternoon."

"Yes, Parker Sahib, but now it is two o'clock and still clear. Maybe today will be different."

Quickly we downed our meal, packed up and were back on the trail by three o'clock. We set out rapidly along the khola, hoping to regain some of the distance we had lost that morning. Two hours on, we rounded a bend in the river valley and saw dozens of dark forms on the hillside a mile away. Excited by what they might be, we hurried closer.

Yaks. A whole hillside full of grazing yaks. The sight made me want to cheer. For where yaks grazed, yak herders watched over them. Yak herders needed to eat, food would be available. Pressing forward rapidly, we approached the yak herd. An unearthly howling greeted us. Three hundred yards away and closing in, a black animal hurled himself in our direction. We stood transfixed, gripping our ice axes, not knowing what we would do if he reached us. The large black mastiff barked ferociously as he tore across the slope towards us. When he was a hundred and fifty yards away, the porters hastily dropped their loads.

At fifty yards he pulled up, just on the far side of the *khola*. A huge animal, more bear than dog, he had jet-black hair and a thick mane that stood straight out as he barked. As he guarded his domain, he set our teeth on edge with a cry that seemed to come from beyond the grave. So furious were his howls, so loud his bark, so unexpected his appearance before us that he seemed to me to be a dreaded reincarnation of the Hound of the Baskervilles.

We backed two hundred feet up the hillside and made our way along a ridge, following the contour of the river. The mastiff matched us move for move, remaining just on the far side of the *khola*. Barking incessantly, he forced us in a wide arc above the river. For a mile we walked like this.

A lone black tent beside a crude stone corral marked civilization. As we descended towards the river and approached to within two hundred feet, the dog raised his protests to a frenzied level. I estimated he weighed eighty pounds, all of that powerful body attached to snapping, lethal jaws. I couldn't imagine surviving an attack by such a ferocious animal.

A dilemma faced us; we did not dare approach any closer yet no one appeared out of the tent. Certainly the dog had done his duty and alerted his owner to our presence, but where was the yak herder? Perhaps he had gone up the hillside to tend the yaks or see to some other business. For fifteen minutes we stood our ground, unsure of what to do as the dog's fervor remained undiminished. Suddenly the tent flap opened and a man stepped out. He whistled shrilly and the mastiff turned and headed towards his master at full tilt. Relieved, we slowly crossed the frozen stream while the yak herder tethered his animal to a stake driven into the ground. The black monster strained against his rope, snapping and growling.

We walked to within one hundred feet and stopped by the corral. The herder approached us and said a few words in a Tibetan dialect that none of us understood. Prem asked him a question in simple Nepali. The Tibetan replied with a shrug of his shoulders. Using a universal sign for food, Prem motioned to his mouth with his hand and showed the Tibetan a few rupees. Understanding dawned. He motioned us to enter the corral where Prem and I dropped our packs. Then the two of us followed him towards the tent.

The dog had continued his delirious howling and now, ten yards from the tent we hesitated. Eyeballing the length of the rope, it seemed to me that the dog could reach us even at the entrance. Seeing the fear on our faces, the Tibetan picked up a large piece of firewood and literally beat the mastiff into submission. The dog, pinned to the ground and impervious to the pain, strained to attack us. Once the dog lay on the ground underneath the short log, the Tibetan turned his head to us and, smiling, indicated we could go into the tent.

Stepping rapidly towards the entrance flap, Prem bent to enter. The Tibetan let the hound up. No sooner was he free than the monster once more leapt toward us but was yanked off his feet by the taut rope only inches from me. The Tibetan entered and smiled broadly. If I thought the village of Tarakot was medieval, Tarengaon biblical, this lonely yak herder's shelter was a holdover from the Stone Age. The tent itself was made of a thin black wool cloth, the weaving coarse enough to let sunlight through. Two of several colorful Tibetan rugs served as a bed. Knickknacks of the usual sort, old and new, useful and ornamental, traditional and modern lay heaped in a jumble in the corners. Our eyes roved over the assortment, seeking what might prove useful, lighting on an urn of fresh butter and a large burlap bag of *tsampa*.

Thinking that this man must have a large food cache, being so far from habitation, we immediately started bargaining for food. He grabbed the bag of *tsampa* and a sack of potatoes from behind him and indicated that he was willing to sell us some of these. We laid rupees in front of him and pointed to a measuring cup. By pointing first at the measuring cup or a potato, he indicated the price of each. We bargained in this silent manner for only a few minutes before we struck a deal. In the end we were able to buy one day's worth of food for the five of us.

Once the goods and money had changed hands, I stood and made a move towards the door. The renewal of fierce barking froze me. The black mastiff attempted once again to attack us, almost strangling himself on his tether. I shuddered at the thought that the frayed yak hair rope was the only thing keeping me alive at that moment. The Tibetan stepped outside, picked up the log and, with several thumping blows to the animal's head and shoulders, once again beat the dog to the ground so we could leave. Meanwhile the porters had collected yak dung from the corral and had a huge mountain of it ready.

"Parker Sahib," Prem said. "We should camp here."

"Good idea. We have fuel, and now that we have food we don't need to push on tonight."

Once we had set our tents in the corral and started to cook, the Tibetan joined us for some tea. He crouched on his haunches near the two-foot-high pile of red-hot yak coals and slurped his tea noisily. Prem tried a few more Tibetan and Nepali phrases, but they found only a few words in common, not enough to carry on any kind of conversation.

We asked, as best we could by gestures, about the route ahead. He responded by pointing up the river, the direction in which we were already heading. We sat in silence, smiling and drinking the salty tea. Finally he put his hands together, bade us goodnight and returned to his tent.

When the sun went down behind a nearby ridge, we quickly huddled into our individual bedrolls for what we knew would be a long, cold night. My altimeter read 16,700 feet.

Luck had run with us that day, to have happened upon the lone yak herder in the midst of this vast desolate area. We had bought food and although we had already eaten half of it, we had some *tsampa* and potatoes left for whatever lay ahead.

* * *

Snow fell once again during the night, adding two inches to the three that already lay on the ground. But by morning, the sky had cleared and we emerged from our tents to another brilliant day. Everywhere a blazing white mantel was offset by a clear blue sky.

During breakfast, which once again consisted only of tea, I dug out the sunglasses and made sure everyone wore them. At this altitude, snow blindness, sunburn of the retina, was a genuine concern. It could be debilitating as well as painful.

We followed the stream for several miles. Ahead, rugged peaks stood directly in our path, blanketed with snow. I assumed we would make our way across them, perhaps that afternoon. We stopped and ate our remaining potatoes, which we had cooked the night before. We washed them down with a large mugful of *suchia*, Tibetan tea made with yak butter, a gift from the Tibetan.

Two miles further upstream, a wall of rock rose vertically out of the water and blocked our way. At this point the *khola* tumbled through a series of rock ledges, thus preventing it from freezing over altogether. Stopping to assess the situation, I shook my head. *Backtrack for a mile to the last safe crossing?*

"Parker Sahib, I think I can go this way." Prem pointed to a narrow band of snow abutting the cliff just at water's edge.

A five-inch-wide path, covered with frost, seemed to stretch from where we stood all along the base of the rock.

"All right, try it, Prem." I stood immediately behind him as he inched out over the rushing water.

Facing the rock, he spread his arms out along the wall for balance. The first few feet of the icy pathway wobbled ominously, but Prem rapidly covered them with two light-footed steps. Next, he took one long step with his right foot. Hesitating only momentarily, he carefully brought his left foot alongside his right. Now he stood with both feet together and his arms outstretched on the rock. He turned back to look at me. From the corner of my eye I saw a subtle motion in the ice at his feet. His eyes grew large and his mouth formed into a small round "O!" So soft was the sound, I could barely hear it. A trapdoor opened and he disappeared.

The water and ice had swallowed him completely. Frantically, I shoved my ice axe as far underwater as I could. The swirling icy water made it difficult to see, but a hand reached out in desperation to grab the axe. I pulled. Heavy weight on the other end told me he had seized the proffered ice axe, but nothing moved. Plunging into the water up to my thighs, I braced myself and yanked on the ice axe again. *Hang on, Prem, just hang on.*

Tugging with frantic power against heavy, wet clothes and the pack on his back, I strained to bring him to the surface. Then the swift current caught him, moving him downstream past the cliff face and towards me. My hand closed on his wrist. Gritting my teeth, I hung on. Suddenly his face popped to the surface, red and contorted with his frenzied efforts. His mouth opened and he gasped desperately for air. He let go of the ice axe and grabbed for my legs. Reaching down, I pulled on his sodden clothes, bringing him into knee-deep water. Quickly we scrambled out.

The porters had not been far behind and now they raced to us. Taking Prem by the arms, they swiftly peeled off his clothes. Untying our loads, we searched for something extra for him to wear. Within a minute he wore dry clothing. But his teeth chattered and his body shook uncontrollably. Akaal Bahadur unpacked Prem's sleeping bag and, wrapping it around him, we sat and watched him closely as he slowly calmed down.

In the panic to find warm dry clothes for Prem, I had forgotten my own plunge in the river. I now realized that my boots, pants and long underwear had been soaked as well. I took them off, then remembered I had nothing dry to put on. Wringing my long underwear out as best I could, I put it back on. I did the same with my pants, but my boots were as heavy and sodden as Prem's. We drained the boots and laid them out in the sun to dry.

Taking stock of Prem's gear, we realized that several items had been lost. His pack had remained firmly on his back—indeed, had he lost it, he might have come to the surface sooner. But a precious ice axe had gone down as well as a small zippered pouch he had carried on the top of his pack.

Jeet Bahadur borrowed my ice axe and tried to snare the lost axe from the river. The rushing water had cut a trench, easily eight feet deep, just at the point where Prem fell. I thought his valiant attempt to retrieve the ice axe futile, but he persevered for fifteen minutes. When Jeet Bahadur's hands became frozen and unmoving, Akaal Bahadur took over the effort. After thirty minutes, they abandoned the search.

By now, Prem had rewarmed sufficiently to resume walking and we got underway once more, ascending with the stream for several hours. Gradually, the stream became smaller; then, at 17,000 feet it narrowed to just a trickle running down the center of a broad valley bounded by low rolling hills. The sun had melted all the snow from the south-facing slopes; wiry yellowish brown grasses and lichens covered the ground. Just up from the stream, we stopped in a cave to rest and have a cup of tea. Leaning against his pack, sipping his steaming mug, Prem turned to me with a smile.

"Parker Sahib, you saved my life. I must say 'Thank you.' Now you are responsible for me."

Akaal Bahadur nodded vigorously at this remark and repeated it to me in Nepali.

I smiled and didn't say anything. I had heard of this way of looking at saving someone's life, but I thought it a joke. The water had been deep just where Prem fell in, but the current would have brought him to shallow water soon enough. I had pulled him out, but if I had not been there, I doubt if he would have drowned. Maybe not, possibly not. Anyway, now safe and dry, he walked in our company.

The stream we followed became nothing more than a narrow ribbon of ice, then it vanished completely. We climbed another two hundred feet of gentle rise and found ourselves on a broad, flat expanse running due east, perhaps half a mile wide and two or more long. Sloping ridges a thousand feet high bounded us to the north and south.

Dead ahead beyond the eastern edge of this broad plateau we saw the upper reaches of snowy peaks, great sedimentary layers tilted at sharp angles into the sky. From what we could see, their bases lay far below where we stood, as though, at the far end, the plateau fell precipitously away. A *chorten* appeared several hundred feet ahead, just where the slope leveled off.

We stopped to rest beside the *chorten*, dropping our loads and leaning against this lone man-made object in the midst of stark wilderness. Having expected a high and dangerous crossing of the mountains, I found myself surprised and relieved at having reached this remarkably gentle pass. Taking out my map, I turned it first one way, then another until I had succeeded in roughly orienting myself. Although it was obvious that the map contained glaring errors, I nevertheless convinced myself that we stood on the Sangdak Pass, at 17,600 feet above sea level.

From the western edge of the pass emerged a frozen stream which drained another broad valley to the south. I wondered if this was perhaps the northern terminus of the Hidden Valley described by the 1950 French Annapurna Expedition during their reconnaissance of Dhaulagiri. If so, the Dhampus Pass lay somewhere in that direction. To the southeast, lost in the rapidly building clouds, loomed the brooding north face of Dhaulagiri.

CHAPTER FOURTEEN

▲

SANGDAK PASS
Sunday, April 8, 1984

TWO O'CLOCK; TIME TO MOVE OUT. A MILE AHEAD, I SAW a faint ribbon of trail ascending the ridge to the north. It was the first trail we had seen since leaving the Barbung Khola at Daragaon, and I was determined to be on it. Even though that meant climbing another thousand feet, something the porters were sure not to like, I believed it the best route to take.

While I lingered at the *chorten* for ten minutes, taking some photos and changing a roll of film, Prem and the porters headed off along the broad expanse of the Sangdak Pass. Finished with my photos, I hurried to catch up with the others, already nearly half a mile ahead, moving slowly towards the jumble of snowy peaks. As I caught up with Prem, walking last in line, I saw that the porters had passed the point where the faint trail headed up the ridge to the north. Prem had stopped and was sitting on the ground.

"Prem," I demanded. "What in the hell is going on? I thought we decided to take the trail. Now the porters are heading straight."

"They don't want to climb any more, they want to go this way, straight to the edge, not up."

I looked angrily at the porters continuing onto the far side of the plateau.

"We agreed to head up the trail to the ridge. Who's in charge here anyway, us or the porters?"

"I don't know, Parker Sahib," Prem said, his normally assertive voice strangely faint and lethargic. "I just don't know."

"What the . . ." I started to shout, turning to look at him seated on the ground. The words stuck in my throat as I peered into his face. Something was wrong, *very* wrong.

Prem lay propped against his pack, eyes closed, hands pressing on either side of his head. He grimaced with pain.

"Prem, what's wrong?" I bent closer.

"I have a headache. And everything is dizzy."

"You've probably got altitude sickness. Come on, the best thing is to go down."

Gripping him firmly under his elbow, I helped him to his feet. He stood unsteadily, took a few steps and faltered. I grabbed his arm again, trying to keep him up and on a straight course.

Although I was still steamed up about the change of route, I could not manage to hold on to Prem and also run ahead to stop the porters. They had now reached the far end of the pass and I could see only the tops of their baskets as the ground slowly fell away. I had to accept the fact Prem was in no condition to climb anymore. The porters were beyond recall. Powerless to change our course, I let them go. Supporting Prem with one arm, I guided us slowly towards the far end of the plateau. The uplifted mass of the Himalaya drew closer, dwarfing us with its bulk. The glaciered flanks caught intermittent shafts of sunlight.

Two solitary beings, three miles above sea level, we trudged on across the vast, barren plateau. Hunger and fatigue gripped me; I felt mentally aloof, my mind oddly separated from my physical efforts as I focused on the mountains ahead. After two months on the trail, we were lost, lost on a trackless crest of the Himalaya, virtually without food. I felt beyond the point of rational thinking, as though my mind had gone through the wall. Yet the cathedral spires pushing upward through the broken clouds were inspiring beyond anything I could imagine.

In crossing the pass, we drew closer to one of the great faultlines of the Himalayas. The geological plate of India, in its timeless trek northeast, had slammed into Asia 25 million years ago. Continuing its thrust, the Indian subcontinent had crumpled and broken the earth's surface, forming the vertical landscape of the Himalayan range. Ahead of us, the ancient sea bed thrust skyward in a mass of unconsolidated rock.

At the eastern terminus of the pass, we began a gentle descent. Dull yellow lichens and short wiry grass covered the tundra. A trickle of water emerged from the ground, cutting a shallow depression in the soft soil. Rivulets from both sides soon merged with the trickle to form a small stream. Following this stream, we descended several hundred feet as the slope steepened.

Where the slope dropped off, the porters had stopped and set down their loads. They sat cross-legged, holding their knees, contemplating the terrain ahead. As Prem and I approached, they ignored us. They sat motionless, eyes fixed forward. I let Prem down gently next to Akaal Bahadur's *doko*, propping him against the basket, and started to join the porters. When I got my first glimpse of the route ahead, I froze.

Below us, the landscape changed abruptly. Geological mayhem, total destruction of earthly order faced us. Cascading precipitously into a rock-strewn chasm, the stream dropped over several rock shelves and then cut down amidst boulders and slide debris. Near-vertical walls rose on either side, rotten and crumbling, cut at frequent intervals by rock slides.

"Holy shit," I whispered to myself.

Removing my pack, I sat down next to the porters as we all stared silently into the gorge. Intermittently, rocks broke away from the sheer walls, falling, bouncing, tumbling to the stream bed before coming to rest. The smaller ones made short staccato cracks like rifle fire, the larger rocks rumbled like distant cannons. At that rate of erosion, it seemed not long before the whole mountainside would fall, piece by piece, to the stream bed. Perhaps the earthquake we had felt the week before had precipitated this bombardment of the canyon.

Climbing back to the pass seemed out of the question. It lay at least six hundred feet above us now, and I doubted that I could convince the porters to make the climb. I turned to Prem, who was half-lying against Akaal Bahadur's basket, his features twisted in pain, his eyes closed. I knelt beside him, asked where it hurt, touched his now-feverish forehead. Slowly, weakly, he described a severe headache, with pain extending down the back of his neck. The porters gathered around me, sensing serious trouble.

"Prem," I said gently. "Open your eyes, let me see them."

"No, Parker Sahib, no," he mumbled. "It hurts, the light hurts to see."

"Prem," I said. "It is very bad going ahead. Do you think you can make it?"

"Yes, I will try. But my head hurts so much. I can barely see. Something is not good, Parker Sahib."

"Something is not good," I echoed.

I ran the symptoms and possible implications through my mind. It didn't appear, as I first thought, to be classic altitude sickness. All signs pointed to a central nervous system infection. A word flashed into my head, and I tried immediately to oust it. But it crept back and I could not dislodge it. Endemic in the Himalayas, highly contagious, often fatal: meningitis. A flash of fear engulfed me. Meningitis, I knew, was no joke in well-equipped western hospitals. Now all of us had been exposed. Had we struggled across nature's wild and treacherous terrain only to succumb to an infection picked up from a fellow human? *What should we do now?*

We had only one choice, to continue on.

I helped Prem to his feet and started to distribute the contents of his pack among the rest of us.

"No, no, Parker Sahib. I can carry my pack."

"Prem, this is stupid. We can go faster, all of us, if you let us carry some weight for you."

"I can carry my own pack." He pulled the pack from my hands and struggled with it. I relented.

We hoisted our loads and started our descent. Just then, the clouds that had been building steadily all afternoon closed in around us. Large flakes began to fall.

Scrambling, sometimes slipping along the course of the stream, we followed it down the middle of the canyon, but after only two hundred yards we saw the folly of this plan. A barrage of rocks cascaded and crashed around us. It would be only a matter of time before one of them hit and injured someone seriously.

We switched to the north side of the slope, heading for the protection of an overhanging cliff face. Scrabbling through loose rock debris for a hundred feet, we stopped directly under the crumbling rock wall. We studied our situation while partially protected. Finally, we made the decision to continue along the base of this cliff as far as we could rather than stay with the descending stream bed. While this gave us a more or less horizontal trail, it actually took us higher and higher above the stream that continued to fall away at the bottom of the gorge.

Prem slumped beside me and took little or no part in the decision-making, now done by Akaal Bahadur and me. During this short pause, he weakened still more.

"Parker Sahib. My arms, they are hurting here." He indicated the backs of his arms and then pointed to the front of his thighs. "And here, my legs. It is so difficult to walk."

Sympathetically, I grasped his shoulder. "We've got to keep going, Prem. We have no other choice."

Once more I helped him to his feet, and we started to wend our way along the rock face. Our trail was little more than a two-foot ledge, with a sheer cliff rising so high on our left we could not see the top and, falling off to the right, a steep drop to the winding stream. The porters, walking together in front of us, helped each other over the more difficult spots.

Prem moaned and groaned with every body movement, and I stayed close to him, keeping up a one-sided conversation, encouraging him at every tortured step he took. Then abruptly, the porters stopped and we all stared ahead at a fifty-foot section of nothing but crumbling, rotten rock. The narrow ledge we had been following had disappeared.

Somehow we had to cross that gap.

Akaal Bahadur crossed first. He carried a less bulky load, and he was more agile than the others. With surprising quickness he picked his way across, finding the best hand- and footholds. Once across, he dropped his load and returned to help Jeet Bahadur and Auri Bahadur make the same precarious crossing. Once all three porters had crossed safely, Akaal Bahadur hoisted his *doko* and the three moved on around a bend in the cliff and out of sight, walking in a close single file. With their bulky loads, they could do little to help Prem cross. That task fell to me.

I took a step out onto the rock. My heart pounded, my mouth went dry with fear. Immediately I realized I had to put Prem in front of me and spot him across. It was a desperate maneuver I didn't want to make, but I could think of nothing else. Without ropes, it was the best hope we had.

I backed off the rock. Behind me, Prem leaned against the wall, his eyes closed. Grabbing both shoulders, I shook him gently. Trying to penetrate the fog that surrounded him, I shouted, "Prem, you *must* pay attention here. This is *very* dangerous. You cannot fall. Do you understand?"

He made no response for several seconds, then, pulling in a deep breath and summoning willpower to overcome his drained state, he whispered. "Yes, I hear. But you must help me, Parker Sahib."

Help him? How could I help him when fear filled my chest and my knees trembled? I was afraid of falling, but I couldn't tell him that. Fortunately, Prem took my silent nod as confidence in my ability to get us both safely across. Prem faced the cliff, easing himself out onto the steep rock, feeling his way tentatively, his eyes half-closed. I looked down at the gorge, a straight drop of three hundred feet, and I felt sure he would fall. I gripped the ice axe loop on the bottom of his pack and slowly pushed him out further along the gap. The gray-and-buff conglomerate rock wall looked and felt like a crumbling cookie, breaking off in small pieces at unexpected intervals. Faces pressed against the cliff, we shuffled along, inching our way across. I shouted encouragement at every step.

"Go, Prem. Good. One more step. You're doing it."

An interminable ten minutes brought us back onto the narrow ledge on the other side of the gap. Exhausted, we slumped against the wall, large wet flakes of snow hitting our faces. Drops of sweat rolled down my back and off my forehead, stinging as I wiped them out of my eyes. Peering across the chasm at the opposite wall, I saw that we had now worked our way three hundred feet above the stream bed.

Pzing. A small rock whizzed by, bouncing off the protecting rock above us. *Pink, pink, pzing.* Smaller ones followed, deflected by our shield. Groaning involuntarily with every breath, Prem lay precariously on the narrow ledge, his eyes closed. Watching the snow accumulate on his chest, I felt anew the urgency to keep going. It was already late afternoon, and darkness threatened. I pulled Prem to his feet and half dragged him along. Two more trailless traverses, shorter but even more precarious than the first, brought us to a corner. Rounding it, we found the porters stopped in a small cliff shelter.

Jeet Bahadur had untied the top of his load and fished out a few precious yak patties. He started a small fire and brewed some tea. Reaching deeper into his *doko*, he produced a cloth bag of dry, floury *tsampa*. We mixed this with our tea and ate greedily. It provided only a few mouthfuls each, but the heavy *tsampa* filled a portion of the emptiness in our stomachs.

We were now completely out of food.

During that break, Akaal Bahadur and I weighed the danger of continuing along the ledge partway up the cliff. As the stream dropped down towards the river, we were left higher and higher along the wall. I feared that by following our present route we might come to a dead end, leaving us trapped hundreds of feet up on a sheer face. Looking across and down the deep chasm, we saw that the gorge had vertical faces thousands of feet high. A half mile ahead, the gorge bent to the left. Akaal Bahadur shared my concern about being stranded, so we decided that he and I would go ahead to reconnoiter the route.

Free of our loads, we clambered swiftly onto the conglomerate, traversing along the ledge. Occasionally, we climbed a hundred or more feet up steep, loose rockfalls, then down again in our desperate attempt to find a passage. Akaal Bahadur was out in front, and as on that day several weeks earlier when we looked for my lost necklace near Hurikot, he set a blistering pace. Humbled once again by his stamina, I gasped for breath trying to keep up.

A half mile ahead, we found ourselves once more traversing near-vertical walls of dirt and loose rocks. But from our position, it appeared we could go on, although the last half mile we had just crossed would be treacherous with loads, and even more so with an ill Prem.

Quickly we returned to the others and immediately started on our way. Prem's legs had stiffened while he sat and now he hobbled, unable to extend his leg muscles fully. Once again I spotted him through the difficult parts, grabbing him by the back of his collar and by the ice axe loop on his pack, forcing his face against the rock.

He had particular trouble with the climbs up the loose rockfalls. At the worst places, I climbed just ahead of and above him, braced myself, then instructed him to hang on to my feet just over his head. I feared we might both go at any moment, that Prem would pull both of us into the void below. I didn't say anything about it. I was not being stoically macho; I simply saw no point in speaking about a situation that I couldn't change.

Akaal Bahadur led the group through slides and across crumbling walls. Being the most sure-footed, he went across each one first and, having done it once, dropped his load and returned to help the others. One especially bad section stretched one hundred and fifty feet, and it took an hour for the five of us to cross it. After the porters carefully inched across, Akaal Bahadur returned to help me with Prem. Akaal Bahadur grabbed Prem from the right side, I took him from the left. Between the two of us, we were able to maintain our balance as we pushed and pulled him across. After fifteen minutes, we had covered half the distance, but Prem begged us, "Stop, stop. I cannot go anymore."

His legs shook uncontrollably and his eyes were clenched shut.

"Prem, you *must* go on! We will help you. But you cannot stop now," I urged him, agonizing over his predicament.

Akaal Bahadur spoke to him in Nepali, words of encouragement, admonishment, whatever would keep him going. Prem moaned and allowed us to push, pull and drag him across the rock, helping us as much as he was able. And finally, after another muscle-straining fifteen minutes, we got Prem to the opposite side.

Not far ahead the chasm turned left and headed almost due north. Here was evidence of a great faultline, which had formed along the interface of the Indian and Asian tectonic plates. On our left the cliffs rose up until they disappeared in clouds, the sedimentary layers horizontal. To our right, a hundred yards away on the opposite side of the gorge, great sections of the earth's crust had been forced upward, with the layers now vertical. They had been crumpled so violently that some soared almost straight up, then turned in tight spiraling arcs and dropped straight down.

The stream below merged with another emanating from an even narrower and deeper gorge to the south to become a tumbling river. At this point, we made our way down to the river, then followed its banks. Boulders and immense piles of debris often blocked our passage, testaments to powerful floods that swept through these desolate canyons. We wound our way around them. On level ground Prem could move faster, but his condition continued to worsen. I walked close behind him, guiding him along the riverbed.

Then, when it seemed that we would have easier going for at least a while, we hit a wall. Impenetrable. Or so it looked. Ahead of us we saw a two-hundred-foot-high rock wall that appeared to block the canyon completely. The *khola*, however, seemed to disappear into the base of the rock. Standing deep within the gorge, we searched the walls for a way to get through. Then Akaal Bahadur's sharp eyes found what seemed to be a solution.

"*Baato!*" he shouted, pointing to the faint remnants of a trail that climbed up through the scree slopes on the left side of the gorge.

"Let's go," I said, wanting to be on our way without losing any more daylight.

We lost the trail several times as it disappeared under rock slides and fallen debris. We knew it went through this section because we kept recovering faint traces of it, only to lose them again. Eventually we found ourselves once more at the river side, the rock wall closer but still blocking our way. Just ahead we saw the river disappear into a five-foot-wide fissure in the rock wall, leaving us with no more bank to follow. Our passage along the river was terminated. We huddled together with nowhere to go. Great blocks of ice which had fallen from the cliffs above littered the ground around us. From the overcast sky, more snow threatened. The grains of sand in the hourglass of this day were running low. We had to find a way out.

"Sahib." Jeet Bahadur pointed.

Lost in the swirling clouds and camouflaged by the same dun color as the surrounding rocks was a thin dark line more than two hundred feet above our heads.

A bridge! A bridge spanning the fissure through which the river flowed. By scrambling up the steep scree slope to our left, it appeared we might get over the massive rock wall that blocked the river and approach the bridge. As we climbed, we had to urge Prem on continually to make him keep up. His mind wandered. He stopped constantly, but we pushed him on again and again until we came upon the trail that lead up to the bridge.

Akaal Bahadur reached the bridge first, and when I arrived moments later, practically holding Prem upright, I found him standing still. Without his load, Akaal Bahadur stood on the edge of the bridge staring hypnotically down into the roiling waters deep in the chasm two hundred feet below. A quick glance to the other side of the bridge revealed why he stood so still.

Clearly a great deal of time and effort had gone into building the bridge. Starting fifty feet below the lip of the gorge, from stone shelves on the far side, forty-foot-high rock buttresses had been built up. The next ten feet on both sides consisted of thick rough-hewn logs projecting towards each other, each layer extending further out than the one below. A ten-foot gap remained between the two sides.

Although at one time a sturdy bridge, now the gap was spanned by two aging pine logs six inches in diameter, a foot and a half apart. Neither old log gave much assurance. One seemed sure to roll if anyone stepped on it. The other had worked loose from its mooring on the opposite bank. Some flat stones balanced on the top of the logs for a walkway. But many were missing, leaving a space of about six feet with nothing but the unsteady logs and a terrifying view to the void below. Standing as close as I dared to the edge, I peered down two hundred feet to the churning river, which roared through a narrow fissure in the rock.

To cross this bridge with our loads would have meant taking a horrifying three or four steps balancing only on the two loosened logs. The thought made me shudder. We would have to repair that part of the bridge. But although flat stones of the proper size lay strewn about, very few were on our side. I saw plenty of good bridge stones on the opposite bank and thought anxiously about how to get at them. Akaal Bahadur obviously had the same thought.

Suddenly, Akaal Bahadur began to walk, carefully and slowly, out onto the bridge. Arms out from his body to help him balance, he stepped cautiously onto the first flat rock. It moved under his weight, so he quickly went down on his stomach, stretched full-length on the stones. Fearlessly, it seemed, he crawled towards the gap. There he stopped and looked down through the logs to the empty space below.

"Ayaaah!" he uttered balefully, then without hesitation crawled all the way across the bridge. On the other side, with a sheer release of nervous energy, he jumped up and ran towards a pile of stones.

Now, with Akaal Bahadur pushing stones out from his side, we worked for a good half hour, carefully rebuilding the center portion of the bridge, shoring up the loose spanner log and filling in the gap with flat rocks. When we had done all we could, it was still not as sturdy as we would have liked, but neither was it so terrifying. Akaal Bahadur tested our reconstruction project by crawling across towards us on his knees. Then he hoisted his load and nonchalantly walked back across to the far side. Jeet Bahadur and Auri Bahadur followed.

I went back to Prem, who had been lying propped up on a rock this whole time, unable to help. I got him to his feet. His legs had stiffened again and he walked stooped over with shuffling, unsteady steps. He still wore his pack.

"Prem, take off your pack and give it to me."

"No, Parker Sahib, I can carry it," he answered, slurring every word.

"Prem, it will be no disgrace. Don't be stubborn. Let me have your pack."

But an iron core of pride would not let him do it. "No, Parker Sahib. I can carry it."

Finally, I turned, exasperated, and waited for him to move.

As he neared the first large flat stone, Prem hesitated. He tried to lift his leg to place his boot onto the rock. But his foot, not raised high enough, snagged the lip of the rock and he crumpled, pitching forward towards the yawning chasm.

"No, Prem," I yelled, leaping forward.

His dark form sank, the top-heavy pack pulling him towards the edge of the precipice. I threw myself towards him, arms outstretched, and I pulled him back as we slammed together into the dirt.

We had cheated death again.

Still gripping Prem tightly, I twisted my head around and looked down. I could hear the river thundering and crashing wild, far below. I also could see it; my head hung over the edge of the first rock of the bridge.

"Prem, Prem."

"O Parker Sahib. I am sorry."

I pulled him to his feet and, carefully coaxing him back from the edge, made him sit down away from the bridge. Calling out for Akaal Bahadur to help me, I took off Prem's pack.

With as much authority as I could muster, I said, "Don't

move, Prem. Akaal Bahadur and I will help you across the bridge."

With my own pack on my back, I slipped on the shoulder straps of Prem's pack so it rested on my chest. I turned towards the bridge and without looking down, held my breath and walked across to the other side. Once there, I shed both packs and returned.

With Akaal Bahadur's help, I again got Prem up to the edge of the bridge, this time on his knees. Akaal Bahadur got in front and I got behind, and we tried to coax him across as we had done on the crumbling conglomerate walls. But his cries of pain as he tried to crawl on all fours forced us to retreat.

Once more on the edge of the bridge, I racked my brains. *How were we going to get Prem across? Could we carry him?* I wished we had a rope. Finally, I visualized a way that might work.

"Akaal Bahadur," I instructed, "you stand here." I stood him in front of Prem, facing in the direction of the bridge. Sandwiching Prem between our bodies, I grabbed Akaal Bahadur's arms tightly, locking Prem between us, all facing forward. Slowly, we shuffled across the bridge.

Thankfully, the going turned easier on the other side of the bridge as the chasm opened up and the trail followed high above the river on relatively level ground. I continued to help Prem. Several times I urged him to stop for a rest, but each time he insisted that we move on. After two hours, we stopped in a small cave and brewed tea. We were all exhausted, and the small shelter beckoned us to spend the night there. But we had no food, and our only hope of finding any was to reach the village of Sangdak. By my reckoning, the village lay another twelve miles ahead on the other side of the river. Given Prem's condition and the state of the weather, it seemed important to keep moving as long as we could.

Now the trail climbed steadily away from the river. Prem

kept up with us on what must have been sheer willpower, grunting with each step, his legs no longer completely supporting his weight. I half carried, half led him along, talking to him constantly.

"Come on, Prem," I yelled. "We've got to make it."

"Yes, we must make it," he replied in a hoarse whisper, parroting my words. His legs moved mechanically though ineffectively beneath him.

After climbing a thousand feet, the trail slowly descended onto slightly easier terrain. Twilight was closing in. I heard Akaal Bahadur and Jeet Bahadur talking excitedly ahead. They stopped and I came up behind them, Prem supported by my arm. They pointed to a ridge a half mile ahead. Two *chortens* stood side by side. *Chortens* meant a village.

"We must find the village," I said to Akaal Bahadur.

There must be a village. I will believe in a god if there is.

But with Prem it was torturously slow going. I carried him on my back for about fifty yards, but then, panting with exhaustion, I put him down again. He took feeble steps, legs flailing, eyes closed, grunting with every effort. His inner strength, an iron resolve that had kept him moving all afternoon—even that seemed to dissipate. I could not rid myself of the thought that wherever our tiny caravan finally halted on this gray evening in April 1984, would be his burial place.

It was dusk, gray fading to black, when we finally reached the *chortens*. From below, I could see that they were old, rounded by the elements into nondescript mounds. Akaal Bahadur and Jeet Bahadur stood silhouetted against the ridgeline, their large baskets clearly visible against the fading light. I watched intently as they slowly approached the ridge from where they would be able to see what lay ahead. Prem leaned against me, his breath heavy and labored. Step by step, the two porters struggled to reach the top. Then they stopped and stood still for fifteen seconds. I saw Akaal Bahadur's figure move. He shook the *doko* that was attached to his head back and forth in great sweeping motions. No. No village. No fields, no more *chortens*, no sign of man. A great sigh of anguish escaped from me. Drained, empty, all of my desire and power to move evaporated. *How could this be happening to us? We had come so far, endured so much, how could we lose now?*

No answers came. My only thought was to get to those *chortens* and collapse. Why struggle anymore? I didn't know. But somehow, reaching them meant not giving up.

"Come on, Prem," I said loudly to the form slumped against me. "Dammit, we have *got* to make it to those *chortens.*"

"Uhhh," was his rasping reply.

One step, one more step. Then two steps. Another step. I thought only of reaching the *chortens*, forcing Prem to move his feeble legs one at a time. Finally, we reached them.

Standing on the crest of the ridge in the dwindling light, I looked out upon an open side canyon, gently sloping towards a vertical drop of undetermined depth into the black gorge of the Cha Lungpa Khola. I could just make out the porters resting in some trees a short way down the slope. Afraid that if we stopped here we wouldn't be able to go any farther, we continued without resting. After fifteen minutes, just as darkness fell, we reached the porters. The ground was covered with four inches of loose, dry dirt. Immediately this powder insinuated itself into everything, compounding our misery. I pulled a tent from a *doko*, spread it on the dirt and laid Prem out on it.

Because we had firewood, the porters soon had a roaring fire going. But we needed water. Akaal Bahadur and Auri Bahadur volunteered to find some. They hoped that a stream ran at the bottom of this side canyon somewhere below us. Within half an hour, they returned with water.

We drank it in great thirsty gulps. Too tired to set up the tents, we spread them out in the miserable dust and laid down on them. I helped Prem to take some codeine to ease his headache. Perhaps it wasn't the proper medication to give him if he did have meningitis, but his low cries of pain made any such concerns irrelevant. I spoke to him and his answer came back slurred, almost incoherent. Frightened, grieving over Prem's misery, I said good night and lay beside him. As I lay back, I saw that the sky was now clear and full of stars.

There was nothing more I could do, with us so far away from anywhere. I didn't know if he would still be with us in the morning. I tried not to think of his death, but the inescapable facts of his condition made me do so. Twice that day he had escaped, but would Death come this night to claim him?

Pain and sorrow overcame me and compounded my exhaustion. My companion for the last six months, Prem meant more to me than just a *sirdar*. He had been my guide to the mountains as well as to the people who lived there. He had loved the great towering white peaks as much as I, the blue sheep, the Tibetans in their wretched villages. Weariness—and hopelessness—overwhelmed me. My eyes closed and I drifted into a troubled sleep.

CHAPTER FIFTEEN

▲

I WOKE JUST AFTER TWO O'CLOCK TO FIND EVERYTHING COVered with two inches of heavy wet snow. I rolled over and looked at Prem. I could hardly see in the dim light, but I could tell it was not a gray, lifeless corpse lying there. It was Prem, still alive. Too exhausted to set up the tents, I woke the others and we crawled underneath the tents and tarps. Lying in the loose dirt, we fell back asleep.

Gray dawn light filtered through the snow that floated from the sky as I pushed back the tent that covered me. My watch said six o'clock. Eight inches lay on the ground and it was snowing heavily.

"Prem?" I said.

He opened his eyes and turned slightly towards me. "Parker Sahib."

"How do you feel?" I leaned close to hear his words.

"My head hurts and my legs." His slurred speech and continuing pain concerned me.

Great wet flakes drifted down, adding to our misery. Everything was soaked and because we hadn't set up the tents, only crawled under them, the moisture-laden snow mixed with the loose dirt to create a clinging, gooey mud that caked everything it touched.

We were reluctant to do anything, but our only option was to get up and move on. As best we could in the driving snow and sticky mud, we packed the baskets. Because he was still unsteady, I helped Prem to his feet. We had nothing to eat or drink.

Visibility extended no more than two hundred feet in any direction. We followed what we thought was a path as it contoured along the broad side canyon. When we reached the canyon's far side, the terrain once again became steep. The snow and mud made our progress slow and risky. To fall here was too easy to do, too dangerous to contemplate. The winds picked up and blew snow into our faces. Visibility dropped to one hundred feet. We hoped that the trail would descend to the river. The map showed the village of Sangdak on the opposite side, no villages at all on this side until the Kali Gandaki Gorge, still twenty miles away. But as we plodded along, the storm's fury increased and the trail contoured up and away from the khola, now far below us.

We came to a small stream. Akaal Bahadur and Jeet Bahadur dropped their loads and disappeared into the rock-strewn depression. If we could follow this stream down to the river, we thought, we might find a way across. But after a few minutes they returned with bad news. A short way below, the stream tumbled over a precipice into the Cha Lungpa Gorge. The porters had not been able to see beyond the edge of the stream's spray.

Exhausted, disheartened, I could not force my mind to hold more than one thought at a time. And my obsessive thought was *We must find Sangdak.* Somehow we must get to the other side of the river, we must find a way to do it. I could not imagine our condition getting any worse. We were lost, without food, a raging snowstorm blew around us. It seemed a miracle to me that Prem was still alive, but how much longer could his iron will carry his ailing body? I helped him walk, as he could no longer do so by himself. I had no way of diagnosing his condition; I knew only that he was not getting better.

Despairing utterly, I didn't know where to turn. We were abandoned in the fury of the wilderness that we had had the temerity to enter, to challenge. Man, nature, the gods—all had withdrawn their help; none offered us refuge or even hope. Alone now, just the five of us, how much longer could we struggle? The snow swirled white around me, but blackness possessed my soul.

A gust of wind blew stinging flakes of snow into my eyes. I stopped and Prem stumbled against me. We had to get to the other side of the river, we had to find the village of Sangdak. "Akaal Bahadur," I called out.

We talked. We would have to change our direction and head down towards the khola. Akaal Bahadur nodded and turned to lead us down the slope, intending to bushwhack a trail.

Then, Jeet Bahadur let out a yell. I looked up the slope and through the swirling snow flakes I saw the dark shape of his slender body and the bulky basket on his back. One arm, a gray, shadowy arrow, pointed upwards. I blinked twice through the blowing snow and the dim shape at which he pointed slowly focused into one I easily recognized.

A *chorten*!

"Prem." I grabbed his arm tightly. "There's a *chorten*. There must be a village here somewhere."

As we slowly drew closer, I could see that it was new and brightly painted. Pulling Prem's arm, I tried to walk faster, anxious to learn what lay beyond the *chorten*.

Fields, neatly terraced. They came into view slowly through the billows of snowflakes. A village—there must be a village nearby. I began to feel a hope that perhaps we had not been forsaken after all, maybe I could start to believe in a god, in *something*.

Through the driving snowstorm, we did not see the flat-roofed houses until we were only two hundred feet away.

Then we saw a few figures on the rooftops as we staggered towards them. Giddy, elated with this seemingly miraculous appearance of a village that wasn't even on our map, I hobbled towards the nearest stone house.

Two women on the roof looked down as we stumbled into their view. With looks of fear, they quickly scrambled down into the house and we could hear the scrape of log bolts barring the entrance. I could imagine our appearance, covered with mud, looming suddenly out of the storm. But this was no way to react to strangers in need. Akaal Bahadur and Jeet Bahadur knocked on the door, calling to those within. In a stupor, too tired, cold and hungry to fight anymore, I slumped against a wall, leaning Prem against a basket. The snow fell and began to stick on our silent, still figures.

The porters returned, saying that no one would open their doors to us. Looking up at them, I blinked stupidly. *How could they leave us sitting outside in the snow? How could they ignore us?* I dug into my pack.

"Here," I said. "Here are two hundred rupees. Give it to them."

"Okay," Akaal Bahadur answered, taking the wad of bills from my hand.

"Tell them we will buy many things from them."

"Yes, Sahib."

I slumped back against the wall, then turned to look at Prem. His eyes were closed, his face lined with fatigue, his breathing shallow and uneven.

Ten minutes later we climbed a ladder to the entrance of the nearest house. As in Jumla when J.B. had needed a plane ticket, money talked.

The sound of oil crackling and the sweet smell of potato cutlets frying on the hearth just a few feet from my head woke me. My watch told me it was just after 6:00 P.M. Wrapped in homespun blankets, my feet inches from the fire, I felt truly warm for the first time in a week. Over my head I saw our gear; tents, sleeping bags, jackets, pants, socks, hung off the rough-hewn rafters to dry. The smell of the food caused me to salivate, to yearn for the salty, spicy taste of it, to feel it on my tongue, to fill my mouth.

Although this was the second meal we had had since arriving at eleven that morning, I saw the others gathered around the fire with the same anxious looks on their faces as mine.

We had been settled into the main floor of a sturdy stone house, just at the bottom of the entrance ladder. A six-foot square hole in the flat roof served as both door and chimney. The gray sky above gave notice that the storm still raged. Periodic gusts blew swirls of spindrift through the hole. Although lying directly below the door/chimney that opened to the sky, I felt warm and secure. Twenty-four hours before, our situation had been perilous; now in this warm enclave, everything seemed safe.

I turned to Prem. Propped up on one of the baskets, he sipped a constantly renewed cup of tea. His eyes shone brighter and were more alert than earlier in the day. *He will live.* If he survived the night and the desperate walk this morning, he would live.

The owner of the house had taken the 200 rupees from Akaal Bahadur before letting us inside that morning. Whether he considered it prepayment for our food and fuel supplies or *baksheesh* was not immediately clear. At the moment, it didn't matter. But with the money in hand, he had become gracious and welcoming, placing us close to the fire, piling on oily pinewood that gave off acrid smoke. Normally this would have irritated us, but it made no difference; we were warm and out of the storm. Our hostess made a huge meal of rice and with it we downed glasses of *rakshi*. Then came blissfully dry and warm sleep.

With all our wandering, we had at last reached the village of Sangdak. If Jeet Bahadur had not noticed the *chorten*, we would have headed down the hill towards the river. If the *chorten* had been another two hundred yards further on, we would have missed it entirely. Just luck? The reward of men refusing to give up, pushing on, searching? Someone, it seems, had watched over us that day.

As we waited for our meal, four heads appeared in the hole above, backlit against the stormy sky. As my eyes adjusted, I made out the faces of four teenage girls, perhaps fifteen or sixteen years old. They peered down intently at us, their brilliant white teeth offsetting smudged dirty faces, black eyes and oily black hair.

Akaal Bahadur saw them immediately. He nudged Jeet Bahadur, and the two porters began to flirt. While some villagers spoke Nepali, most spoke only an odd Tibetan dialect. The language barrier hindered verbal communication, but the porters managed nicely with the girls despite this.

Giggling enticingly, the girls grew braver and moved through the hole to sit on the steps hacked out of the log. We could see that although they were quite young, each carried a baby strapped to her back. Exquisitely beautiful, they captivated us with their strong Tibetan features, flashing smiles and youthful exuberance. The harshness of their precarious existence in the inhospitable Himalaya had yet to dull their love of life.

It seemed to me a long time since I had seen or even thought of beautiful young girls. During the last few weeks my mind had been too frequently occupied with simple survival to permit any room for such thoughts. Now I smiled and enjoyed their company as much as the porters did.

We ate heartily of fried potato cutlets and boiled potatoes washed down with *chang*. A feeling of contentment washed over me as I finished.

I turned to Prem. The food had revived him as well and a smile lit his face. In answer to my question, he indicated that his thighs and upper arms were still painful and swollen. I thought this most likely the result of myositis, involvement of the muscles in the infection. But his speech was no longer impaired, and he had a request for me.

"Parker Sahib, could we stay here one day? The porters would like to celebrate."

"No problem, we could all use the rest."

"They want to buy one goat, from their own money. We will have a feast."

"Good idea. I will buy *chang* and *rakshi*. And potatoes."

"*Very* good, Parker Sahib."

I glanced up at the hole in the roof, now dark and vacant. What other motives might the porters have in wanting an extra day and planning such a feast? *Who cares? We could use the rest and food—and entertainment.*

The heavy meal made me drowsy, and I curled up near the hearth. I had long since given up on the large, heavy-bound journal and now, in my small notebook, I made cryptic notes on the events of the last two days. The last note for that day read, "First night below 14,000' in a week."

I tucked the notebook back into my pack, curled up and fell soundly asleep.

I woke late the next morning, still tired. Eating our morning meal of rice and potato *tarkaari* took energy I didn't have. A combination of queasy stomach and sixty days of the same diet permitted me to eat only a few mouthfuls. I crawled back to the comfort of the fire and my sleeping bag and drowsed the morning away. By midafternoon I finally felt rested enough to think about exploring outside. From the bottom of the ladder, I could see intensely clear blue sky overhead. I climbed the log ladder to the roof but the brilliance of the sunlight made me quickly duck back in. I searched for my sunglasses and then, properly protected, I reemerged.

Looking back towards the Sangdak Pass I saw snow sparkling on the peaks, receding as the mountains fell away to the black gash that marked the Cha Lungpa River. In the pristine Himalayan air every detail etched itself clearly.

Sangdak perched 1,500 feet above the *khola*. Just two hundred feet below the village, the canyon dropped away.

On the other side of the canyon, the sun had already melted the snow on the south facing slope and I could now clearly see an abandoned village. Directly across from where I stood lay "Old Sangdak." A desert now, its terraced fields had long ago slid into the canyon, buildings had returned to the earth from which they had been built. This was the Sangdak marked on my map. Prem had told me what the villagers had said. "It was too hot and too dry there. There was no more firewood for cooking. The soil would not grow any more barley. So all the people left and they came here. They built new houses and made new fields."

I cursed the map makers. Old Sangdak had been abandoned for decades. I thought about what might have happened if we had crossed the river and found that pile of rubble. And what if we had ended up there? What would I be thinking now standing on the opposite side of the canyon and looking at the new village of Sangdak? All those what-ifs bothered me so much, I forced them from my mind.

Akaal Bahadur and Jeet Bahadur had spent much of the day bargaining. Finally, they arranged to buy a small goat for 200 rupees. A runt, the goat was missing an eye and unable to forage for food as well as the others. The owner was pleased to be rid of it. Now came the time to slaughter it, and we brought the animal down into the house.

While the porters made preparations, I held the little animal. I wondered how this species had managed to survive. They seemed defenseless, with horns too short to gore anything. Perhaps they survived by running away from danger. Yet, when I stood him up and pushed against the front of his head, his knobby head pushed back. I repeated my push, he repeated his. I realized then that if I stood there for half an hour pushing, he would continue pushing back. Maybe they didn't run away. I smiled at his cute antics and his spunk, and then a twinge of remorse hit me. We were famished and he was to be our dinner.

While Jeet Bahadur carefully sharpened his *kukri*, Akaal Bahadur picked the goat up by its hind legs and suspended it over a wash basin. Jeet Bahadur motioned for me to hold the goat's mouth shut with the neck extended downwards. As soon as I did this, he took his *kukri* and sliced into the underside of the throat. Blood spurted from both carotid arteries and splashed into the wash basin. There was no noise but a sucking sound as Jeet Bahadur cut through the windpipe. The goat showed no sign of pain, nor did it struggle as we waited for it to lose consciousness. Soon its eye closed. Jeet Bahadur, with a few swift strokes, severed the head and it fell into my hands. The jaw and neck muscles twitched as I held the still-warm cranium. I felt a sudden queasiness, and I looked around for a clean place to put the thing down. Finding nowhere, I continued holding it upside down in the palm of my hand as I watched the rest of the butchering.

Jeet Bahadur stuck the knife in the underside and with one quick stroke sliced the goat up the belly, through the sternum and chest. Quickly locating the heart, he hacked it free and set it aside, waiting for the carcass to clear of blood. When the flow of blood eased, Akaal Bahadur lowered the body and the butchering began in earnest.

First the organs were removed, the lungs, liver, spleen, stomach, small intestine, kidneys, pancreas all placed in a large bowl. The only item discarded was the large intestine. Next Jeet Bahadur removed the limbs. He pulled the skin back from the joint, then with a few sharp blows severed the front and hind legs at hip and shoulder. The limbless carcass was laid on its back. As Akaal Bahadur grabbed the ribs and pried them open, Jeet Bahadur sliced them free from the skin from the inside. The skin remained attached to the rest of the body. The tenderloins were removed from just near the spine. Finally the rest of the carcass was hacked into small pieces with a few dozen rapid *kukri* blows. Total elapsed time: four minutes.

Akaal Bahadur now cut the lower spindly portion of the legs from the upper meaty portion. He relieved me of the head, which I still held, and with the legs, he placed it just above the hearth to smoke. I couldn't imagine what Akaal Bahadur thought he was going to do with a smoked head and the bony lower legs.

Auri Bahadur picked up the bowl of innards and disappeared up the ladder. He returned a half hour later with everything washed thoroughly. The small intestine had been sliced lengthwise and chopped into small pieces. The other organs also had been washed and hacked into chunks. Mixed together the pieces no longer were identifiable as heart, liver, intestine or other innards. Each part of the animal had been set aside, including the blood, for the upcoming feast.

The owner of the house came around to offer us some of his *rakshi*, much of which he obviously had imbibed already. I had tasted it the night before and now politely declined. It reeked of kerosene. I decided to hold out for more of his wife's tasty, thick *chang*. Earlier I had felt the rumblings that preceded the intestinal ailments to which I had become so prone in Nepal. Perhaps it would have been better to drink the *rakshi*; I knew that it was distilled, whereas they made the *chang* with whatever water they had available. I decided it didn't matter, I would drink the *chang* and worry about the consequences tomorrow.

Our host lurched from side to side as he meandered into the next room where he slumped down against a pile of old blankets. He would probably sleep the rest of the afternoon away, as he did most days. A tall man, apparently of pure Tibetan stock, he possessed one gold tooth which he showed us repeatedly with generous smiles. A great piece of coral dangled from one ear.

I felt it unkind to note that his wife, now off tending the goats and yaks, was homely as sin, with eyes that seemed

painfully crossed. But what she lacked in beauty, she com-
pensated for by a generous heart and boundless energy. At
five o'clock when she returned, she scurried about tending
the fire, making food, fetching water, blithely stepping
around her drunken husband. I doubt she complained about
her condition, as most of the village men appeared to be
plastered by midafternoon every day. The women missed
this dissipated lifestyle since they all left for the pastures
early each morning.

As I watched the domestic comings and goings of the
household, I heard giggling. Looking up, I saw six heads
outlined against the sky through the hole. A smile creased
my face and I felt warmed by the sight before me. Beside me,
Prem stirred, and I saw him smiling too. I knew then that he
was well on his way to recovery.

The girls sat around the chimney hole and on the ladder,
whispering quietly to each other, multicolored homespun
blankets wrapped around them like shawls. Their babies
made no sound; we were aware of them only as bulges on
each girl's back. Akaal Bahadur and Jeet Bahadur began to
sing Tamang folk songs. The girls responded by singing two
songs in Tibetan. As the porters launched into another song,
Prem leaned over to me. "Parker Sahib. This is a marriage
song. First the men sing and then the women sing."

The porters had finished the men's part and started to
sing the women's part, when the Tibetan girls picked up the
melody and sang with them. Astonished, Akaal Bahadur and
Jeet Bahadur stopped. Pleased with themselves, the girls finished the female part with a flourish as the men picked up
the next verse. Prem and I laughed with amazement as the
Tamang porters sang their part in Tamang and the Tibetan
women sang their part in Tibetan. The end of the song
brought smiles and laughter from all.

After an hour, the Sangdak girls placed the palms of their
hands together in front of their faces and drifted off without
a word. Hastily, Akaal Bahadur, Jeet Bahadur and I clam-

bered up the ladder and watched them disappear into their houses. They looked back at us several times, coyly laughing.

Wistfully, with bittersweet smiles, we watched them go. We had truly enjoyed their company. The women of Sangdak clearly were much more interesting and full of life than the men. Our judgment may have been prejudiced from being on the trail for two months, but the presence of these simple girls had certainly changed our demeanor. That day in Sangdak, they seemed to me the most enchanting women in the world.

The porters climbed back down into the house to prepare our feast. I stood on the rooftop in the twilight, the halo of happiness left by the singing girls still warm around me. I missed Clara. It would be only a few weeks now before I would see her again. Her shining black hair, those exquisitely shaped, expressive eyes. Her shy smile and her whispered words of goodbye when I had left. *Soon.*

Our feast began with a mixture of fiery chilies, garlic, liver, heart, kidney and lungs. Our hostess offered no *chang*, so we washed it down with the kerosene-flavored *rakshi* firewater. For the next course we had the small intestine fried in blood. Finally we ate the meat with fried potatoes. We ate until we nearly burst and drank *rakshi* until we passed out.

Dawn found me desperately searching for a "toilet." Every village had a spot—not too close, not too far and generally not easy to find. My guts rumbled as I hastily searched below the village, crossing terraced fields just above the drop-off into the gorge. I found the open-air spot in a cul-de-sac only yards from where the cliffs began. Feeling lousy and hung over, I still couldn't help but notice the scenery. It was stunningly beautiful this morning, not a cloud obscured the sky. After I had taken care of my urgent problems, I fetched my camera and spent an hour photographing the village and its occupants.

Returning to the house, I found the rest of our band badly

hung over and downing cup after cup of strong tea. As we slowly packed up the *dokos*, Prem and I turned our attention to a woman who told us about our route.

"Parker Sahib, she says we have one day to Jomoson."

"That's great, Prem. I'll be so glad to see the Kali Gandaki. We're going to have to forget about going over the Thorung La and through Manang. We'd never make it. Instead we can head down the Kali Gandaki and get to Pokhara in a few days. Ask her where the trail is."

Using hand signs and a few words of broken Nepali, Prem questioned her at length. He turned to me.

"There are two ways to go. This one is the Lekh Baato." He pointed up towards the 17,000-foot lekh behind us to the south. "It is shorter this way."

"I don't know, Prem. There's at least three feet of new snow up there. I don't like it at all. What's the other way?"

The woman used a snakelike hand motion to describe the other route.

"The Khola Baato. It is longer and we will follow the river," Prem interpreted.

I looked towards the black gorge of the Cha Lungpa Khola. Gently sloping hillsides, like the one on which Sangdak perched, stretched atop the steep cliffs that fell sharply to the river. Although deep snow covered the higher slopes, most had melted at this elevation. It looked passable. Our map showed a straightforward route to the Kali Gandaki.

"We'll take the Khola Baato, even though it's longer. You agree, Prem?"

"Yes, Parker Sahib. The snow would not be good for me."

By eight o'clock, we were ready to leave. Still sated by our feast on the goat the night before and immensely relieved at being so close to our destination, we said our goodbyes and left, turning many times to look back at the ocher-colored buildings of Sangdak.

CHAPTER SIXTEEN

SANGDAK

Wednesday, April 11, 1984

WE LEFT SANGDAK, CLIMBING UP OUT OF THE VILLAGE FOR several hundred feet, then headed for a low ridge that separated two drainage areas on the southern side of the canyon. Prem had recovered somewhat. His fever had lowered and his head ached less than during the previous three days. His thighs and upper arms, however, were still swollen, forcing him to walk in a stiff-legged shuffle, using his ice axe as a cane. We kept an eye on him, ready to help if he faltered.

Reaching the ridge, we looked northeast through the canyon and caught our first glimpse of the snow-covered Damodar Himal to the northeast on the far side of the Kali Gandaki. We were sobered, however, by the view of the terrain that lay between us and the Kali Gandaki. The Cha Lungpa Khola formed the most rugged canyon I had ever seen. The river had cut a narrow vertical notch through the steep, mountainous terrain. From where we stood, eight hundred feet of the vertical rock walls were visible, their upper ramparts in some places only a hundred yards apart. The river was easily another thousand feet below, lost in the depths of the canyon. Although the locals called the trail we were attempting to follow the Khola Baato, we could see that getting down to the waters of the Cha Lungpa would be out of the question.

Above the vertical walls, the mountains rose steeply several thousand feet and were cut into by numerous side canyons. Our intended route looked impassable. Several slide areas cut across what we could see of the trail ahead, wiping it out completely for long stretches. I feared that we would not see Jomoson that day.

We made our way along shifting scree slopes, contouring as best we could into a great side canyon above the gorge. A stream ran down its center. Because we had water here we stopped early for our first meal.

That's when I realized that we might once again run out of food. Because the villagers assured us that we could reach Jomoson in one day, and because we wanted to travel as light as possible, we had brought only a minimal supply of food from Sangdak. Akaal Bahadur and Jeet Bahadur had asked Prem how much food to bring and he had told them one day's supply. It had slipped my mind to check on how much we had before we left, and now I didn't know with whom I was more upset, them or myself.

Still, I ripped into Akaal Bahadur and Jeet Bahadur and then took my bowl of potatoes and _tsampa_ off to eat in angry silence. They seemed surprised and offended by my raised voice, and a pall descended over the group. Soon I felt guilty about berating them after all we had been through. In exchange for a few rupees a day they had done everything asked of them and more. Nevertheless it seemed unthinkable to me that after all our food shortages we could be caught short once again. If I had known, I would have carried the damn food myself.

Despite my tinge of guilt, I sank deeper into a black mood. Looking at the terrain ahead, I felt we had been duped once again. Hadn't we learned yet that what people told us didn't always correspond to reality? Yes, maybe in the best weather, with the trails in excellent condition, with a light load and strong legs, someone had made it to Jomoson in a day. But that person's easy walk to Jomoson might be two or even three days for us. I felt incredibly weary, physically and mentally run down, having thought that the worst was over only to be confronted with additional trials.

As we sat among bushes next to the small stream, we could see across to the next slope. An almost constant bombardment of rocks crashed down, one after the other or several simultaneously, loosened from their frozen perches by the brilliant sun. A few landed in our midst and we scattered, clutching our food bowls. As we finished our meal, we contemplated the next slope, its thick ice covered with loose gravel.

Akaal Bahadur and I headed out to the slope with our ice axes and began cutting a trail for the others to follow. Auri Bahadur kept watch for falling rocks, whistling when he saw danger coming. Several times he whistled shrilly and we dove for cover, watching rocks bounce by. We were playing a deadly game, knowing that a rock the size of a baseball could kill when hurtling down from above.

Fortunately, one at a time, we all made it across that slope, a dangerous dash of more than three hundred feet, without being hit. Near the end, Prem's pace slowed to a crawl. His thighs, now badly swollen, froze up on him. He could hardly bend his legs. We took his pack from him despite his weak protests and that helped, but not much.

More side canyons snaked ahead, making this kind of travel terribly disheartening. We could see that from one side to the other was only a half mile, but frequently we had to travel two or more miles in a long descent followed by an arduous ascent to get to the other side. The canyons cut through hundreds of feet of rock and dirt conglomerate, and in places the trail disappeared, carried down into the deep gorge below by water, snow and earthquakes. At times we could see far into the gorge, a 2,000-foot vertical drop to the white, foaming waters.

We climbed down and up four more side canyons before meeting the dividing ridgeline of yet another canyon. Looking down, we saw the deepest and widest yet, and after just a few feet the trail simply ended. Water and wind had carved the compacted rock and dirt into free-standing spires and knife-edge ridges, a labyrinth through which we had no idea how to make our way. This couldn't possibly be the route. At least it wasn't any longer, if it ever was. But with nighttime approaching and our anxiety to make progress increasing, we didn't stop to think this through. We started down into the canyon, edging our way along, clinging with hands and feet to the conglomerate.

Two hundred feet along, we came to a small depression in the steep slope, a slanting ledge just large enough to support a lone pine tree. We stopped to rest and consider our next move. Once again Akaal Bahadur and I went ahead to scout while the others waited. Beyond the tree, we were relieved to see the semblance of a trail reappear just ahead and slightly above us. We climbed up and followed this track around a corner and further into the morass. I followed close behind Akaal Bahadur as we came to yet another corner. Here, the slope fell away in a sheer wall of dirt and rocks before merging with a steep slide a hundred feet below. The path appeared as little more than an indistinct strand, working its way along just above the drop-off.

Akaal Bahadur began to cross this area, but I held back. An oddly familiar feeling, centered somewhere between the butterflies in my stomach and the deep pounding throbs of my heartbeat, gave me pause. I broke into a cold, clammy sweat. Adrenaline pumped a what-am-I-doing-here queasy kind of feeling into my veins—a feeling I knew only too well from rock-climbing. The feeling you get on lead and forty feet out from the last protection, hand and foot placements tenuous at best, when your legs begin hammering up and down like synchronized sewing machines. As forearms cramp and hands start losing their clawlike grip on the rock, you dream of a flat piece of real estate and make a pact with the gods that you will gladly live in Iowa City for the rest of your life if you are just spared the ankle-breaking, skull-crushing fall that you feel sure is coming. I had been out on that "pointy" end of the rope enough times to heed the feeling before the nasty stuff began.

But Akaal Bahadur was already thirty feet along and now perched just above the vertical section. I didn't want to tell him the truth: that I was beginning to lose the mind game. That I was half paralyzed with the fear of falling off the slope, bouncing and scraping and thudding to the bottom of the canyon over two hundred feet below. So I asked him if maybe this wasn't the trail after all, but maybe just an animal path. *"O Akaal Bahadur, baato ho?"* I said weakly.

He looked first at what lay ahead, then took a furtive glance downward. For the first time since I had met him over six months before, I saw fear in his wide eyes. Finally he grasped the fragility of his position, with arms spread too wide and feet barely gripping the crumbling rocks. He remained frozen in place for half a minute, looking at the wall inches from his face, at his feet, at the drop below. Slowly he edged back towards me, one foot and one hand at a time, testing each placement gingerly before shifting his weight onto it. Reaching the rock where I stood, he let out a long, airy whistle and waited for his breath to return to normal.

"No good, Sahib," he finally gasped in English.

Then, in Nepali, *"Yo baato kahaaho?"* ("Where is the trail?")

"Musalai kaideo," ("The mouse ate it.") I replied.

Akaal Bahadur burst out laughing. He laughed until he could no longer breathe, and I laughed along with him, thinking that the joke had finally come full circle. *"Musalai kaideo,"* I repeated.

"Yiss, Sahib," Akaal Bahadur replied, chuckling again at the joke.

Satisfied that I had made the point about the trail ahead,

we worked our way slowly back to the others waiting beside the tree. I talked with Prem. We agreed that we should return to the stream that cut through the previous canyon, the last place we had seen any semblance of a real trail. We would follow the stream uphill in hopes of getting above this series of side canyons blocking our way. First we had to retrace our steps back two hundred feet from our current position to the ridge that bisected the two canyons. Because we had consistently gone downhill while traversing, we were now faced with an uphill climb, a decidedly unpleasant prospect.

Akaal Bahadur took the lead, followed by Jeet Bahadur, Auri Bahadur, Prem and then me. Akaal Bahadur crossed the section rapidly, dropped his basket and then came back to help Jeet Bahadur, who was having trouble keeping his bulky load balanced. I helped Prem as best I could as he limped along. He groaned every time he had to stretch to reach the next foothold.

Fifteen feet before the ridgeline and safe ground came a particularly difficult section. We had to face the near-vertical slope, making three reaching steps onto three rocks protruding from the conglomerate. I went ahead of Prem, dropped my pack and returned. He made the first step with my help, then the second two with Akaal Bahadur's help. I followed directly behind him. In my hurry to cross back again I stepped onto the first rock facing away from the wall instead of towards it. My foot touched but did not hold on the sloping sand-covered rock, and slipped off into the void.

Instinctively I spun around as I fell, arresting my fall by bearhugging the rock from which I had slipped. My chest and chin slammed into the rock, knocking the wind out of me and driving my teeth into the side of my tongue. I sucked for breath that wouldn't come. My feet flailed in empty space. I started to slip. Frantically grabbing for a more secure hold, my hands met only grit, sliding across the uneven rocks. Sand trickled off the rock onto my face. I stopped slipping, my hands clutched something firm. My feet still dangled though, and I swung them around blindly, desperately searching for purchase on anything.

Realizing I had nothing below me, I pulled myself up until the side of my face pressed against the wall. With a contortionist's maneuver I pulled one foot up onto the rock. Slowly, taking shallow gulps of air, I pushed and pulled myself to my feet. Prem and the porters watched all of this in utter silence, their mouths agape. Auri Bahadur, who was closest to me, finally spoke. *"Bistaari, Sahib."* ("Go slowly, sir.")

I stood until my breath returned and my forearms began to uncramp. I couldn't bring myself to look down, I didn't even want to know what I had missed this time.

Half of my tongue was numb where I had bitten down on it and now I hacked great pink globs of blood and spit into the air. Along with the blood came a few bits from a front tooth. Finally, I brought myself to make my way cautiously back the remaining ten feet to where the others waited.

Silently we picked our way back a mile to the stream at the bottom of the preceding canyon. Although it remained the only logical place for the trail to be, we saw nothing but dense brush lining the stream. We pushed our way through, looking everywhere for any hint of a path. A third of a mile up the stream bank Jeet Bahadur let out a yell. *"Baato ho!"* His words were music to our ears.

We converged on him and found ourselves staring down at what might be called a major thoroughfare for this part of the world. It came in above us from the west and followed along the stream uphill in the direction we were going. Buoyed by our good fortune, we followed the trail upstream for more than an hour until it veered off to the east, heading up a scree slope in steep switchbacks.

Prem announced wearily, "Parker Sahib, I cannot go any further today." Even though we had less than one full meal left, we had no option but to set camp here near this source of water. Akaal Bahadur and I began our daily ritual of putting up the tents. As we did, he puzzled me by muttering beneath his breath. I could catch only a few words but knew they were derogatory and apparently aimed at the rest of us.

Quietly, I asked Prem about Akaal Bahadur's mumbling and he answered with a sigh, "Akaal Bahadur is calling us all fools. He swears at us and curses our relatives."

"But why should he do that?"

Prem shrugged. Perhaps Akaal Bahadur was upset because we had lost the trail that afternoon. More likely, it was just frustration and the friction caused by all of us being together for so many months. There had certainly been enough frustrations to cause anyone to curse; it just wasn't pleasant to be the object of his swearing.

Carefully, we ate our last meal of *rotis* and potatoes. My tongue was swollen and sore, making it impossible to enjoy my bit of food. After we were finished with our small meal, I searched out the last remaining piece of Afghan hash from the bottom of my pack. Taking Akaal Bahadur's last *beedie*, I carefully removed the tobacco. Breaking the hash into small pieces, I mixed it with the tobacco and refilled the dried leaf skin of the *beedie*. We smoked it in silence. When it was gone, I worked myself into my sleeping bag. My mouth still throbbed, but I no longer cared. In my hash-induced haze, I fell into a fitful sleep.

The next morning, the switchbacks led us up a small hill—steep, rocky going. With only tea and a small amount of chicken bouillon in our bellies, lack of food began to sap our strength. We stopped frequently, and I found myself drinking pint after pint of water trying to fill the void. This didn't do much to assuage the hunger pangs, however. It only contributed to the aching of my distended stomach.

But from the top of the hill we could see eastward and our first view of the waters of the Kali Gandaki. To the north and east across the vast desert of the upper Kali Gandaki stretched the barren region of Mustang. Far below and a few miles ahead we could see the Cha Lungpa Khola, its energy spent, now a gray ribbon on its final journey to join the Kali Gandaki River. At the confluence lay the village of Tangbe. Its irrigated fields formed a tiny green emerald in the sea of parched brown earth.

The trail was easier now, and our pace quickened. We walked downhill, down towards the Kali Gandaki, which had been our destination for the last two months. Prem increased his pace to a stiff-legged trot. He gouged parallel tracks in the sandy soil as he shuffled from side to side with the help of his ice axe. But an hour later, we rounded a promontory and looked down into yet another side canyon.

I felt utterly drained. With an almighty groan, I threw myself backwards onto a large flat rock. Dolpo, it seemed, would loosen its physical hold on us only with the greatest reluctance. Having wrung us dry, having squeezed from us the last drops of our physical, mental and spiritual strength, it now threw up one last obstacle to overcome, this final deep gorge between us and the Kali Gandaki.

But we *had* glimpsed our destination. To be certain that we chose the best way through this canyon, we paused to rest and discuss the route ahead. The side gorge was several hundred feet deep and the far slope, sheltered from the sun, lay blanketed in snow. Bypassing it completely by making our way down to the Cha Lungpa Khola looked possible from where we sat, but the khola ran east and a little north towards the Kali Gandaki and Tangbe. This would have added several miles at least to the route between here and the town of Jomoson. We decided to follow the trail as it contoured into this side canyon, betting that this would be the last such canyon before we found ourselves on the slopes heading down into the Kali Gandaki Valley.

Making our way to the stream that cut through the center of the canyon was straightforward, and within an hour we stopped along its banks. The opposite snow-covered slope revealed that an ascent of seven or eight hundred feet awaited us. Above the ridge crest shone a brilliant blue sky. Lack of food and the bright warm sun sucked the strength out of us.

To heat water for some chicken bouillon, we built a small fire from thorny scrub. We all watched intently as Prem unwrapped our last few bouillon cubes and threw them into the boiling water along with some salt, pepper and the last few chilies. Then he turned to Akaal Bahadur and said something quickly in Nepali.

Akaal Bahadur untied the length of yak rope that held the top of his load, removed a piece of plastic and laid it out on a flat rock. Then he reached further into his basket and extracted a small package wrapped in tattered bits of homespun. He put the bundle down on the plastic and slowly, teasingly untied the bit of wool yarn that held it together.

"Hungry, Sahib?" Akaal Bahadur asked in Nepali, showing a crooked little smile as he removed the cloth.

The goat's head! I had forgotten it, or rather more accurately, I had put it out of my mind, along with the goat's stringy lower legs, which Akaal Bahadur now held up. Grabbing his *kukri*, he hacked at the head with great swinging blows, crushing the skull and leg bones into dozens of pieces. He carefully picked up the plastic and slid the entire blackened mess—bones, skin, brains and feet—into the boiling chicken broth.

We gathered around the fire and sat on our haunches without speaking, staring at the mysterious dark chunks of goat rising and falling in the roiling liquid. I found myself not the least bit reluctant to down my share of this meal. I was literally starving, the hunger coming from deep within me, a primitive need for food that overwhelmed all my other sensibilities. Although we had gorged ourselves on the more palatable portions of this goat only two days before, that feast came nowhere near recouping the long-term food debt of the last few months. I would never again speak those empty words, "I'm starving," without a twinge of remembrance as to how starving really felt.

Waiting expectantly, we watched as Prem carefully ladled out each portion. I salivated—literally drooled—as a bowl was passed to me. I held the steaming bowl and looked at the dark fragments of skull and a few lighter chunks of what I took to be brain. How strange it was, how great and transforming my struggle had been, that I could at this moment relish the sight of a steaming bowl of goat's head soup. Life was stripped of any complexity except the simple overpowering need for food.

Taking my bowl a few feet away from the others, I ate my share as if it were a feast. I savored the still hairy skin, played with the small gobs of fatty brain with my tongue, chewed the bones until they were pulp, extracting every last bit of nutrient. All too soon I held an empty bowl; I stuck my face in it to lick it clean. The others also finished quickly, and Auri Bahadur collected the bowls to wash in the stream. Except for the large intestine, we had now eaten that entire goat. I wondered who had eaten the eyeball from the poor one-eyed creature. I was thankful that it had only had one and that I hadn't found it in my portion, because it was the only body part that still made me queasy.

Soon after leaving the stream we passed through a large stand of gnarled birch. It was now early afternoon, and the sun had finally found its way onto the snowy slope. The foot of snow that remained had turned to mush and the ground underneath it had melted into a slick layer of mud. The powerful reflection of the sun pushed the temperature into the eighties.

Because Prem had lost an ice axe in the accident at the stream on the other side of the Sangdak Pass, we were left with only two. So from the birch around us, Akaal Bahadur and Jeet Bahadur cut three additional staffs for the climb. Without them, it would have been nearly impossible to climb up the steep muddy slope. Even with the aid of ice axes and staffs, we all fell several times.

The trick of eventually making it up the hill, not losing any more than we gained, was to stop ourselves as quickly as possible after falling. We knew the best method was to try to lie completely prone and perform an ice axe arrest or dig a stick into the mud. Even so, twice Jeet Bahadur fell and wiped three of us out with him. Soon we were all soaked and covered with a freezing mixture of snow and mud.

But the sun warmed us, restoring at least some energy, and two hours after the first slippery step, Prem reached the top and turned a corner out of view. I followed five minutes behind him. Rounding the corner, I was confronted by a lone *chorten* and a breathtaking panorama of the land we had been seeking for so long. I stopped, almost with a foot in midair, transfixed by the view before me.

To the north lay an eroded desert landscape leading to Mustang and the Tibetan plateau. The Tibetan border stood clearly demarcated by the snowy peaks of the Damodar Himal. Directly across the vast basin of the Kali Gandaki, the dry barren plateau rose gently and then in a great rush to the snow-covered *V* of the Thorung La, gateway to Manang and the region north of the Annapurna Himalaya. Further south was the massive thrust of the Himalaya of central Nepal, with Tilicho and Niligiri forming a sheer 10,000-foot wall of rock and hanging glaciers. Unable to turn away from the sight, I dropped my pack and sank down next to Prem, who was leaning against the *chorten*.

The porters rounded the corner, one by one. Akaal Bahadur came first and I watched his expression as he approached me. The tumpline on his load kept his gaze downwards, permitting him to take only fleeting glances ahead. But each time he raised his eyes I could see his expression change as the beginnings of a broad smile creased his face. He jogged the last few steps before squatting down to drop his load.

Then he stood with his hands on his hips, looking out across the great valley below.

"*O Akaal Bahadur, Kali Gandaki ho!*" ("This is the Kali Gandaki!") I exclaimed.

Pointing to the scene he asked in an incredulous voice, "*Kali Gandaki?*"

"*Ho, ho,*" I answered, beaming like an idiot.

"*Ahhhhh,*" was his only reply.

Jeet Bahadur and Auri Bahadur arrived in close succession. Dropping their loads, they flopped down against the *chorten* beside us. We sat and gazed to the east for several minutes without speaking, all moved by the scene before us, relieved, happy beyond words to have finally reached this spot for which we had struggled so desperately for so many weeks.

I finally broke the silence with a half-whisper. "We made it, Prem, we made it through Dolpo."

Saying nothing in reply, he pursed his lips and nodded slowly, still looking straight ahead. After a while he looked at me with a crooked smile and I smiled back. We shook our heads in wonderment. I turned away to regain my composure.

By God, we had made it. Almost.

CHAPTER SEVENTEEN

▲

"*Jaau*," Prem called, our signal to be up and on our way.

We hoisted our loads and followed the long, contouring trail down towards the riverbed. We lost altitude in great gulps, as though unseen forces were sucking us deeper into the vast watershed of the Kali Gandaki. The land was a barren, treeless desert.

Late in the afternoon, we came to a lone yak herder's hut set amidst a series of stone corrals. A Tibetan man and his small boy emerged from the low doorway and motioned us inside. They offered us Tibetan tea and minutes later we gratefully accepted bowls of the salted, buttery broth. We bought some *tsampa* from the yak herder and mixed it into the steaming liquid.

Immensely tired and wanting to be alone, I stooped through the hut door and climbed a log ladder to the roof. I propped my dusty pack against stones that formed a low wall around the roof edge, sat down and leaned against it. I ate slowly, scooping the salty mixture of tea and *tsampa* out of the bowl with my fingers, savoring each mouthful. Absently, I scanned the same Kali Gandaki view we had seen earlier in the day, only now much closer at hand. Directly across from me was the Thorung La, framed to the north and south by

21,000-foot snow-covered peaks. Nearer and far below the pass lay Muktinath, a holy pilgrimage site, an island in the sea of brown.

I scraped out the last of my simple meal, laid the bowl aside and licked the remaining *tsampa* from my fingers. My hands were filthy, still caked with mud from the slippery climb a few hours earlier. But it didn't matter. After eating the blackened, smoked goat's head, a little Himalayan dirt didn't seem so terrible. My tongue snatched up a bit of cracking mud and I ground it gently between my teeth. Earth, no doubt about it.

I sat quietly, staring at the scene before me, the raw and untouched earth. Soon the bright rim of the moon appeared from the *V* of the Thorung La. I watched, mesmerized as the first half appeared. Then, with such surprising speed it seemed the earth had squeezed it forth, the whole moon floated free, suspended in the sky. Almost full, a barely perceptible yellow, so beautiful it made me think of my camera, of taking a photo of this familiar companion. So often during the last few weeks, I had struggled against exhaustion to record my journey on film. Now, with all energy spent, a numbing weariness gripped me and my camera remained buried in my pack. No strength left to even lift it to my eye.

My mind wandered to other moons. I was at Thyangboche five months earlier at the Mani Rimdu festival, when the full moon had risen directly out of the summit pinnacle of Ama Dablam. I was in Surkhet in February, at the beginning of this journey, with all of us still fresh and strong. In Gum Gadhi, passing silently in the night. In Dolpo, where it was cold and hard, reflecting blue white off the Dhaulagiri Massif. This same moon had been my light through all those dark nights.

Kathmandu. She had risen as a yellow ball, impossibly large, out of the Khumbu Himalaya far to the northeast. Clara, our first words. *Your Full Moon*, she had called herself.

I wanted desperately to be with her now, to hold her in my arms.

"Claaaarraaaah!" The cry rose in anguish from deep within my chest, the sound quickly dissipating in the vast open valley.

A few moments passed in silence, then Prem stuck his head above the roof. "Okay, Parker Sahib?"

"Okay," I answered softly, still gazing off towards the Thorung La. I felt him watch me for a long moment, then disappear into the hut below.

I continued to drift, my eyes open but only half conscious of what I saw. Now, with the Kali Gandaki so near, I felt a lifting of weight, a letting down of barriers, a dissolution of emotional control. The visceral emotions I had experienced on this journey emerged as tears that filled my eyes and flowed down my cheeks. Frustration, anger, pain, grief; an emotional maelstrom rose up from my subconscious. With a dirty sleeve I rubbed tears from my face.

Why had I come to the Himalayas? To conquer them? Had I been the quintessential American simply assuming a conquest of these storied peaks? Had I been *that* naive? Those magnificent and beautiful mountains had barely let me through alive. "There are no conquerors—only survivors." That phrase whispered through my mind, taunting me.

I recalled the vision of Akaal Bahadur, water streaming down his face as he dug a trench for my tent; felt the rain drops from his wet clothes when he came in smiling, satisfied in having done his job no matter what. Jeet Bahadur kneeling by the stream, washing my clothes in the freezing water, his hands purple with cold but his work dignified by his satisfaction. Had their culture given them a different view of life, one that saw not a need to conquer but rather a need to view all life as transitory, and that therefore found prizes of little value? And had I, in all my years of collecting awards, titles, degrees; and in my ambition for material success—had

I "conquered" nothing of lasting importance? Had Akaal Bahadur, Jeet Bahadur and Prem begun to teach me that true satisfaction lay not in prizes won, but rather in the doing with competence and decorum life's daily work, whatever it might be?

Yet they had gone beyond a simple day's work, for we *had* defied these Himalayas, struggling through where natives feared to trek and warned us not to go. We *had* conquered. But perhaps here lay the meaningful difference; we now held no prize. Only a shared honoring of the indomitable human spirit, a bond that crossed our cultural differences and united us.

Asia. A kaleidoscope of images flashed through my mind. I saw a beggar child in Delhi, her withered stump of a hand pinned to her chest by her parent for a extra rupee or two of pity. I smelled the stench of feces, heard the buzzing of flies, saw the children of Mandu. Bloated bellies, thin reddish hair falling out in clumps, uncomprehending eyes, the handless child. Puraba's children, caked with dirt, minds dulled, destined for a life of toil in a forgotten canyon of western Nepal. Would they experience any joy in their lives? How long would they live? Would their short lives be filled only with pain, despair, affliction?

Death. Memories of my own confrontations with it. Warm salty blood from my tongue where I had bitten down on it; sand on the sloping rock grinding into my fingers as I slipped towards the void. The freight-train roar of the mountainside crashing down to the river and about to take me with it. The smell of dust filling my nose. My brain frantic, my head feeling light and dizzy.

I saw Prem, just a few days before, that night below the Sangdak Pass. I felt his weight on my arm as I half dragged him onwards. I had felt certain he was dying, that he wouldn't survive the night.

Those close calls had shaken me to the core. I had tried to suppress my fear then, tried to accept the possibility of dying. But those experiences had confronted me for the first time with the understanding, the internalization of the idea that someday I would die. The adolescent sense of immortality ended on that rock, in that landslide, on that bridge. And with it went the childish notion of self-importance, the idea of occupying the center of the universe, to be replaced by an acceptance of myself as a mere member in the family of all living creatures.

The tears slowed, I looked out once again at the magnificence of the scene before me. In the stillness of the early evening, in the absolute silence, my emotional turmoil ebbed. Then, as the background noises of my mind quieted, a peacefulness, a clarity emerged from deep within me. For a moment, I sensed an understanding, a harmony. As though the earth and my self were one, inextricably tied together, bound in the cycles of life and death.

With incredible clarity I felt this. My mind, with all its senses sharpened, went beyond weariness to a new level of awareness. Though I had prepared myself for physical hardship—plunging into the icy rivers, scaling crumbling canyon walls—I had not imagined how my experiences would twist and challenge my mind. I had taken a mental journey through frustration, exhilaration, fear, despair and hope to new perception. Facing the tenuousness of life and death, I had experienced the body as it confronts mortality, the mind as it confronts immortality.

The clear silence brought peace, a singular harmony to body and mind. And then, unexpectedly, a sense of sadness, a loss of something. A melancholic network of feelings, tenuous and vague, crept into my small clear silence. Would something be gone forever as I moved on?

Never having adequately answered for myself the question of why I had come to the Himalayas, I felt I had found something of an answer. At least a beginning of one. Yes, physical challenge had brought me here and spurred me on, but something much deeper had happened. My physical journey now almost over, I sensed I was embarking on another odyssey, a journey of the spirit.

I looked again at the rising moon, now glowing in the washed-out blue of the evening sky. From below, I heard the scrape of the hut door and the porters' voices speaking softly. The log ladder creaked a protest as someone climbed it.

"O Parker Sahib," Prem stuck his head above the rooftop. "It is time, we must go."

CHAPTER EIGHTEEN

▲

DARKNESS ENVELOPED US AS WE DESCENDED THE FINAL 2,000 feet into the Kali Gandaki Gorge. By the moon's light we saw the tightly clustered buildings of the village of Kagbeni across the river. A police checkpost guarded the restricted routes north to Mustang and west into Dolpo. We scanned the silvered moonlit buildings for any signs of activity, then cautiously descended to the river's edge. Reaching the second of two bridges that led to Kagbeni, the porters dropped their loads and we rested in the shadows.

As we sat quietly in the darkness, I thought of the long discussions back in Kathmandu in January about our trekking permits. Two major problems had arisen. First, our intended route and projected time on the trail would put us past our visas' three-month limit. This we could easily correct with judicious use of *baksheesh*. But the second problem had no such easy solution. The route we planned to follow would take us to both Jumla and Jomoson. "Not possible," the government officials told us. "One or the other."

We had opted for the route to Jumla. From the perspective of Kathmandu in January, Jomoson seemed lost in the distant future anyway and other obstacles loomed much closer. We had decided to worry about the Kali Gandaki if and when we ever reached it.

Now I held an expired visa and no permit for trekking in this region. One option was to pass by night all the checkposts between here and Tatopani, two days' travel to the south where the route from Jumla joined this trail. Jeet Bahadur had passed through here some years before, and Prem questioned him closely about the number and placements of the police *chaulkis*, but unfortunately he remembered little.

Now, on stiffened legs, Prem leaned against the bridge abutment and scanned the broad floodplain that formed the floor of the gorge. It extended far to the south, flat and strewn with rounded stones.

"Prem, what are you thinking?"

He replied without turning. "Ahead is a much-traveled trail, even at night, Parker Sahib. And maybe *chaulkis* before Jomoson. We should cross this bridge quickly and leave the trail. Walk on the riverbed."

"Sounds good to me. Let's do it."

In single file we wended our way across the river plain, lit blue-white by the brilliant moon. A steady warm breeze washed our faces, the air at only 9,000 feet syrupy-thick in our lungs. Although hungry, I felt alive, energized by my time spent on the roof of the shepherd's hut.

An hour later Prem stopped and pointed south to glimmering pinpoints of light, the electric lights of Jomoson. We now found ourselves on the most heavily trekked route in Nepal, from Pokhara to Muktinath. And where there were trekkers, there were teahouses ready to offer shelter and food.

Hunger consumed us, dominated our thoughts, and a mile further on we diverted towards the main trail to Jomoson. To find food, we would take our chances with the police. In making our way back up to the trail, now seventy feet above our heads, we climbed through a steep, boulder-filled gully.

Jeet Bahadur, always so steady and strong, was now so weak he needed help with his load. And we had to hoist Prem up and over boulders to get him onto the trail. A mile on, we came to a teahouse.

I entered first, stepping into a large, open room lined on one side with a dozen single bunks. The fire from the sooty kitchen beyond cast grotesque, flickering shadows on the earthen walls. Round tables and chairs cluttered the remaining space. I sat in a blue aluminum chair with "Dhaulagiri 78" stenciled in now-faded black lettering on the back, an expedition relic. A shy adolescent girl with lovely almond eyes brought menus, a plastic yellow bucket of *chang*, a bottle of *rakshi* and five dirty water glasses. I scanned the menu. "Toste," "nudels," dozens of other goodies. Unabashedly I ordered "pancaks, omlait and *momos.*" Prem and the porters ordered their favorite meal, *daal bhaat.*

Apprehensively, I turned and looked at the two rows of bunks full of sleeping trekkers. Two, in bright orange bags, read by the light of a single candle. They eyed us curiously. I thought about what they saw; decrepit bodies, matted hair, smelly, blackened clothes. I had a momentary urge to charge over to their corner to say hello, to talk, to ask about the outside world, to speak English with someone besides Prem. But I held back.

Prem, Akaal Bahadur, Jeet Bahadur and Auri Bahadur chatted easily. As I watched them, I felt the bonds among us, bonds forged by months of putting one foot in front of the other, leading up and down trails unimagined by any of us a year before. Bonds that we would remember for the rest of our lives. Together we had endured privation and physical hardships, experienced frustration and soaring exhilaration, traversed a rugged land, survived on little food, traveled day and night, dodged bandits and soldiers alike.

As I contemplated the westerners asleep in their bunks only a few feet away, I sensed that contact with the outside world would pull us apart, splinter our tiny band, make us individuals again. I turned back to my Nepalese companions, warmed by our present kinship and content to remain with them for a while longer.

With our bellies full, we talked quietly. About the women of Sangdak, the frozen rivers, Lama Dorje, and of J.B. Despite our disagreements before Jumla, which I now attributed to nothing more than the stresses of trekking, I felt acutely his absence from our group.

After a lull, I turned and spoke to Prem in English. "Prem, you can hardly walk. I'm worried that you might become sick again. I want you to fly back to Pokhara. I will pay." I said this knowing that we didn't have enough rupees for the flight. I would borrow from other foreigners if necessary.

I could have predicted his response. "I will not fly back, Parker Sahib."

I opened my mouth to argue, then closed it. I knew he meant it. By the light of the flickering fire, I studied his profile and saw beyond the dirt, the grime, the thin, weakened body, to the man's soul—to his inner strength and dignity.

Just before 11:00 P.M., we hoisted our loads and continued south. Once on the trail, we stopped to discuss our plan for getting through the checkposts. Although I knew that the scheme we used for Dunai had worked, it still seemed far-fetched to me. Yet we decided to try it again. Akaal Bahadur and I walked ahead, with Prem, Jeet Bahadur and Auri Bahadur a hundred yards behind us. Surprise would be our strategy.

Taking our positions, we approached the cluster of buildings that straddled the trail a few hundred yards ahead. The guttural bark of a dog sounded menacingly in the darkness ahead. As we drew closer, several dogs surrounded us. But after the mastiffs of Dolpo, these scrawny beasts seemed pathetically harmless, and Akaal Bahadur and I took a sort of revenge for our previous troubles with others of their species. Swinging bold, windmilling strokes with our ice axes, we broke their ranks, chasing one and then another as they backpedaled, whined and scattered in retreat. But the commotion awoke the occupants of one of the houses, where lights blinked on. Akaal Bahadur gave me a warning look, along with a big-jawed grin as we reluctantly ceased our attack and moved quickly on into the dark.

Ahead stood a brightly lit cable suspension bridge and, beyond that, a small enclosed booth with a bell, a *chaulki* for reviewing trekking permits. No one in sight. So I pulled my Chinese hat down low over my brow and we stepped out onto the bridge. Swiftly and silently we crossed it, passed the *chaulki* and made our way up the hill past shuttered shops.

Ahead two figures appeared in the trail. They watched us approach, then spoke sharply to us. Ignoring them, I stepped in the shadow of Akaal Bahadur's basket and hurried on by, picking up the pace. After fifty yards I looked back, and with relief saw no one following. Fifteen minutes later, we came to the southern edge of town and yet another checkpost. A gate, a booth, a bell and under a single bright bulb, a police guard. I hid behind the *doko* once more, but just as we came abreast of the guard, I glanced up. For an instant our eyes met. Immediately my heart pounded with a rush of adrenaline. But the guard made no move to stop us and we sped on. For half a mile we walked, then stepped off the trail to rest.

As my heartbeat slowed, I wondered why the guard had done nothing to stop me. Perhaps he didn't recognize me as a foreigner, or maybe he had just been caught unawares, not expecting anyone past midnight. Twenty minutes later, several figures approached from Jomoson. We recognized Prem's halting gait and went out to meet them. Prem bent over and rested his hands on his knees, sucking for breath.

"I think they are coming after us!" he said. "They stopped us three times. At the bridge, in town and just back at the government post. They questioned us. I told them I was a student in botany coming from Manang, walking all night because of a leg injury, after a rest in Muktinath. They did not believe me. They wanted to open our loads to check for the number of people with us. To search for stolen art objects. Finally they let us go. Each time I told them the same thing."

He looked back along the trail, pointing at half a dozen lights bobbing a hundred yards away. "See there. They're coming."

For several seconds, I stood rooted, staring back up the trail, not willing to believe that once again we would be chased by the police. But the bouncing lights were real and coming closer. I grabbed Prem's arm and we ran as best we could, stopping every hundred yards to look back and take a few breaths. But on they came. A mile later, at the small settlement of Syang, we stopped once again, waiting for the porters. A quick glance back told me our pursuers had not yet abandoned the chase.

"Quickly," I whispered. "Let's leave the trail and go behind those buildings. Get over by the river."

The porters joined us as we hurried down an embankment and over a dilapidated stone wall. We settled in close against the wall and waited in silence. No one came.

I awoke at daybreak, shivering, huddled against the cold stones, covered by our unrolled tents and sleeping bags. The others lay asleep, buried under gear and our makeshift cover. I looked towards a building thirty yards away and saw a young man squatting in the doorway, watching us. With daylight our secure hiding place had vanished. I woke the others. Hastily we packed our gear.

Less than an hour later I passed two trekkers on the trail. I had spotted them when they were still a quarter a mile away and had eagerly awaited my first contact with foreigners and some conversation about the outside world. I smiled as they approached, but they passed by without so much as a nod, eyes averted. To them, I supposed, foreigners were to be avoided as intrusions into their "Nepal experience." A few minutes later, we stopped at a teahouse in Marpha. Three Americans sat at a nearby table, but now I felt out of sorts, hungry and in no mood to talk to anyone.

Another hour and a half brought us to Tukuche and another rest stop at a small lodge. I walked into the front room to find several trekkers sitting at a long table. I sat with Prem at the far end of the table as the porters continued through to the sunny interior courtyard.

I spotted them right away—several warm bottles of Golden Eagle on a shelf behind Prem, the first I had seen since Surkhet. A smiling woman in Sherpa dress approached and asked what we wanted. I greedily ordered two Golden Eagles while Prem ordered *chang* for himself and the porters. I popped the cap on the first large bottle of beer and almost drained it in a single draw. After a prolonged and satisfying belch, I looked over at the other foreigners, who watched us with a peculiar mix of curiosity and revulsion. They had the latest in equipment, bright multicolored packs of red, blue and green; new boots, fresh clothes, scrubbed faces. I had lived in my clothes for three weeks, my hair was uncombed, greasy and matted. I looked at Prem. That fastidious Nepalese was filthy and unkempt. When the porters came in and sat down, our stench filled the room.

After a meal of *daal bhaat* and more beer, the porters went outside to unpack our gear. I lingered at the table. Sated with food and drink, my eyelids closed.

I woke to find one of the foreigners sitting across from me. "Where have you come from?" He spoke with a Scandinavian accent.

It took several seconds for his query to penetrate my haze. "To the north and west."

"From behind Dhaulagiri?"

I paused, then nodded weakly.

"But I heard you cannot go there, that it is restricted. And dangerous."

After fifteen seconds of silence, he looked away. But he didn't leave. *This guy really wants to talk.* I asked him about the Olympics, about what was happening in the world. But he obviously wanted to talk about other things, and the conversation soon petered out.

Then I rose unsteadily and entered the white sunlight of the courtyard, finding Prem checking supplies and Akaal Bahadur washing clothes at a water tap. Rummaging through Jeet Bahadur's basket, I found a scrap of soap at the bottom and decided to wash. I stripped off my polypropylene shirt. White skin, brown forearms, *Bodhissatva* ribs. Removing my long underwear for the first time in weeks, I was shocked at the sight of my legs. So thin. I took my hands and completely encircled one thigh.

"Prem, what have you done to me?"

Prem studied me with his crooked smile, then grinned broadly. "Now you are Asia thin, Parker Sahib. Like the rest of us."

Moving to the tap, I sluiced my body with frigid water and washed head, arms, legs, toes, every inch several times over. While I scrubbed, Akaal Bahadur took my pile of clothes and washed them, then wrung them out as best he could. Having handed out my extra clothes weeks ago in Dolpo, I put the damp clothes back on and lay down in the midday sun.

An hour later swirling winds and dark clouds forced me inside, where I slept until Prem roused me.

Our plan was to hurry south and pass the checkpost at Lete under cover of darkness. Towards dusk, however, the clouds lowered and yellow flashes lit the sky. Large drops spattered on the rounded rocks of the floodplain. We dashed ahead, looking for shelter and finding it in a small lodge in Dhumpus.

At 4:00 A.M., Prem and I set off to pass the checkpost at Lete before dawn. The porters would catch up with us later in the day. Roosters announced the coming day as we moved silently past the checkpost, which sat ghostly in the predawn twilight. An hour later, we waited for the porters under the shady porch of a teahouse.

At eleven, the porters arrived, sweatsoaked in their mountain clothes. That day we would drop another 4,000 feet down through the twisting Kali Gandaki Gorge. From the cold windswept reaches of Dolpo to the sultry green subtropics in two days. I found myself still wearing my long underwear, wool shirt and jacket, my second skin for so many weeks. But before heading for Tatopani, I changed into shorts for the first time since Surkhet.

Prem, the porters and I lost sight of each other and I walked alone. Not alone, really—the trail was crowded with an odd assortment of locals, trekkers and Indians on pilgrimage to Muktinath. After the stark isolation of Dolpo, I found the stimuli of civilization disorienting. My eyes and thoughts darted to one exciting sight after another, so many villages, so much humanity. Within the spray of a waterfall a short distance off the trail a large group of trekkers bathed. White, blubbery paunches jiggled as they splashed in the tumbling waters, Germanic-accented shouts accosted the surrounding silent beauty. *What species did these creatures belong to?* Loud, gaudily clad, defiantly obese in a land of hunger.

The porters, I knew, had stopped somewhere for food and the lodges along the way tempted me with their signs. "Welcom! All you can Eat!" proclaimed one. "Tasty Western Snaks Served Here" said another.

I stopped at one and looked up and down the trail for Prem and the others. Not seeing them, I ducked inside. I sat at a table covered with a white linen tablecloth and holding salt and pepper shakers, an ashtray and pink rhododendron blooms in a earthenware vase. A menu of more than fifty items boasted Nepalese, Chinese, American and Japanese cuisine, right down to sukiyaki fritters. I ordered a double stack of apple "pancaks" with powdered sugar and coffee.

Around five o'clock I met Prem at the outdoor restaurant of the Namaste Lodge in Tatopani. I took off my pack and sat down. "Prem, where are the porters?"

"Don't worry, they are behind us. They will come later. The *chaulki* is at the edge of town. We can bypass it by going out the back door of the kitchen and heading to the river. We can follow the river to the hot springs. From there we can get back on the trail beyond the *chaulki*."

In celebration we ordered beer and *suggotti*. After the porters passed by, we left, going out the back door past two smelly outhouses and down to the river. A half mile later we came to an open-sided building and a small concrete pool filled with dirty tepid water, the hot water from whence Tatopani got its name. Earlier, we had thought of soaking in the hot water, but the sight of the pool now made us reconsider. We left the spring to two dreadlocked *saddhus* (holy men) and found the path back to the main trail. Congratulating ourselves on bypassing the checkpost, we cruised on up the trail. Stone walls lined the path as it wound between houses and small fields.

I rounded a bend to see a uniformed policeman sitting on a wall only thirty yards ahead! My mood sank immediately. Another checkpost. Prem saw him at the same moment I did and whispered, "Wait just a little, then come."

Prem went ahead. The policeman stopped and questioned him. As the policeman was thus occupied, I started to walk on by, hoping he wouldn't notice me.

"*Namaste*, this is a checkpost. Please show your permit." He pointed to a chair on the porch of the low building on the other side of the trail. I sat down, took off my pack and rummaged through for my passport and permit, which I presented to another officer seated there.

"I am coming from Jumla." I assumed a false bravado.

"Jumla?"

"Yes, I came past here from the south last night looking for a place to stay in Tatopani. I was very tired."

He looked at my passport and inspected my permit carefully. "But your permit is expired by ten days, and your passport also."

"Yes." I kept up the false front. "We had a very difficult time coming over the Thakurji Lekh. Lots of snow and it delayed us for two weeks."

The policeman turned to Prem and spoke in Nepali. "Do you know this *bideshi* ("foreigner")?"

"No," Prem said. "I met him on the trail just last night. He was lost so I showed him the way to Tatopani. His porters are just ahead."

To my relief and surprise, the policeman stamped my permit and returned it. "Okay, but you must get a new visa in Kathmandu. It will cost you several hundred rupees."

"Yes, I know. I am just happy to have made it back from Jumla."

"Yes, a very bad place," the officer said. "I used to live in Jumla. And that Dhorpatan is a dangerous place, so many *dacoits* ("bandits")."

"Yes, the people were unfriendly," I said over my shoulder as I headed down the trail. I waved goodbye to Prem.

I waited a quarter of a mile down the trail, and shortly Prem followed.

"That's it, Prem," I said with a big grin. "I'm legal! They stamped my permit."

"Yes, Parker Sahib, we're almost home."

For two days we walked with the other trekkers along the well-trodden paths, eating and drinking our way from teahouse to trekker's lodge. We went down 6,000 feet to Birethanti, 2,000 feet of it consisting of steep stone steps that left my legs aching, yearning for an up of any sort. After six hundred miles on the trail I surprised myself—I didn't know there was anything my legs couldn't handle easily. That night we celebrated with chicken and drank *chang* into the wee hours.

The next day's ascent through hot, muggy weather intensified my hangover, headache and queasy stomach. I hadn't discovered until long into the night that the *chang* had been made with water drawn directly from the Modi Khola. Hot, frustrated, reeling with fever, I left Prem and the porters and rushed on to Naudanda, where I planned to cash my last traveler's check at the bank.

At the Nepal Rastra Bank I found a long line snaking out into the street. For forty-five minutes I waited in the stifling sun, straining to keep my bowels from exploding. And when I finally handed a teller my traveler's check, he looked confused and referred me upstairs. Why, I didn't know and didn't care. All I wanted was my money and a toilet, maybe in reverse order. After another half hour, I emerged to find Prem waiting for me.

I opened my mouth to speak, then thought better of it and rushed off to the relative privacy of some nearby bushes. An hour's walk and a forty-five-minute jeep ride brought us to the edge of Pokhara, where we waited still another hour to board a packed local bus. Once aboard I scrunched into a window seat and concentrated on not soiling my shorts for the trip into town.

Soon we found ourselves stopped in the midst of the bazaar, caught in a gridlock of cows, cars, lorries, bicycles and *tongas*. Two arguing drivers traded fists as a swarming crowd surged around for a better view, shouting encouragement and groaning with each well-landed blow. Inside the bus, the hundred-degree heat made me claustrophobic, and I leaned out the window for a fresh breath. Instead I got a lungful of noxious diesel fumes. Feverish and queasy, with the din of the crowd and honking horns, the polluted air, I leaned my aching head against the window frame wanting nothing more than to be back amidst the mountains of Dolpo.

When we reached the Himalayan Lodge, Prem and the porters made plans to hit the town. This outing had been planned for some time, but I was too sick to go with them. I asked Prem to buy me a bus ticket to Kathmandu for the next morning. The four of them would stay in Pokhara for a few days and meet me later.

I awoke before dawn to catch my bus. My head ached from only two hours' sleep and my stomach still felt queasy. I swallowed two codeine tablets and Prem fed me two large mugs of steamy sweet tea, then made sure I got on the bus.

At four that afternoon the bus crested the last switchback and the Kathmandu Valley stretched out before me, just as it had during my first approach from the plains of India seven months before. Back then I thought I had reached Nirvana. I laughed to myself. Was that only seven months ago? It seemed like seven lifetimes. The countryside, then cloaked in twenty shades of green, lush from the lifegiving monsoon rains, now lay brown and dormant, the terraced hillsides awaited the nourishment of summer rains.

As we rumbled down into the valley, two Tibetans in black *chubas* pushed their way into the aisle of the bus. Gesturing excitedly, they raised their arms overhead and bowed towards the great *stupa* of Swayambhunath atop an isolated hillock above the city. I, too, revived at the sight of the *stupa* and those great brooding Buddha eyes that had surveyed our departure two and a half months earlier.

I had come full circle. I closed my eyes against the dust billowing in through the open window and let my forehead rest against the window post. My thoughts wandered and I found myself once again lost in the mountains of Dolpo. Prem, Akaal Bahadur, Jeet Bahadur and I had literally stumbled there, not knowing where we had come from or exactly where we were heading. Lost within a massive geological backwater, isolated from the world by the crumpled crust of the earth. Was I ever really there? Or did I create that place in a warped dream?

I opened my eyes and looked down at my shrunken body, sinewy muscles, taut skin. It had been no dream. But even with its vision vivid in my mind, Dolpo remained somehow secretive and aloof. As though our circuitous passage through Jumla and Dalphu had been a necessary prelude, a hardening of the body, softening of the mind, a shedding of values and preconceptions to prepare us for those stark and mysterious mountains, the utter desolation, the awesome and frightening power of the earth.

I thought again of Tibrikot, Dunai, Tarakot, our brushes with the police and military. Lama Dorje, who had appeared from nowhere to tell us of a route through the mountains, our Dorje Route, the Path of Lightning Bolts. Sangdak, into which we stumbled in a raging blizzard, on the "wrong" side of the Cha Lungpa Gorge. All just happenstance? Perhaps. I thought so at the time, for I was no believer in Fate or God. But the time on the shepherd's roof, watching the moon, had challenged my beliefs. Now I knew nothing.

The bus crossed the bridge spanning the Bagmati River and entered Kathmandu. Left off at Ratna Park, I headed on foot through the crooked streets towards Asan Tole. In the sticky afternoon heat, rickshaw wallas approached and circled me, hungry for a few rupees. But I was determined to walk the last mile by myself and told them to go away, perhaps more sternly than I should have. Turning the corner in Thamel, I spotted Pema at the same moment he spotted me.

"Parker, my God!" he said. "You are so thin!" Taking me inside his cramped shop, he pulled the dirty worn pack from my back and found a place for me to sit among the piles of ropes and sleeping bags. Summoning a boy from the street, Pema pressed a few rupees in his hand and sent him scurrying in search of *chang*.

"We were so worried. J.B. did not think you would make it. He was already planning how to look for you if you did not come back by May first."

"We were lucky many times, Pema. Many times."

The *chang* arrived and we ceremoniously drank three glasses in toast of my return.

"Where is J.B.?"

"At the same hotel. He went to pick up the extra supplies you left in India last year and returned only two days ago."

"I should go find him." I stood to leave. "Will you have dinner with us tonight?"

"Yes. Yes, of course."

I paused, the one question I really wanted to ask burning on my tongue. "Oh, Pema. Have you seen Clara?"

"She is in Darjeeling. Some letters came for you. They are at my home. I can give them to you tomorrow."

"Thanks." I desperately wanted to read her words, but persuaded myself tomorrow was soon enough.

I found J.B. in his second-floor room. I rattled the window. He looked up, startled, then his face softened and he jumped up to greet me. "Parker, good to see you."

He took my hand in both of his. The warmth of his greeting was a welcome relief. I felt guilty about the turn of events in western Nepal, and I knew that our differences on the trail were as much my fault as his. In my mind, these were events of the past, and I was relieved to sense that they were to him, too. We feasted that night on buffalo steak and apple pie. After dinner, I went back to our room and slept for fourteen hours.

Four days later, Prem and the porters showed up. Our gear —the cooking pots, kerosene stove, tents, tarp—was all neatly packed into two baskets. We sat on the balcony and talked for a time about our extraordinary trip together. But it surprised and disappointed me how soon the status of westerner and hired help returned, and the intense closeness faded. I thanked and paid them all, including large tips. Auri Bahadur had decided to take a bus back to Surkhet and walk home from there. Flying in the iron bird scared him too much. Prem planned to remain in Kathmandu and regain his health. Akaal Bahadur and Jeet Bahadur were to leave for their village the next morning. I found out later that Prem had gone to a doctor in Kathmandu who gave him some pills. Prem, as is the custom in Nepal and much of Asia, never bothered to question the doctor but took the pills and subsequently recovered his health. His symptoms resembled the symptoms of meningitis, but I never found out whether that was what he had. In any case, I'm grateful that he got better.

When the time came for them to leave, they walked down the stairs and crossed the open courtyard, Akaal Bahadur last. Before he disappeared from view, I called out to him.

"O Akaal Bahadur!"

He turned. I raised my hands, palms together over my head. *"Dhanyabaad!"* ("Thank you!")

For a moment he stood there. He was dressed once more in his lavender pantaloons, his long-sleeved shirt and blue sweater vest, and I took a mental picture I will never forget. "Yiss, Sahib, thank you. *Namaste."* He bowed slightly, turned and moved into the street.

During the following days, J.B. and I discussed the possibilities of continuing our trans-Himalayan traverse through northern India in the summer. But they were futile discussions because J.B.'s ankle had been examined in Delhi, with a grim diagnosis. He faced the possibility of further damage and he still walked with a limp. We both knew his trekking days were over.

I could have gone alone, but the prospects looked poor. Sporadic news reports had reached Kathmandu about unrest in northern India. The Sikhs were agitating for an independent state and there was also trouble in Kashmir. Neither the Nepalese newspapers nor the Indian embassy could supply any reliable information. Our only hard sources were contacts within the British embassy. And they gave ominous news; Indira Gandhi's government and the Sikhs were headed for a showdown at the Golden Temple.

Beyond the political problems, I had personal doubts

about continuing. My finances were low, and after months on the trail I felt physically and mentally drained. My journey through western Nepal had left me with a sustained glow, but it had also taken its toll.

A week after I returned, I ventured up to the fourth floor where we had stayed in December and January. Deserted now in the off-season, the place that had been so vital and alive only a few months before now seemed tired and disheveled. Those few weeks around New Year's had been a special time, a random union of unique personalities and circumstances. Americans, Swiss, Belgians, Canadians; trekkers, wanderers, seekers, smugglers. Through a concatenation of circumstances, we had all found ourselves in Kathmandu, and the result was a release of euphoric, synergistic energy. Now the others had scattered over the globe and only J.B. and I remained, a day late for the party. I felt their ghostly presence as I walked along the balcony, then sat briefly in a worn rattan chair.

I climbed the creaking steps to the roof and sat on the low wall that surrounded it, looking out over the rooftops of Kathmandu to the brown fields and hills beyond. It all appeared so different now. Back then, the January sun, lower in the sky, had cast a cool, exotic aura over the valley. Now in the brighter light, the city stood naked to my view, imperfections exposed. The bamboo scaffolding of new construction sprouted everywhere, especially in the tourist area of Thamel. The day before, during a conversation overheard in one of the new upscale bakery-restaurants, I had heard Thamel referred to as a "tourist ghetto." An apt label for a place fast becoming insulated from the people and culture of Nepal.

I remained on the roof for two hours as the sun set, a pocketful of chocolates and two letters from Clara my companions. More and more during the last weeks she had filled my thoughts. I relived the delicious sensual frustration of our time together in January. In my memory, I replayed bits of our conversations and actions. Slowly I began to see the essence of what had happened. And, as I did, I began to feel what I was not seeking: doubts about the vast cultural differences between us. Could we overcome them?

During our descent of the Kali Gandaki, I had tormented myself. I feared Clara had forgotten me, written me off as just another foreigner tramping through her country. By the time I reached Kathmandu, these doubts and fears had pitched me into a deep well of depression. But she *had* written, using Pema's address, and now I reread those letters. Through anguished pages she pleaded with me not to forget her, to visit her in Darjeeling as I had promised. As I watched the sun set to the west beyond Swayambhunath, her presence next to me was palpable.

On the first of May I said goodbye to J.B., who had decided to head for the northern Sahara and Morocco. We made plans to meet in the U.S. when we both returned. I boarded the overnight bus to Kakarvitta on the eastern border with India.

The next day I crossed the border and hitched a ride with a tea plantation manager in his Land Rover. We left the Indian plains and drove up along the twisting road into the lush Himalayan foothills. In the town of Darjeeling I wandered through the crazy winding hillside streets, and soon stood before the modest cottage Clara's parents rented not far from the Mall.

Nervously, I opened the gate and walked up to the door. As though expecting me, Clara opened it before I could knock. Our eyes met and a rush of emotion flushed my face. Then she smiled, black eyes sparkling, deep dimples piercing her cheeks, black hair brushed and glistening. Standing in the doorway, she looked the part of an English schoolgirl in a plaid pleated skirt, white blouse and knee socks. Her mother stood behind her in a traditional sari.

I smiled at her mother and put my hands together. She

returned the greeting. She spoke no English, and although functional, my Nepali wasn't up to the subtleties of social conversation. Clara led me to the sitting room and we sat stiffly on a couch, knee to knee. When her mother left the room to get tea, I leaned towards her. She turned demurely and I gently kissed her cheek.

"Oh Parker, when I saw you at the door, it gave me such a start. I thought you had forgotten me." She spoke quietly in the Nepali British accent I found so appealing.

"And I was so afraid you had forgotten me," I said. This time she leaned towards me and I reached out for her. We embraced in a long, lingering kiss.

"No, I didn't forget," she whispered. "How could I forget?"

Clara's mother brought tea and cookies, then left us to our conversation.

"Just a few days ago, Praven's brother came here along with a friend, looking for a place to stay. I could not turn them away, so they are staying here with us. Just now they are out, but they may come back any time. Please, I will take you to my cousin's house. You can stay there until they leave."

More complications. For a week I stayed in her cousin's cottage, confined inside so as not to risk running into Praven's brother on the street. Once again I found myself near Clara but able to see her for only an hour a day, when she could slip away unnoticed. After a week, Praven's brother left for Kathmandu and I moved into the guest room at Clara's house.

There I spent two of the most peaceful weeks I have ever known. The monsoons had arrived, leaving the days overcast with intermittent afternoon showers, the foggy nights cool and damp. In the mornings I awoke from under heavy blankets to the delicious scent of steaming tea and warm flatbread. During the days, Clara and I spent long hours together talking about our childhoods, our backgrounds and our hopes for the future. I learned of her Catholic upbringing, attendance at the local schools run by nuns, the repressive atmosphere of the narrow-minded town of Darjeeling. She told rather ugly stories about nuns beating and tormenting students, instilling lifelong guilt for what seemed the smallest actions. Darjeeling society itself seemed a peculiar mix of the restrictive Catholic school atmosphere, the stifling British tradition and the timeless stratification of Indian culture.

This restrictive social system was particularly hard on women, most of whom had resigned themselves to its strict rules of behavior. But Clara had not yet totally given in. She longed for an escape from the guilt she felt about many things, including her attraction to me. More than anything else, our time together proved to both of us that Kathmandu in December and January had been more than just a brief interlude. Our mutual attraction seemed guided by forces outside either of us; in each other's presence we found ourselves uncontrollably drawn together.

Through the groundswell of emotional and physical longing, however, I sensed that different needs and desires motivated each of us, some embedded in the very cultural differences between us. I recognized that for Clara, I represented a chance to escape, a way out of this society. I knew that dealt me the upper hand in our relationship, but I saw that as a responsibility, a reason to be extra careful with Clara, not to mislead her—or myself.

Evenings I usually spent with Clara's brother, since it was expected of the men to socialize together. Invariably we would go to a friend's house for dinner, then drink glass after glass of warm scotch or rum. Our conversation ranged from politics early on, to drunken ramblings by men who also felt trapped, resigned to living boring lives in a repressive society.

Occasionally Clara and I took advantage of the late-night veil of darkness and fog to walk through the streets of Darjeeling. Just as in Kathmandu, for her to be seen with me would have raised eyebrows and sent vicious rumors scurrying through the streets of this small, provincial town.

After three weeks I had to leave, my special Darjeeling permit having been renewed twice already. On the last afternoon, Clara took me for a walk along the Mall, the promenade set on the ridge above town. She linked her arm with mine and we walked through town. Walking thus, the statement she made was an act of defiance for which I knew she would pay a stiff price in jealous comments from "friends."

That night she sneaked into my room for a time and we spoke quietly in the darkness. We made plans. I had been thinking seriously of staying in Asia; even if I couldn't continue my trek in northern India, I wasn't ready to go home. And now, with Clara so close, what other thoughts could I have but to stay? I knew a number of foreigners working in Nepal, and I thought I could find a job. Clara also thought she could find work in Kathmandu.

"We could live together," she said quietly after a long pause. "And if you go trekking in India, I will find a place to live and wait for you. I will write to Pema's mailbox at the post office to tell you when I arrive."

This suggestion both surprised and pleased me, because it would give me something I longed for—to be alone with her. For her it was a major step, perhaps an irrevocable shift in her social status. Maybe these plans came from the heart and not from the mind. But we were intoxicated with each other, and emotions easily overpowered logic. And that night, we truly believed in our plans.

In the morning, I packed my rucksack and headed off with Clara's brother for the taxi stand. As I reached the front gate, Clara and I parted with just a wave and goodbye. Without telephones, and with poor postal service, long separations with little or no means of communication were a way of life in Asia. I had grown accustomed to it. Besides, we had made our plans the night before.

Back in Kathmandu the monsoons had driven the tourists from Nepal. Landslides and leech-infested jungles do not lend themselves to comfortable trekking. By the first of June, events in India had degenerated into near-civil war. Gandhi had sent troops into the Golden Temple, hundreds had been killed, martial law and curfews had been ordered throughout northern India. Reports trickled into town of hijacked buses with all passengers killed. Such news dashed my hopes for continuing on to northern India.

So I looked for work. USAID had no openings for biologists, but the U.S. Embassy school needed a middle-grade science teacher, and I applied for the job.

Clara wrote that she was having trouble returning to Kathmandu. Forbidden to come alone, she waited until her friend Sera could leave Darjeeling. Finally, early in June, I received a letter saying she was now in Kathmandu, staying with her aunt in Dilli Bazaar. She did not give me an address.

"I want to see you so much," she wrote. "But certain circumstances beyond my control prevent me from doing so. Please to understand. Your Clara."

Please to understand? What was she talking about? I was desperate to see her and all she could ask of me was to understand some unexplained reasons for not being able to see her. I was puzzled, angry and hurt. But the best I could do was an exchange of letters via Poste Restante at the post office. She asked me to be patient. And I waited, though not patiently. Finally, two weeks later, we arranged a rendezvous. She would come to Pema's shop and I would wait for her in a nearby restaurant. She feared that Praven or his friends would see us together.

At the appointed time, I waited upstairs by the window in a second-floor restaurant. I watched the narrow, crowded street below. Pema stood in the doorway of his shop.

Then I saw her, walking with her friend Sera. My frustration and resentment disappeared, for Clara seemed the most beautiful woman I had ever seen. She found Pema, who pointed up at me. She turned and waved and then came up to the restaurant.

"Please," she whispered as she sat down. "Could we move away from the window?"

We moved to the other side of the table, which was crowded with my friends. We talked quietly but with constraint, unable to speak of what was most on our minds. I wanted so much to be alone with her. Still, we managed to communicate that our plan was still on. But her aunt was very strict, so she was trying to find a place to stay with Sera. First, she had to return to Darjeeling and hoped to return by mid-July. After fifteen minutes she said she had to go. I walked downstairs with her. Just inside the doorway, she turned and leaned back towards me.

"Do you have something to say to me, Parker?"

I whispered in her ear. "I love you."

"Thank you!" she smiled at the answer she wanted to hear and stepped out into the street. Then she was gone and I was left wondering when I would see her next.

Trekking in India was out of the question, but my impatience wouldn't let me sit in Kathmandu and wait. I decided to return to Khumbu and try to climb a couple of peaks I had missed the previous fall. I hoped that by the time I returned a month later, something would have happened. Wind and weather once again foiled my attempts, and after a long slog through mud and leeches, I arrived back in Kathmandu by the last week in July.

More letters awaited me. Clara had arrived in Kathmandu and was once again staying in Dilli Bazaar. Again she left no address. I left a letter at Poste Restante and waited impatiently. A week later she had not come to check for mail. I fumed. *What was going on? What kind of game was she playing?* I didn't know what she was doing, but I suspected I was being toyed with. Finally the letter was picked up. She wrote back saying she would meet me at a restaurant near Ratna Park. "Four o'clock, the day after tomorrow."

Two days later at three-thirty, the streets were jammed with people leaving work and heading home. In a downpour I walked through the crowd and arrived at the restaurant fifteen minutes early, excited at the thought of seeing her. At last we could talk again about our future.

I found a table near the door, ordered a beer and waited. By five she had not appeared. I went outside and stood across the street in the steady rain, watching the entrance to the restaurant, scanning faces on the street. At seven I walked back to my hotel, both furious and frightened that I would never see her again.

I left letters daily at the post office. No reply. One afternoon I rented a Chinese bicycle and rode under threatening skies through Dilli Bazaar, looking, searching. Mud splashed up at me from the wet street. Strangers' faces haunted and mocked me. A quixotic gesture, but I had to do something. Riding back to the hotel, my mind and stomach were in turmoil from the internal fight between my pride and my passion. To think I had once worried about not misleading *her*, not falsely raising *her* hopes. What was she doing to *me* now?

I arrived wet, discouraged, frustrated. I flung open the door to the extra room I had rented to store all our expedition gear. Searching once again, digging through the mounds of rucksacks and *dokos*, pulling out tents, sleeping bags, extra socks. Smelly kerosene stoves rubbed soot on my hands, plastic bowls tumbled around my feet. I *knew* it was there, it had to be there somewhere. But I could not find it. I had lost Clara's good-luck charm.

In a rage of frustration, I hurled a cooking pot against the wall, then slumped into a chair. *Stop and think. About yourself instead of her.* Was this a fantasy I created? To live and work here in Kathmandu, was that a realistic thing for me to even think of doing? What about my education, all those years in graduate school, training for highly specialized research? Being a teacher was an honest occupation, a needed service, especially in Nepal, but couldn't I put my knowledge to better use elsewhere?

What about Clara and me? Could we really live together in Kathmandu, or anywhere? Was the cultural chasm too deep and wide to bridge? With the way she left me hanging, did she really love me? She could not—or would not—tell me why she couldn't see me. I wanted to believe it wasn't because she didn't care, but what signs had I had lately that she did? She asked for understanding, but how long did it take for understanding to turn to foolish hope? I suspected she saw me as her savior, a way out of an unhappy situation in her life. And I was willing, in part, to play that role—but would I be satisfied with that for very long? I didn't know. I could no longer sort fantasy from reality.

Finally, I knew that I had to get out of Kathmandu, try to develop some sensible perspective on the situation. Our cultures clashed with a violence that had shattered my equilibrium. Hers was infinitely patient, willing to wait for events to happen, for years, for lifetimes. Mine was impatient, and I could not wait.

I bought a plane ticket and wrote her a letter saying my father was ill, that I had to return home immediately. I felt foolish lying, but I couldn't put into words the uncertainties, frustrations and doubts that were tearing me apart.

And so I boarded the plane—the hardest thing I have ever done.

EPILOGUE

▲

DARIEN, CONNECTICUT
Late September, 1984

I ARRIVED IN NEW YORK AFTER DETOURS TO THAILAND, NEW Zealand, Hawaii and San Francisco. Around the world in just over a year. For two weeks in Darien I cut grass, painted and chopped wood around my parents' home, readjusting to life back in the U.S. But I was broke and needed a job.

So on a crisp fall morning in early October, I took the three-hour train ride to Philadelphia. From the Thirtieth Street Station I trekked a mile and a half through urban streets to the University of Pennsylvania campus. The ivy-covered entrance to the medical school seemed as impressive as I remembered it, the colonial portraits of the school's founders and the huge Thomas Eakins painting still lined the marbled halls.

On the second floor of the Anatomy-Chemistry building I paused for a few moments to go over the list of reasons why I should be rehired for my old job. Then I walked in, unannounced, to the office of Howard Holtzer, my graduate school mentor. My rehearsed lines proved unnecessary. Although only three months earlier he had written a glowing letter of recommendation for the teaching job in Kathmandu, I discovered he had also, on a hunch, kept a position open for me in his lab. I signed a few forms and slipped behind my old desk, surrounded by the same labeled bottles of chemicals and solutions I had abandoned fourteen months before.

In West Philly, I found a dirty, roach-infested apartment, and tried to continue my work as though I had never left. I glided through the first few weeks, trying to believe I was happy and that in coming back I had done the right thing.

The pretense proved shortlived. It ended the day the first thick envelopes, taped together to hold all the pages, arrived from Darjeeling. Long, anguished letters from Clara, crying out her shock and sorrow at my leaving, telling of how she had been helpless in the face of events she could not control, pleading again for understanding, saying what she did not say while I waited futilely in Kathmandu.

Clara's letters cracked my veneer of calm and brought roiling to the surface memories of painful and emotional experiences that had fundamentally altered my outlook on life. Once again I sat dirty, half starved and dead-tired on a shepherd's roof, staring at the Kali Gandaki. Physically and mentally extended by my ordeal, emotions laid bare, I had found myself torn by questions about pain and suffering and death—things I had never contemplated during my comfortable, cocooned life, but that so dominated the Third World.

All the questions I had pondered on that April day came back as on a page of a long-ago-written diary. Though I soon came to realize that over the millenia others had grappled with these same questions, that made them no less real to me. How could there be so much poverty, disease and ignorance on the same planet with the upper-middle-class postcard towns such as the one in which I grew up? Why had no one—my teachers, my parents—told me that other worlds existed beyond New England stone walls and freshly mown grass? Perhaps they had tried but I hadn't been ready to hear it. Not with soccer games to play and proms to attend.

But now I spent long, sleepless nights haunted by visions

of hollow-eyed children with bloated bellies, of ghostly wisps of smoke from burning *ghats*. I passed, in a predictable progression, from immense sorrow to searing guilt.

I had assumed that by leaving Asia, by returning to my old and familiar surroundings, I could regain some equilibrium, some perspective. But my experiences in the Himalayas had altered the framework in which I lived my life. And back in Philadelphia, the people, the sprawling ghettos and gritty streets seemed more alien than the desolate peaks of Dolpo. My old values and aspirations lay in tatters; new ones had yet to emerge.

And even my closest friends, who lacked an experiential framework for understanding my point of view, sat stone-faced while I ranted anxiously about our distorted values, our selfish lives. It was as if I were speaking in tongues.

I needed to do something. I found the pace of my biomedical research work maddeningly slow and the results abstract. I longed to do something tangible, where results could be seen now rather than through some obscure ripple-down effect generations hence. I wanted to save the world, or at least work at it until I exhausted the guilt inside of me.

And I missed Clara. The frustrations of not being able to see her during those mysterious months in Kathmandu had begun to fade from my memory, replaced by guilt at having left her. How could I not have made a last bold attempt to see her just one more time? To talk with her, to ask her why. Should I have stayed? With her? This question troubled me most of all. I dwelt on it at length, and with despair. For finally I came to accept the truth that leaving Kathmandu had been the best thing for both of us. The cultural differences were, at least for me, insurmountable. My expectations of relationships between men and women, between husband and wife, between individual and society were too different from hers. In August in Kathmandu my emotions had swallowed my rational thoughts. Now I began to see that this relationship needed more than emotions to survive.

We drew some comfort from each other's letters, hers anguished, mine sorrowful. But with pen and paper, I could not adequately tell her what I felt.

I had to return. To see Clara once more and tell her how I felt. I needed to see Kathmandu again. To somehow reconcile with my life the immense guilt and sorrow I felt for the suffering I had witnessed. To find a reason for my medical research and to validate my choice of career. I also had to retrieve a part of me that had not come back with my body, a piece of my spirit without which I felt I could not go forward with my life.

On September 15, 1985, I arrived in Kathmandu. A group of friends, including J.B., who had taken a job a few months earlier as the Nepalese judo coach, met me at the airport and drove me into town. It was great to see them all again.

The next afternoon I sat talking with Pema in his shop, surrounded by the dusty paraphernalia of trekking. With no warning, she appeared in the doorway. I jumped up to greet her and Clara's eyes smiled their welcome as her lips said hello to me.

Pema had rented the top room of an old Edwardian house on the edge of Kathmandu. For three weeks Clara and I met every afternoon in his apartment. We listened to music and talked. She explained how her spinster aunt had prevented her from coming to meet me that day at the restaurant, how desperate she had been to see me. Hearing this, feeling the depth of emotion in her words, I knew that the rift between us had simply been our inability to communicate during those summer months. I couldn't help but wonder, with some despair, how different our lives might have been had she kept that one rendezvous.

We also talked of little things. I told her of life in Philadelphia; she spoke of events of the last year, a protracted illness and how difficult it was to be an old maid at twenty-six.

One afternoon we sat on the balcony and watched dozens

of brightly colored kites play tag over the lush green rice fields. The last of the monsoon clouds had wet the valley an hour earlier, and now the slanting rays of the sun set the emerald paddies aglow. We talked for a time about nothing in particular.

For more than two weeks we had carefully sidestepped the major issues between us. So happy were we to have even these few weeks together, we pretended that I was not going to board a plane soon and fly back to another world. I had come halfway around the world to tell her that I could not spend the rest of my life with her. That the cultural chasm was too deep. We had to talk, I needed to explain, to make her understand. I wanted to make it all right. I summoned my courage and turned to her.

"Clara, we need to talk about what is going to happen between us. You know that I . . ." She put her hand over my mouth to stop me.

"Please, Parker, I know what is in your mind. Please don't say anything. Let's just watch the kites. There are so many beautiful colors."

I held her hand and she leaned against my shoulder. It was another example of the gulf between us. For me, explanations were necessary, we had to talk it out, to make neat, wrapped ends. For Clara, her culture gave her the patience and wisdom to know that we cannot control our destiny, to accept what life gives.

I watched the kites through tears until the colors blended, red, yellow, green against the blue sky. Never before had I felt such helplessness. Wanting desperately to take her away, to remake her life, but knowing that I could not. Within the week I would escape. But she would remain, born into the confines of her culture, someday to die within them.

My last night in Kathmandu we had a private party in K.C.'s restaurant. At nine o'clock, I found a cab and rode with Clara to her aunt's house. The taxi halted at the end of a rutted dirt road and I walked with her the fifty yards to the house. Stopping in front of the gate, we turned towards one another and fell into a final embrace.

"No, don't, Parker. Others may see." She unwrapped my arms from around her.

I started back towards the taxi. Knowing that I would never see her again, several times I stopped and turned to capture the memory of her brilliant white jacket shining in the beam of the taxi's headlights. At the taxi door I stopped and held up my hand. She raised hers for several seconds, then disappeared behind the gate.

Distraught, I returned to K.C.'s. My friends tried to buoy my spirits and kept me up all night, ending with a dawn rickshaw ride through the awakening streets of Kathmandu. At seven in the morning I stumbled to bed. My flight left at six that evening.

In the early afternoon, I woke and packed my belongings. Fighting a cold and nursing a hangover, I stumbled around my room, trying not to think of having to leave.

Suddenly she was there, climbing the stairs in a brilliant white dress, a red ribbon in her hair. She had never looked so beautiful. I had not expected to see her again and this extra time together was like a gift. Having accepted the sorrow of our parting, expressed all we could, given her way and mine, we were at last at peace. For two hours we talked and watched the clouds build over the Himalaya to the north.

When it was time to go, Pema performed the traditional Buddhist ceremony. He placed a white scarf around my neck, and dipping into the small bowl of *chang*, flicked droplets first one direction, then another. I downed three quick glasses of the milky *chang*. We piled into two taxis and headed for the airport.

We sat in the large, open visitors' pavilion set up across the road from the terminal entrance. For a while I talked with my friends, and then it was time to go. I moved down the line of chairs, saying my goodbyes to Pema, J.B., my Peace Corps friends, Bob and Sean. And last of all, to Clara.

I wanted to express all I felt for her, the joy she had given me. But now the final moment had come and I couldn't speak. I leaned down and kissed her on the cheek, then turned towards the terminal.

She stood, grasped my hand and walked with me across the road, right to the entrance.

I climbed the first two steps, then turned towards her. Our eyes met, she tilted her head and smiled. I tried to return her smile, but couldn't. We moved apart, her hand slid from my grasp, but I paused. For a moment we touched by just an outstretched fingertip.

I turned and left.

GLOSSARY

Note: Tibetan terms are indicated with a (T).

A

achar	chili sauce
alu	potatoes
aulo	malaria
ausadhi	medicine

B

baato	trail
baksheesh	tip, a gratuity given for service, or a bribe
beedies	small, cheap cigarettes that are hand-rolled from tobacco leaves with no paper
bhaat	rice that has been cooked as opposed to uncooked rice
bharal	blue sheep (pseudois nayaur), sheep-like in appearance but exhibiting the behavior of a goat; found north of the main Himalayan range

bideshi	foreigner
bistaari	slowly
Bodhissatva	an enlightened being, one who, on the verge of reaching Nirvana, chooses instead to be reincarnated and returns to the world to help all other sentient beings achieve enlightenment

C

chang	homemade beer, found throughout the Himalayas, it is made from whatever grain is available, rice, wheat, barley, millet
chapattis	unleavened flatbread made from flour and water and cooked on a flat metal pan or plate
chaulki	checkpost for checking trekking permits and to control outsiders
Chetri	a caste
chha	there is, it is
chhainna	negative, not, no, none
chillum	pipe
chitto	hurry
chorten (T)	Buddhist funerary monument, the same as the Sanscrit "stupa"; built with a square base and dome shaped upper portion, they are repositories of relics of *lamas* or other important personages; found on the approaches to villages and *gompas*, one should always pass on the left
chu (T)	water or river

chuba (T)   Tibetan overcoat; nomads wear chubas of sheepskin with the wool on the inside; country-dwellers have ones made of homespun, townsfolk from black machine-made cloth, the wealthy from silk; the sleeves are long, the garment loose-fitting with a sash around the waist, the extra room is used as storage for personal items; traditionally worn off the right shoulder to free the arm for work or warfare

D

daal   thick lentil soup, a staple in the Indian subcontinent, nutritious when combined with rice

dacoits   bandits

dahi   yogurt

daura   firewood, logs, branches or sticks

dhanyabaad   thank you, used to communicate sincere gratitude

dhauliya   protective spirit figures found in the area around Jumla; generally seen in pairs, a male and a female, they guard the fields, houses and especially bridges; believed to be holdovers from pre-Buddhist, pre-Hindu religious practices, they are generally carved from wood; because they are often unclothed and sexually explicit, they are frequently referred to as "pornographic" or "erotic."

dinos   give me

doko   funnel-shaped bamboo basket carried by a rope around the forehead called a tumpline

dorje (T)	lightning bolt, also a religious object symbolizing lightning
Drokpas (T)	nomads
dui	two
dzong (T)	fort, built on hillsides, usually with a commanding view of the approaches

E

ek	one

G

ganja	marijuana, grows wild in the hill country of the Himalayas
ghat	platform by the river used for washing and for cremating bodies
gompa (T)	Buddhist monastery, literally "high place," frequently built on top of or into the side of a mountain
Gurkha	caste, ethnic group known for being mercenary soldiers

H

himal	mountain or range of mountains
ho	there is, it is

J

jaanasakchha	possible
jaau	let's go (colloquial)
jane	go

jodhpurs	cotton trousers loose in the waist and hips, narrow around the ankles

K

kahaa	where
Khampa (T)	Tibetan from Kham, eastern Tibet, known as fierce warriors and nomadic traders
khola	stream or river; also the canyon formed by a river
korsani	chilies
kukri	traditional Nepalese knife, generally with a wide flat blade that is curved

L

la (T)	pass; in thanksgiving for going over a pass, Tibetans build *cairns* or *chortens* and string prayer flags; travelers traditionally add a stone or prayer flag as they pass.
lama (T)	Buddhist monk
lekh	hill or mountain; long winding ridges under 20,000 ft. found across Nepal south of the main Himalayan peaks.
linos	take it

M

maanchhe	man
Magar	a caste
Manangi	villager from Manang, an isolated village behind the Annapurna range
manna	unit of measurement, about one pound

mate	high
momos (T)	potstickers, Tibetan raviolis, filled with meat or vegetables and boiled or steamed
musalai kaideo	"The mouse ate it!"

N

na	no, not, negative
nah (T)	blue sheep (see bharal)
namaskar	formal greeting to an important person
Namaste	greeting, literally "I greet the god within you"
Newari	ethnic caste from the Kathmandu Valley
Nirvana	a state beyond suffering, free from reincarnation

O

Om mani padme hum	Hail to the Jewel in the Lotus

P

paathis	a measure, about five pounds
pani	water
pradhan panch	mayor or village headman responsible to outside authorities and consulted by the villagers

R

rakshi	distilled spirits made throughout the Himalayas in homemade stills with whatever grain, vegetable or fruit is available

ramro	good
rotis	flatbread
rupee	unit of money, approximately Nepalese Rs17 to U.S.$1 in 1984

S

saddhu	Hindu holy man who has frequently taken vows of poverty and therefore begs for all his worldly possessions
sahib	sir, form of address used for all foreigners as well as high-ranking Nepalese
sakdaaina	not possible
Sherpa	Tibetan from the Khumbu region of Nepal, known for being Himalayan climbers, guides and high altitude porters
sirdar	guide, head of the trekking group, liaison with the locals, translator
sisnu	a dish made from cooked stinging nettles
stupa	funerary monument, see *chorten*
suchia (T)	Tibetan butter tea made by churning together hot tea, butter and salt or baking soda
suggotti	dried buffalo or yak meat

T

tarkaari	curried vegetables
Tamang	caste from eastern Nepal
tapaai	you are
terai	plains of the Indian subcontinent
Thakuri	a caste
thangka (T)	Buddhist religious painting

thugchen (T)	long brass horns with a deep, bass sound, blown on ceremonial occasions by Buddhist monks, frequently from the *gompa* roof
tin	three
tonga	two-wheeled horse-drawn carriage
topee	Nepalese brimless cloth hat
tsampa (T)	roasted barley flour, a staple for Tibetans, made into flat bread or mixed directly into butter tea
tulo	big

V

Vishnu	Hindu god, the Preserver

W

wallas	workman, e.g., the worker who peddles a bicycle rickshaw is a rickshaw walla

Y

yak (T)	member of the cow family adapted to high altitudes, cross-bred by the Tibetans with cows; the milk has a high butterfat content and is used for cheese, in making tea and for butter lamps